TONY GREIG
LOVE, WAR AND CRICKET

In loving memory of

Anthony William 'Tony' Greig

Foreword

ANTHONY WILLIAM 'TONY' GREIG DIED ON THE MORNING OF 29 December 2012. It was a terribly sad time for our family. The days and weeks that followed his death were filled with mixed emotions. On the one hand we were all trying to come to terms with life without the person who had been such a dynamic and intrinsic part of our lives, while on the other we were so incredibly touched by the host of wonderful tributes that came in from around the world.

As we read and listened to these tributes, we realised that the making of this special person began with our darling 94-year-old mother, Joycie. This was a very special relationship, in which our mother had successfully imparted her philosophy of building a close-knit and united family to her eldest son – a philosophy he embraced until his last breath.

From the time he confided in his sister Sally Ann and brother-in-law, Phillip Hodson, in Sri Lanka that he had been diagnosed with cancer, we all assumed that with this early diagnosis he had plenty of time to take on another huge challenge in his life and beat it. This was not to be. After his diagnosis, I made numerous trips to Sydney to be with him and his family, and we shared many rewarding hours chatting and reminiscing. My elder sister, Molly Joy, also made the long trip from the United Kingdom, and I know he really appreciated this precious time with her.

Tony's children, Samantha (Sam) and Mark, found themselves faced once again with a parent suffering from cancer. They both spent as much time as they could with Tony in his final months and helped care for him. Sam would leave her young family in Gunnedah and fly each week to Sydney to be with her dad and support his family. He had the love of family around him.

Molly Joy had always intended to write a book about our family and its wonderful history of love and adversity. It is a fascinating life story that provides an insight into the values and character traits that made Tony who he was. This was the legacy of his upbringing in South Africa, and the strong sense of family instilled in his soul by his mother.

Since the death of their father, Sam and Mark have discussed with the family their desire to record the many stories they have been told over the years by their parents, both of whom sadly lost their lives to cancer. Tony was the best storyteller of all, and had so much to tell given his amazing life. Sam and Mark want these stories preserved for their younger brother and sister, Tom and Beau, and also for future generations of our family.

Living in South Africa, so removed from all the tribulations, Joycie found it very difficult to come to terms with the loss of her son, despite having the love and attention of Molly Joy and Sally Ann who were both by her side. Sam and Mark put their own grief aside and flew to South Africa to visit her and attempt to help her overcome her dreadful loss. As they were by their father's side when he died, they were able to give Joycie great comfort in knowing that her son did not experience the terrible suffering that cancer often inflicts in the final weeks. They also discussed with their grandmother how they wanted to honour their father's memory by way of a family memoir, combining it with her own incredible life story – a story filled with love, war and, of course, cricket. This unbelievable story includes that of our late father, Sandy, a highly decorated World War Two RAF navigator in Bomber Command. Sandy formed a huge part of the person Tony became.

So the idea of a family memoir was born, and who better to take a leading role in telling it than the person who had known Tony the longest, the person who had shared and supported him through all his ups and downs in life – our mother, Joycie.

Sam and Mark, with the help of Molly Joy, spent hours helping our frail and grieving mother and grandmother to recall the early years of her life, meeting and marrying Sandy and bringing up their four successful children, all blessed with her loving family philosophy. Tony, of course, went on to achieve great things in his life. He loved cricket from an early age, became one of England's best all-rounders and captains, and revolutionised the sport through his involvement with World Series Cricket. He then went on to become one of the most respected commentators and analysts of the modern game.

Joycie, Molly Joy, Sally Ann and I are thrilled and grateful that Mark has picked up the second half of the story. Mark was only a couple of years old when the news of World Series Cricket shook the cricketing world to its core, but over the years Tony shared with him many of the critical moments and events. In addition, Mark has also acquired extensive access to the records of Tony's long-time manager, confidant and friend over a period of 40 years, former Australian opening batsman Bruce Francis. Many books have been written about World Series Cricket but none have contained some of the stories to which Tony was privy. Mark also understands from his childhood experience the unique friendship that developed out of World Series Cricket between Kerry Packer and his father. The two men were kindred spirits, both wild adventurers and madly competitive.

As a family, we all have our own special memories of Tony. We shall all treasure these forever. Tony will never be allowed to fade. To me he was everything a younger brother could ever wish for. He was one of those exceptional people who had the ability to make things happen, whether on the cricket field, in the commentary box, or at home. I admired him for his achievements, his motivation, his wise counsel, but for nothing more than his total devotion to all of us, his close family.

Molly Joy, Sally Ann and I want to thank our wonderful mother for sharing so much of her life story and her feelings with us, and also Mark and Sam. Without such passion and drive this wonderful family memoir would not have been possible.

Tony was, and always will be, the wind beneath my wings. As in life he drove me to greater heights, his memory will continue to inspire me in everything I do and his love for me, the younger brother, will remain with me forever.

Ian Greig
October 2013

Contents

Appendices

'You need talent, but you need more than that. You need this special thing that some people have which makes them play above themselves, a little better than you perceive they should be based on talent alone. You need to relish confrontation. I adored backs-to-the-wall situations.' – Tony Greig

Preface

My uncle, Ian Greig, who like my father is also a former England Test cricketer, has outlined in the foreword how the idea for this book came about. We wanted to record not just my father's wonderful stories, but those of the remarkable family from which he came.

There is also another motivation for me – a desire to recognise some important people in Dad's life. Some people might think it silly to say so but Dad always believed that Kerry Packer, or Mr Packer as I always called him, didn't receive the right kind of recognition for creating World Series Cricket (WSC). Dad was deeply concerned that over the years Kerry had come to be characterised as a bully, a man of incredible wealth who wanted not only his own boys' toys, but the other bloke's toys, too, and didn't care too much about how he got them.

Kerry Packer, to those who really knew him, was a man of great generosity, integrity and loyalty. He was also a deep thinker, particularly in respect of his many business interests. In WSC, he was the brains behind virtually every initiative. WSC didn't just happen overnight; it was the result of an astonishing amount of research and planning undertaken by Kerry and his right-hand man, Lynton Taylor. Kerry travelled to America to learn how professional sport was being packaged there, especially for television.

He picked the brains of every expert he could find. He then channelled it into making the Nine Network a world leader in the way it covered not just cricket, but most major sporting events in the world.

It also annoyed Dad that cricket historians and the establishment-loving media had airbrushed out of history the single event that caused the 'war' between the cricketing establishment and Kerry's WSC. In early 1976, the Australian Cricket Board had agreed to give Kerry the opportunity to bid for exclusive rights to televise cricket in Australia. In June of that year, the ACB reneged on that agreement, granting non-commercial rights to the ABC. This was done without giving Kerry's Nine Network the opportunity to bid for the exclusive rights, not just the commercial rights. It was this duplicity that caused everything that followed.

Dad was also angry that the former PBL boss Lynton Taylor had been written out of the events. Lynton was involved in everything from the moment of conception right through to the extraordinary settlement deal with the ACB he secured for Kerry. I don't think it is stretching things to say Dad became obsessive about Lynton receiving the recognition he deserved for getting WSC up and running, particularly in its first year. The logistics of finding grounds, organising transport, hotels, staff and overseeing drop-in wickets were monumental enough, let alone all the silky negotiation skills Lynton produced almost on a daily basis.

In addition to Kerry and Lynton, there are other people Dad always felt needed to be recognised – his parents. His father, Sandy, had been honoured for his war service with a Distinguished Flying Cross (DFC), presented by King

George VI, and a Distinguished Service Order (DSO). He had also fought against apartheid in South Africa in his capacity as a newspaper editor, and at a personal level he had won a long battle against alcoholism.

Dad idolised his mother, Joycie, even more than he did his father. He deeply admired her for the way she kept her family together in the most difficult of circumstances as her husband dealt with his demons. Dad also respected the open way Joycie talked about her relationship with her first husband, Charles Barry. He felt that if everyone were as open and honest as his mum, the world would be a much better place. I chuckled when my grandmother said that she was writing her chapters as a 94-year-old and didn't want someone tarting up her words so that the style was consistent with the other contributors.

Finally, this book is about recognition of what I might call the 'real' Tony Greig. When he wasn't being the man who taunted Australian cricketers on the field, or stuck keys into cricket pitches as a commentator, he was the wonderful father who taught his children the simple game of 'unders and overs' when we went to Bondi Beach. To people watching, it must have been an amusing sight, all six foot seven inches of my dad holding hands with his young children and yelling out 'over' or 'under' as the waves rolled in, and then either jumping or diving with us. He was also the man who gave us so much joy taking us fishing, kite flying, on holidays, to the park, or to the cricket.

Despite Dad having his fair share of adversity in his private life, we admired him so much for the way he took his challenges head-on, and we want to share the whole of him with the world.

Another question I have been asked almost as many times as 'Are you any good at cricket like your father?' is why Dad was so close to Kerry Packer. Simply, the two men were kindred spirits, always up for a challenge. As was the case with Dad, the private Kerry I knew was considerably different from the public one. So this book offers the opportunity to peek over the back fence into the world of these two extraordinary men.

Because Dad's African roots played an enormous part in shaping the man he became, Granny Joycie and I also thought it was important to sketch some of the history of southern Africa, particularly for non-South African readers. Australians and South Africans share the Southern Cross, a love for sport and have fought alongside each other in two world wars, but there are aspects of the histories of the two countries that set their peoples apart.

Whether you liked him or not, my father was a larger-than-life figure in stature, achievement and personality. He was an amazing man to countless people, one who helped change the world of cricket in so many ways. The first was through World Series Cricket, something I hope every young millionaire cricketer of today recognises. Also, I want people to know how Dad fought for better recognition of India, and more recently Sri Lanka, on the world stage. He believed you had to 'stand up and be counted' and in recent years he went out of his way to do this for Sri Lanka. Just months before his death, when he gave the 2012 MCC Spirit of Cricket Cowdrey Lecture at Lord's, he was still urging changes to improve the game. He just loved cricket.

Sitting down for hours with my grandmother has taught me a great deal about my family and why Dad was the person he was. I feel privileged to have had this opportunity and encourage everyone to connect with the older generations of their family. I have also come to realise through the writing of this book how highly regarded my father was in his private and public life.

The story begins with Joycie's account of her early years, her marriage to Charles Barry, then to my grandfather Sandy. I take over around the time I can first remember the name 'Kerry Packer' and the words 'World Series Cricket'. Between us, Joycie's and I paint the portrait of the man we knew and loved. I have attempted to bring these two lives into one through this family memoir, and I hope you enjoy reading about my dad's life as much as I have enjoyed writing about it.

Dad was a cherished son, husband, brother, father and grandfather and for many, many people around the world, as we saw at the time of his death, a friend, a mate – Greigy.

I love him and I will miss him forever.

Mark Greig
October 2013

Acknowledgements

BOOKS OF THIS TYPE DON'T GET WRITTEN WITHOUT THE assistance of a wide range of people.

The Greig family would like to thank Tom Gilliatt, Samantha Sainsbury, Jacquie Brown and all the team at Pan Macmillan for the opportunity to work with them, and for the assistance they provided in putting together the final publication.

We would never have got this far without the generous access that Bruce Francis, Tony's friend and former manager, gave us to his extensive files. These included hundreds of letters between Bruce and Tony; Bruce's diaries; Tony's contracts; drafts from the biography Bruce was writing about Tony; transcripts and notes from meetings with Kerry Packer; minutes of meetings and telephone calls with Tony; and minutes of meetings with Kellogg's, Waltons, TAA, Ford, Leyland and other companies with which Tony worked.

I would also like to mention Max Kruger and Shiran Manukulasuriya, two very close friends of Tony's. Max has put in writing some wonderful anecdotes about Dad, including his unique insight into his relationship with Bill Lawry. Shiran has provided the Sri Lankan perspective, and shared stories about Tony's affection for Sri Lanka and its people.

We thank Channel Nine for providing us with access to their photo collection.

Thank you also to Rina Hore and David Wells at the Bradman Museum in Bowral, New South Wales, for providing us with access to the photo collection of the late Viv Jenkins. Viv was the official photographer for World Series Cricket, and his widow, Jan Johnson, kindly donated in excess of 1,000 transparencies to the Bradman Foundation.

We acknowledge the work of the cricket writers David Tossell and David Lemmon.

There were so many wonderful tributes written around the world to Tony following his death. It would be impossible to include them all, but we wanted to include in the Appendices at least ten tributes we felt described Tony so well. For these kind words we would like to acknowledge some specific people: Mike Selvy, Bill Lawry, Mike Atherton, John Etheridge, Peter Lalor, Malcolm Conn, Robert Craddock, Vic Marks, Kersi Meher-Homji, Rex Clementine and Avijit Ghosh.

Finally, we should like to thank another writer, Warwick Hadfield, who worked tirelessly to help us pull together a huge amount of information from more than 90 years of family history.

Joycie and Mark Greig
October 2013

Prologue:
A Legacy to be Proud of

'Obviously I am disappointed. The only
redeeming factor is that I have sacrificed cricket's
most coveted job for a cause which I believe could
be in the best interests of cricket the world over.'
— Tony Greig, 13 May 1977

IT SAYS EVERYTHING ABOUT MY FATHER THAT HE ACCEPTED
the consequences of his actions when he was stood down
as captain of England. Although Dad hoped that Kerry
Packer and the Australian Cricket Board would be able to
work through their differences, he knew it was unlikely.
Consequently, he knew, and accepted, that the day he
signed for World Series Cricket (WSC) he would lose
the captaincy. It was a sacrifice he was prepared to make
primarily in the interests of his family, but also in the
interests of the game and his fellow cricketers.

Dad therefore wasn't surprised when on 13 May 1977
the decision was made by the Test and County Cricket
Board (TCCB), the game's governing body in England,
that he would no longer captain England. The TCCB's
secretary, Donald Carr, paid Dad the courtesy of informing
him over the phone of the decision before the chairman of

the Cricket Council, Freddie Brown, released this public statement:

> Captaincy of England concerns involvement with selection and development of England players in the future and clearly Greig is unlikely to be able to do this as his stated intention is to be contracted elsewhere during the next three winters. His action has inevitably impaired the trust which existed between the cricket authorities and the captain of the England side.

Although disappointed, Dad agreed that it was impossible for him to be involved in team selections and long-term planning and accepted the decision with good grace. He also understood the comments about trust from the TCCB's perspective. He believed, however, that during their lives, every member of the TCCB would have acted in the same way he did when negotiating with a potential employer. Dad never accepted the charge that he was untrustworthy. He argued that he, and anyone else in the same position, had no option but to act in the way he did. And he was prepared to accept the consequences.

He might not have been captain anymore, but he was still part of the team, so Dad threw all his energy into helping England beat Australia. His loyalty to England, and to his new captain, Mike Brearley, remained paramount. At Brearley's insistence Dad played in all the Tests in that five-Test series in which England won the Ashes 3–nil. In his landmark book, *The Art of Captaincy*, Brearley acknowledged the support he received from Dad during that series as both adviser and player.

Dad consistently scored runs and took wickets in that series. He particularly enjoyed the 91 he scored in the second innings of the first Test, scoring almost half those runs from 11 boundaries. The whole world against him, his and his team's backs to the wall, these were the situations in which Dad revelled. Australia had a first innings lead of 80. England was struggling in its second innings before Dad, batting at number four, joined Bob Woolmer in a 92-run partnership. It helped England to a relatively healthy 305 and when stumps came on the final day, Australia was struggling at 6–114. The match was drawn, but England had taken a powerful psychological advantage.

Australian fast bowler Rodney Hogg said that Mike Brearley had a degree in people. He actually had a qualification in psychoanalysis from Cambridge University and he certainly would have needed all of his academic skills to unite a side which included Alan Knott, Dennis Amiss and Derek Underwood, all of whom had joined WSC, and Geoffrey Boycott, who vehemently opposed it.

I also have to admire Dad's amazing mental strength to go out and play cricket amid all the criticism, some of it deeply personal. Perhaps the cricket ground became a refuge. There he was no longer a rebel, or a traitor, he was the one thing that he always longed to be, a Test cricketer. Dad scored 76 in the second Test, which England won by nine wickets.

England also won the third Test, in which Dad's contributions were more modest, a couple of wickets, 11 in the first innings and a duck, bowled by Max Walker, another WSC signee, in the second. They might all have been about to work for the same boss, but already there was no love lost between the Australian World Series players and the teams that Tony Greig would lead in Mr Packer's colours.

England required only one innings in the fourth Test, Dad made 43 out of 436 and took the wickets of the Australian openers, Rick McCosker and Ian Davis, in the second innings. The fifth Test was drawn. In the official team photo taken at the end of that game in the shadow of the Gasometer at the Oval, Dad can be seen sitting right next to Brearley, and with a beaming smile. Dad's smile was always biggest when England beat Australia.

Despite the comprehensive victory against an Australian side which was unable to show the same unity between its own WSC and non-WSC players, the English press still went after Dad. He was labelled a traitor, greedy, selfish. He had already developed a thick skin as part of the protection needed just to survive as England's captain. Now it needed to grow a lot thicker. No matter how much Dad argued that cricket would benefit in the long term, nobody in the English media seemed to want to listen. No matter how often he said it would have been selfish to go on as things were – him enjoying the fruits of captaining England, while the game languished and the conditions for the players remained so poor – the criticisms remained ferocious. Even the fact that the game was already benefiting had no impact. As the arguments raged, Cornhill Insurance emerged as a major sponsor for English cricket, the huge sums involved increasing the payments to Test cricketers to £1000 a game.

Dad has many legacies, as a father, as a friend, as a commentator. High among them is the one that should be acknowledged by every international cricketer today, many of whom are millionaires. When Dad decided to throw in his lot with World Series Cricket, he did so because he believed in the end it would be for the good of the game and for its participants. That was Dad: if he believed in something, if he wanted to achieve something, he went for it.

And in the end, all these years on, even his harshest critics have come to accept that on the matter of what World Series Cricket would ultimately do for the game, Dad was right.

1

Despair, Love and War

IF ONLY MY MIND WAS AS CLEAR AS THE BLUE SOUTH African sky.

Instead it was a tangle of agonising emotions.

The day, still etched deeply into my 94-year-old memory, was 22 July 1945. Hitler had been beaten. Victory in Europe had been declared. Victory over the Japanese forces in the Pacific was less than a month away.

For me, however, the celebrations were overshadowed by the hardest decision I had ever had to make in my 26 years – one that had torn apart my family.

I saw my mother's face through the train window, the sadness in her eyes. I saw the man standing there, my husband, whom I had betrayed. The sadness was deeply imprinted in his thin, war-torn face, too.

There were no tears, not from them, they were beyond them. Inside the carriage I was crying my heart out.

At last the train jerked forward on its journey to Durban. I was left to my own thoughts – dark ones. The harsh words of my sister Dorothy echoed in my mind; the silence of my parents had been equally damning, equally hurtful.

I had grown up in a family full of love. Now my parents were barely speaking to me. Dorothy told me that if my mother died it would be my fault because I had 'caused her heart to bleed'.

The train was part of a hastily put together escape plan. I would go to Durban and stay with another sister, Adelaide, who might be more sympathetic. I had reached this state because my husband, Charles Barry, the man who had wooed and married me just days before he went off to war, had come home. World War Two was to have a profound impact on the shaping of our lives, as it did for many servicemen and their wives. After three years in a prisoner-of-war camp, he had returned to a wife who had to confess to him that there was someone else. Alexander Broom Greig, or Sandy, to the host of people he could charm with his good looks and easy ways.

They say honesty is the best policy but as the train gathered speed, I found it hard to agree. Honesty had brought to me, Charles and our families a sense of agony that now threatened to overwhelm me completely.

I was the only person in the carriage. I could easily walk over to the door and throw myself out. End it all. The thought was a brief one, but it was real.

Then the conductor came through the door of the carriage and asked me for my ticket. Commonsense returned. I had been brought up in a strict Methodist home. Taking your own life was considered a dreadful sin, surely an even greater one than my mother and father now thought me guilty of – abandoning my husband in his greatest moment of need.

As the conductor left me, I put my ticket back in my purse, let my head fall back against the seat and closed my eyes. The peace was fitful, with my mind working hard to make sense of it all.

Josephine Emily Barry, née Taylor, had always been a sensible, caring, thoughtful young lady and one most definitely full of life, not thoughts of death. It was time to find her again.

I was born on 15 June 1919 in De Aar in the Northern Cape province of South Africa. My parents were Daniel Vaughan Taylor and Elizabeth Adelaide Taylor. What a coincidence, they both had the same surname before they married. When they met it was love at first sight, a love that has stretched out over generations to my children, and to their children.

My parents were part of the British colonisation of southern Africa. South Africa had gone through two periods of European colonisation. First, the Dutch established a permanent settlement in Table Bay in 1652. Over the next 150 years they were joined by people of German, French and Flemish descent. They called themselves Boers, meaning 'farmers' in Afrikaans, the language that developed among them, with mainly Dutch origins. Over time they pushed north and east into the hinterland from Cape Town to establish their farms. These days there is little or no reference to Boers in the Rainbow Nation. The Dutch South African's home language is Afrikaans and now, in the new South Africa, there are multiple languages that we all accept and try to speak and understand.

In 1806, the British conquered the Dutch in the Cape Colony and the Boers officially came under British rule in 1814. It was an unhappy co-existence and when the British abolished slavery in 1833, the Boers headed north and east in 1834 on their Great Trek to establish their own republic. After many separately fought battles with the indigenous population, the British established a second colony in Natal, and the Boers established two republics, the Orange Free State and the South African (or Transvaal) Republic.

My forebears were of British descent and settled in De Aar in the Northern Cape just south of the Great Karoo desert. When diamonds were discovered in Kimberley in 1869 and gold discovered in the Transvaal in 1886 many British subjects from the Natal and Cape colonies moved north to make their fortunes. Fearing that the British would attempt to annex the two Boer republics, the Boers launched a pre-emptive strike in October 1899. This was the start of the second Anglo–Boer War and it lasted until May 1902. My father enlisted at the age of eighteen and fought on the side of the British. More than 26,000 women and children died in British concentration camps and the resentment among the Boers (Afrikaners) lives on to this day. In World War One it was no surprise that many Boers, even senior military people, sided with the Germans. Even in World War Two there was much sympathy for the Germans among the Boers.

My father first met my mother when she was eleven years old. He was dressed in his uniform and riding his horse high in the saddle like a prince up to the post office store in which my grandmother worked. My mother was the most beautiful girl, a fairy princess with long, golden hair. Daniel Taylor had told my grandmother to 'keep that young lady for me, I will come back to fetch her when she's grown up'. And he did. He married my mother and together they produced eight children. I was the seventh. Blanche, Dorothy, Adelaide, Daniel, Corrie and Toland were all born before me. Basil was our little brother. We called Daniel 'Dummy' because when he grew up to play rugby, he had the best dummy pass. The opposition always fell for it.

Dad worked as a manager for the Singer Sewing Company. In 1922, when I was about three, he was transferred from De Aar to Queenstown in South Africa's Eastern Cape. What a big decision. In those days, people lived their whole lives in the one town. Queenstown is about 360 kilometres away from De Aar – different terrain and a different world.

Established in 1853 as a military outpost during the frontier wars, Queenstown's centre was laid out in the shape of a hexagon so that it could be easily defended by firing cannons down the six thoroughfares. When my family moved there it was a town of about 5000 white people, with about 6000 black people living on its fringes. Although it was in the Bundu (in the sticks as Australians would say), it served as a commercial centre for the beautiful farming country surrounding it. The town is 180 kilometres inland from East London, which is on the coast, about 1000 kilometres northeast of Cape Town and about 760 kilometres south of Johannesburg. Today Queenstown's urban density spans over 180 square kilometres and has a population in excess of 20,000 people. Though the population has almost doubled since my family moved there over ninety years ago, the white population still stands at around 5000 people.

Even though I was so young, I can remember boarding the train to leave De Aar – there was so much excitement among us children. But I still don't know how my mother and father managed it. I just know they did it. My father was such a leader, such a good provider for his family who only ever wanted to do the right thing by them. But he must have been anxious. He didn't know anyone in Queenstown; how would he and his brood be accepted? And where would they live?

The answer to the last question was a little house we rented in Berry Street which had just two bedrooms. We somehow managed to fit everyone in. We had no choice, rental accommodation was scarce at the time and it was the best Dad could do. It was in a good part of Queenstown and right next door to Daphne Rowles. She is the reason I always remember my first day in Queenstown – the day I met my lifelong friend. Only a week older than me, she and I went through school together.

Daphne and I had many an adventure. My big sister Dorothy had married Cecil King and they had a farm at Newtondale, Tarkastad, just over an hour's drive outside Queenstown. Daphne and I went to the farm for a few days when we were supposed to be studying for a history exam. We nearly became history. We didn't open a book. Instead we rode horses and played tennis and had a real holiday. The day before the exam we came up with this crazy way of avoiding it – we borrowed Daphne's father's old pipe, hid under the quince hedge and puffed and puffed away until we'd both turned green. When I arrived home I was violently sick. My parents called the doctor, thinking my appendix was about to burst. I didn't have to do the exam. I was then given the average mark for the class, which wouldn't have been high. Daphne would have dragged it down because she was so utterly unprepared, but still had to sit for the exam. She had had no lasting effects of all that silly schoolgirl inhalation of her father's tobacco smoke.

Queenstown was quick to take a shine to Taylors and we soon came to love it, too. Because it was so high above sea level, the air was fresh and clean and there was no humidity. A place of great beauty, the town is surrounded by majestic mountains. And the roses, they were everywhere: Queenstown is the Rose Capital of South Africa.

From the day we moved to Queenstown Dad had his eye on a bigger house. Having seen one in Livingstone Road, owned by the local doctor, my father went to see him and told him that if it ever came on the market, he would like to have first option. The doctor said to my father: 'Isn't it strange that you have come here today because I am retiring and leaving Queenstown.' It was as simple as that. So we moved to our great new home on Livingstone Road, Queenstown, a place that became a most loved part of our family's story.

It was an enormous house with a beautiful big garden bordered by a long grapevine that produced gloriously juicy grapes every season. We had an abundance of fruit from the orchard in our own back yard – peaches, apricots, pears, plums, oranges, lemons and figs from a huge fig tree. My mother made marmalades and jams and preserved the fruit; our pantry was always laden with bottles and jars of homemade produce. She also made delicious lemonade.

Dad loved working in his large vegetable garden and would also plant barley to feed the soil.

We had so many places to play in the front garden on the large grassy lawns lined with flowers, shrubs and ferns and trees, including a huge palm tree that rustled in the breeze. We played hide and seek, hopscotch and the boys spent endless hours in the blue gum forest across the road from our house, playing cowboys and crooks and making 'foofie' slides – a type of flying fox. They had to be called in for meals because they were so lost in their play. I also loved the veranda at Livingstone Road where my mother and father used to sit and chat.

The house had six bedrooms and an enclosed porch on the veranda where my brothers slept. A long wooden passage wended its way down the centre with my parents' beautiful room on the right. I always felt secure because Basil and I shared a bedroom that had a door leading into Mum and Dad's room. We were the youngest, so we went to bed long before the rest of the family but we could hear them all chatting in the lounge. We used to pester them with our constant calls of, 'Good night Mummy and Daddy … good night all.' At first the response would be warm, but eventually we were firmly told to go to sleep.

The kitchen had a magical feeling, oozing warmth and homeliness. There was always someone busy in there – chopping vegetables, kneading bread, baking biscuits, topping up the coffee percolator, pouring endless cups for family and friends. A big black wood-burning stove dominated the room and I can remember huge loaves of hot bread coming out of the oven. With homemade butter and jam, these were a meal in themselves. It was lovely the way that the smell of fresh, homemade bread drifted throughout the house. There was large pantry next door to the kitchen and the wooden shelves were always heavily laden with flour, meal and other cooking essentials.

We didn't have showers, we had baths. The hot water was produced by lighting a fire under the geyser, an old-fashioned boiler. When Basil and I were young, Mum and Dad washed us in their room in a large zinc bath. Dad would light the fire in their bedroom in the winter and the tub would be placed next to the roaring fire. Dad would wash us and Mum would dry us and dress us in our pyjamas ready for supper. My mother and father did everything together, they were a real team. Mum called him Dan; Dad called her Flossie because of her beautiful golden hair.

Not only did our family move into Livingstone Road, but so did Andries, one of my father's employees who had come with us all the way from De Aar. He was an Afrikaner, a poor man with no family. When he heard we were moving to Queenstown he said to my father, 'What am I going to do without you?' My dad knew he would have been lost, so he asked him to come with us. This was another sign of dad's great kindness. Andries was a great help to Dad, doing many of the chores but ultimately, he felt Andries could manage on his own and helped him to find a job on the railways. Our house was just across the road from the railway station.

Along with Andries, we also had maids who worked inside the house, washing and cleaning. Most foreigners frowned on this aspect of South African life but I believed they did so without understanding the situation. Work was so scarce. Many black African men headed to Johannesburg to work in the mines and their wives invariably headed to

Cape Town to work in service. They only saw each other when they returned for a couple of weeks over Christmas. Children had to be looked after by aunties or grandmothers and those aunties sought income by doing domestic duties for white families. Many were provided with food and lodgings, uniforms, healthcare and a small income.

Our daily routine was a simple but wonderful one for me and my brothers and sisters. It began with our father bringing us a cup of coffee and a dry rusk, a Boer biscuit. We all dunked our rusks into our hot drinks. In the evening we would always sit together for dinner – a big family around a large yellowwood table. I know Dad loved those moments when he had everyone close by.

Although the Victorian era had passed elsewhere in the world, it hadn't in conservative Queenstown and it definitely hadn't passed in my household. My father kept his family very close, especially when his daughters began attracting the attention of the young men of Queenstown. Instead of taking us out, the suitors were encouraged, almost obliged, to join the family for meals, games and our homemade concerts. One of the games was 'Black Market' and my sister Dorothy donated 10 shillings' worth of farthings so we could play. Many years on, my own children would also play this game. My dad also had a game with six little horses. It had a winder and when Dad wound it up, it made the horses race around a track and everyone could have a bet, but only a little one.

Queenstown, and our little bit of it in Livingstone Road, was the perfect environment in which to bring up a family, particularly one as big as ours always seemed to be. It was home to not just my mother and father and siblings but also other family members. As big as our house was, though, I don't know how we accommodated everyone, we just did. My maternal grandmother lived with us and later after the Depression, Ray Hardwick, my sister Adelaide's son who was nine years younger than me, also came to live with us because his parents were living and working in Durban. He moved in with us so he could complete his education at Queen's College. He only went home to his parents in Durban once or twice a year – depending on whether they could afford the train fare. Our domestic staff lived in the 'Location' just outside of Queenstown. Our maids walked thirty minutes each day from the Location to our house on Livingstone Road.

The Depression in 1929 hit people around Queenstown hard, mainly the farmers. But fortunately for our family it wasn't so bad. My father had a secure job at Singer, and my elder sisters all had good clerical jobs, and they brought that money home. While other people still had horses and buggies, we had a car.

There was not a lot of money around, but there was enough. When I was still quite young, if I had a ticky, a threepence coin, I would buy six long toffees. I would eat five, then cut the sixth one in half and while my parents were at the cinema, I put one half on my mother's side of the bed and one half on my father's side. When Basil and I woke up in the morning we'd have a Lucky Packet beside us, put there by my parents to say thanks. Lucky Packets had sweets in them, plus a little surprise.

Religion was another special part of my childhood. I loved going on Sunday School picnics to a place called Flowers Holt just outside Queenstown. We went to church each

Sunday, to the Wesley Methodists church in Queenstown.
I can still remember the song when the collection was taken:

> *Hear the pennies dropping*
> *Listen to them fall*
> *Ev'ry one for Jesus*
> *He shall have them all*
> *Dropping, Dropping, Dropping, Dropping,*
> *Hear the pennies fall*
> *Ev'ry one for Jesus*
> *He shall have them all.*

When I left school I took a commercial course in Grey
Street at Mr Wilkinson's college – bookkeeping, shorthand,
typing, etc. I rode on my bicycle each day to college. I got
my first job through my brother-in-law when he advised
me that Mr Snell (a chemist) was looking for a secretary.
I did all his bookkeeping for him in the back office of his
one-man chemist. My next job was as a clerk at Standard
Bank.

I loved music. From 1937, my nephew Ray and I shared
a bedroom for about two years. I was eighteen and Ray
was nine. I loved having little Ray around. We often used
to listen to my collection of the latest records. Ray would
wind up the gramophone and play them non-stop while I
was getting ready to go to work. I can still remember some
of the music we used to play – 'Moods' by Raie Da Costa
and '(In My) Solitude' by Duke Ellington. Dad also had an
old-fashioned wireless on which we used to listen to all the
hits. He would call out, 'The hits of the week are on!' and
we would all rush to listen.

As the youngest daughter, I benefited the most from Dad's mellowing and slow abandonment of the Victorian age restrictions. Courting was allowed to go on outside the home and I loved to go dancing. According to Ray, I was always saying: 'I wonder if some little fairy will pack my clothes away and tidy our bedroom while I'm dancing.' The little fairy was of course Ray.

Courting back then was so different from what my own children experienced. Women didn't drink in bars. If the boys wanted to see you, they would first come to your house and sit and talk with the whole family. When they did have permission to take you out, they would take you to dances or to the Bioscope – the travelling cinema – and it cost sevenpence for a ticket. I really enjoyed dancing. There were lots of dances in Queenstown and I accepted invitations to go with whoever asked me first, on the condition that they were able to pass the tests set by my family. I never wanted to be tied to one boy – they were all just good friends.

Friends and family, friendship and love: there was so much of it. From those early days in De Aar and Berry Street, through my school days and right up to the day when I would leave school and get my first job, it was the most delightful childhood a girl could wish for.

2

War-torn Bride

I WAS EIGHTEEN, WHEN I MET CHARLES BARRY FOR THE first time. I was standing on Cuthbert's Corner in Queenstown, wearing a pink dress. It must have been love at first sight for him because, he told me later, he had said to a friend he was with at the time: 'See that lovely girl on the corner in the pink dress, well one day I will marry her.'

Charles became persistent in his pursuit of me – and I was happy for him to be persistent. He was a charming man who had moved to Queenstown to work in the Chamber of Mines and soon became one of the regular visitors to Livingstone Road. My parents quickly grew to like him very much. With their approval, Charles and I went out to dances and to the Bioscope and I began to fall in love with him. I couldn't wait for him to come to our house to fetch me and take me out to dance. We had such fun together. We laughed a lot. We just seemed perfect for each other.

At night, my last thoughts before I went to sleep, after I had said my prayers, were of Charles. The moment I realised just how much I had fallen in love with him came when he told me he was being transferred in his job to King William's Town. It was about 160 kilometres away, though distance would not cause our love to diminish. When we met, we would run to each other and hug and kiss and then the laughing would start again. That's how strong our love was. Then the time came to part and as I watched him leave for King William's Town I would feel tears running down my face. I would start counting the days before I could see him again.

Then came the jolt that would alter the course of our lives far more than a transfer to King William's Town. World War Two broke out and Charles did what so many other young South African men, including my brothers Toland and Dummy, did: he enlisted. Even if many Afrikaners didn't, the young men of English descent in South Africa still felt a great love for the Mother Country. In 1940, Charles joined the Kaffrarian Rifles. (Kaffraria was a name given to parts of the Eastern Cape by the British.)

That year, to my absolute delight, Charles proposed to me. He had sought my father's approval, Dad had said yes and there I was, an engaged woman. I couldn't believe it: I was in love with this wonderful man, and we were to be married. It was such a marvellous moment, even with the talk of war all around.

After the excitement of our engagement, Charles returned to Pietermaritzburg, where he was stationed, and I went back to work in Queenstown, daydreaming about being Mrs Charles Barry and wondering if it would ever happen.

Then one day he phoned me from Pietermaritzburg. 'Let's get married, Joycie, and as soon as possible, before I go away!' he yelled down the phone. As much as my parents approved of Charles, they were firmly against the idea. 'There's a war on,' they said, 'and you're too young.' I was distraught. I loved Charles Barry and I loved the idea of being married to him, but I was also their daughter. Charles persisted; he kept phoning me and phoning my parents. Eventually, he convinced them to give us their blessing. We had just enough time to have the Banns of Marriage read three times at church in the three weeks before the wedding, which would be held when Charles came to Queenstown on embarkation leave.

There was no time to send out invitations, so we put a notice in the paper: 'All friends are invited.' In August 1940, at the age of 21, I married Charles Barry. Daphne Rowles, my childhood friend from that first day in Queenstown, was my bridesmaid; my niece Meryl, Blanche's daughter, was flower girl. Charles's best man was Dennis Scott, a captain in the First City Regiment and also a teacher at Queen's College in Queenstown, which my sons Tony and Ian were later to attend. Dennis Scott eventually became my younger son Ian's housemaster at Connaught House.

Since there was little time for a honeymoon, after our reception we went to Kalk Bay to visit Charles's parents. On our wedding night, we only made it as far as Fort Beaufort before it got too dark to drive, and so we stayed the night in a hotel in the little village. The following day we arrived at Kalk Bay, a pretty little fishing village on the coast of False Bay on the southern side of Cape Town. Dad and Mum Barry were the most marvellous parents. Dad Barry was a magistrate in Cape Town and his family was highly respected. They had prepared a great welcome for us and there were presents from all of their Cape Town friends. But still there was the anxiety over the war. The Barrys had three boys, Douglas, Charles and Brownlee. They all served.

We spent a week at Kalk Bay, a glorious week in each other's company in which I went from being a girl to a woman who was deeply in love. Then, before we knew it, that time was up and we had to leave. We said our goodbyes to Mum and Dad Barry. They weren't just saying farewell to a young married couple, they were also saying goodbye to a son going off to war. There were tears and long hugs.

At first Charles and I travelled on the same train, but at De Aar, there came the moment we had silently dreaded for weeks: we had to part, me for Queenstown, Charles for Pietermaritzburg. We hugged and kissed and cried. I told him I loved him and would love him forever. He told me to be waiting there for him to come home. Then the steam train's whistle pierced the moment. My train was leaving. I waited until the last minute before I got on board. I felt my hand slip slowly out of his. When I got on the train, I ran to a seat by the window so I could still see Charles. He had tears streaming down his face and was waving his hand. I cried too. All my happiness at being married was drowned by those tears. I could not help the thought that had been aching in my mind while we were in Kalk Bay. Would Charles come home from the war? Would this be the last time I would see this man?

It wasn't. The weekend before Charles was due to be shipped out, I got a call from Val Wheelwright, the wife of Dudley Wheelwright, a fellow soldier in the Kaffrarian rifles. She lived in Nqamakwe, about 120 kilometres from Queenstown. When she asked me if I would like to see Charles, I told her of course I would. She said all I had to do was get to Nqamakwe and she would take me the rest of the way. My father immediately volunteered to drive me.

Val Wheelwright was full of fun. In those days, very few people had phones. Instead there were phone booths, or ticky boxes – you had to put tickies into the phone to make your call. Just as we were about to meet with our men at a hotel Val had chosen, she said: 'Let's have a bit of fun, Joycie, hide in the phone booth.' She was going to play a trick on Charles. When she met the men, she said, 'I'm so sorry, Charles, Joycie couldn't make it.' Before Charles had much time to feel disappointed, a waiter came up to him and said, 'Excuse me, Corporal Barry, you are wanted on the phone.' Val said, 'Oh that must be Joycie because I told her where we'd be staying.' Of course Valerie was in cahoots with the waiter. When Charles came out to the ticky boxes and saw me standing there, he nearly went crackers with excitement. I got the biggest hug and lots of kisses and he kept saying, 'Oh Joycie, oh Joycie.' After the weekend, Val returned home but Charles asked me to stay because they were leaving soon. He planned to get out of camp to see me as often as he could. We spent every precious moment together we could until one morning I woke up and the camp was gone. It was an extremely lonely and sad trip home to Queenstown.

The Kaffrarian Rifles left South Africa on the HMT *Nieuw Holland*. They became part of the 2nd South African Infantry Division and were sent to the Western Desert in North Africa, Egypt and Libya. The Western Desert was vital because of the strategic importance of the Suez Canal in Egypt and the oil fields in the Persian Gulf. Initially, they went to El Alamein in Egypt, where their first job was to prepare the defences, a job well done as it turned out. The Kaffrarian Rifles then went into action in the attack on the Fortress of Bardia. They suffered severe casualties in that battle but the real tragedy came at Tobruk, a small Libyan village about 130 kilometres from the Libyan–Egyptian border. Tobruk was of vital strategic importance because of its deep-water harbour and substantial fresh water supplies. The Australians, British, Poles and Indians held it from April 1941 until December 1941 against fierce attacks from German General Erwin Rommel and his Afrika Korps and Italian allies. Rommel then withdrew to the west.

On 26 May 1942, Rommel mounted his second offensive, which became known as the Battle of Gazala. It was fought around Tobruk, which was defended by the British 8th Army and two South African infantry divisions. On 21 June 1942, General Rommel launched a surprise attack on Tobruk. Confusion reigned. Nobody knew what the orders were. Some were told not to shoot, others to fight to the death, or every man for himself. Charles didn't fire a shot before he was captured by the Germans.

My brother Toland, who was also in Tobruk, was able to escape. He jumped on a truck and caught up with the British 8th Army, who were withdrawing to El Alamein. Others were not so fortunate. More than 200 were killed. Charles was one of 10,000 South Africans taken prisoner by Rommel's soldiers. Rommel then immediately handed his prisoners over to the Italians, because he needed his best German soldiers to fight the Allies. He apologised to the South Africans as he did it. Rommel thought the Italians were 'miserable soldiers'. They were cruel beyond belief. Prisoners were refused water and food and even shot in the back. Then the Italians turned the South Africans over to the local Senussi tribesmen, who were even crueller.

Eventually, they were sent to Italy. There the authorities were either so disorganised or just so cruel that there wasn't enough food. When Italy capitulated to the Allies, the prison gates were thrown open and this time everyone knew what the orders were: 'Every man for himself.'

Charles, Dudley Wheelwright and Cecil King, my sister Dorothy's husband, set off with a group of Allied soldiers through the countryside. They fought alongside the Partisans, the Italians who had taken the side of the Allies against the Germans and the Fascist Government of the Italian dictator Benito Mussolini. At one point the Partisans hid Charles, Dudley and Cecil under hay on a wagon. It was like a scene from a movie. If they had been discovered, everyone would have been shot – both the soldiers and the Partisans. When it became too dangerous for them to stay, the Partisans asked them to move on. They were on their own. Searching for food, they split up. Charles went one way, Cecil and Dudley another.

Cecil and Dudley's group was caught by the Germans. Tragically, they fell victim to Il Massacro del Grappa, a dreadful slaughter in which the Germans killed more than 200 people – Partisans, civilians and Allied soldiers. At one place, the Germans told eighteen Allied soldiers to take off their boots, dig their own graves and then they shot them. They tried to conceal the identities of the soldiers, twelve of whom were South African. Eventually their names became known and Lance Corporal Cecil Newtown King and DD

Wheelwright were among them. They were both buried in the Padua War Cemetery.

Back in South Africa, we had no knowledge of what had happened. Cecil and Dudley were simply declared missing in action. It was horrible for Dorothy and Valerie, for all of us. Every morning we would all wake up hoping for news, or that no news was good news. The stories of the battlefront and the home front are inextricably linked.

Charles suffered a different fate from that of Cecil and Dudley. Caught by another group of Germans, he was imprisoned in Italy for a short time before being sent to Germany. I received news through the Red Cross that he was a prisoner of war in Germany. The news, and the anguish, was shocking but I can also remember thinking at least I know he is alive, not missing in action.

Since that day at the fall of Tobruk, Charles had suffered the most dreadful of times. I received letters from him through the Red Cross, though sadly they were few and far between. Initially I wrote back regularly but as time dragged on I became very depressed. I would wake up in the morning and my first thoughts would be of Charles. Where was he, was he suffering, was he even still alive? Eventually I convinced myself he was not coming home. When that happened, the black cloud I felt I was living under grew darker and darker. I wanted to keep writing to Charles, but not knowing whether he got my letters, not knowing if he would ever come home, I found it hard to find the words. Soon it became impossible.

3

From Out of the Blue

When Charles was captured for a second time by the Germans in 1943, I was working at Standard Bank's Queenstown branch. On the weekends, I played hockey for Queenstown, which for a brief time took my mind off Charles and his awful fate. It relieved the relentless anxiety of wondering where he was and whether he was even still alive.

During World War Two, Queenstown had again become a military town. We had a training camp for airmen because there was a shortage due to all the heavy losses in Europe. Experienced RAF airmen from Britain were sent there to train young South Africans as aircrew, among them Squadron Leader Sandy Greig, the officer in charge. Everyone called him 'the Skipper'. Though very young at twenty-two, he already had a distinguished career.

Sandy was born Alexander Broom Greig on 5 March 1922, in Bathgate in Scotland. It is a Greig tradition for the males to have either William or Alexander in their names. That's why my eldest son Tony was named Anthony William, and his brother Ian was named Ian Alexander. Sandy's middle name, Broom, was his mother Elizabeth's maiden name. His mother died when he was eight and even though he lost her so early in his life, he never stopped talking about her. He loved his mother, a physical education teacher and a woman of great beauty. He also had a sister, Isobel, five years his junior.

The Greigs have a fascinating family tree. They are related to the world-famous Norwegian composer Edvard Grieg, who wrote 'Peer Gynt'. After the Battle of Culloden in 1746, in which the Scots were slaughtered by the English led by the merciless Duke of Cumberland, Edvard Grieg's great-grandfather moved to Norway. At that time he spelled his surname Greig, the same as Sandy's family, but later changed it to Grieg.

Sandy went to school at George Watson's Boys' College in Edinburgh, one of Scotland's finest schools. Rugby was a big part of the school's activities and Sandy loved the game; however, like so many other young men of his time, the outbreak of World War Two denied him the chance to excel beyond his school years. When he left school, he moved to London to take up a position with the Royal Bank of Scotland.

On 3 September 1939, the British Prime Minister Neville Chamberlain declared war on Germany. Sandy enlisted two hours later. He bluffed his age – he was just seventeen and a half. Like a lot of parents, his father thought the RAF was a safer prospect than the trenches, so he helped Sandy bump up his age. Sandy had said that he wanted to join the RAF and if his father didn't help him, he would wait until he was old enough and join the Army. Having served in World War One, William Greig knew all about the trenches.

Now an enlisted airman, Sandy's connection with Africa began as a trainee pilot when he was sent to Southern Rhodesia (now called Zimbabwe). After he crashed a plane, it was suggested he become a navigator and he was posted to Bomber Command. Winston Churchill said of Bomber Command: 'The fighters are our salvation but the bombers alone provide the means to victory.' Bomber Command crews were asked to fly highly dangerous missions over Germany, bombing city after city while being shot at from the ground and the air. It was their job to break the spirit of the Germans and somehow not have their own spirits broken.

Members of Bomber Command came from all over the world. There were Canadians, Australians, New Zealanders, Poles, Czechs, South Africans, French, Americans, Jamaicans and Rhodesians. The average age of all these brave young men was 22. They suffered awful losses – 55,573 out of 125,000 were killed; 8,402 were wounded and 9,838 were taken prisoner. Only one in six survived 30 missions. One in 40 survived 60 missions. Miraculously, and there is no other word for it, Sandy Greig survived 54 missions. Part of it was due to his navigational skills – he re-wrote the book on that.

Before there could be accurate bombing, there had to be accurate navigation. Sandy and his crew were often forced to fly at night to avoid German fighters and flak. It was his responsibility to navigate his aircraft across Europe to their targets in darkness and through frequent cloud and bad weather.

Once he was able to get his bomber to a target area, Sandy and his crew then had to identify their specific target (for example, a factory, railway yards, or docks). Often cloud, mist, fog, haze, smoke or industrial pollution made the job almost impossible.

He had many close calls. During the attack on Poissy on 2 April 1942, he navigated his plane to do a second run to release the five remaining bombs. His plane had already been damaged from light anti-aircraft fire, but he asked the pilot to take him back in under the radar, the bombs were released and they managed to get back home. During a daylight raid on Lübeck when his Stirling bomber was attacked by five enemy fighters, he navigated his aircraft for twenty minutes down to roof- and treetop height until the fighters gave up the chase.

In September 1942, when he was an Acting Flying Officer in Squadron 218, he was awarded the Distinguished Flying Cross and in 1943, as squadron leader with 101 Squadron, he was given the Distinguished Service Order. He received his DFC medal from King George VI. His father and sister Isobel proudly accompanied him to Buckingham Palace.

In October 1942, Sandy was posted to 101 Squadron at Holme-on-Spalding Moor. In the first two and half years of the war, only one navigator had been made a squadron leader. In March 1943, Air Vice-Marshal EAB Rice recommended such an appointment be made to the Commander-in-Chief, Air Marshal Arthur Harris, as follows:

1. Under the provisions of your letter BC/C 23068/P dated October 1942, authority is requested for Flying Officer (Acting Flight Lieutenant) AB Greig DFC

– 68753, Navigator – No 101 Squadron – Holme
be reposted to No 101 Squadron to fill the post of a
Flight Commander consequent on the formation of a
third flight.

2. This officer has completed one operational tour
[30 sorties] and six sorties of his present tour. He
is an exceptionally able officer and moreover, has
an outstanding enthusiasm for flying, particularly
operational flying, in which he has shown great
ability not only as a navigator but also as an officer.
He possesses pronounced organising abilities and
has powers of leadership and personality which
mark him as fully qualified for the post of Flight
Commander.

3. I strongly recommend this appointment as a
special case.

The promotion to squadron leader came through shortly
afterwards, on 2 April. In less than a month after his
twenty-first birthday, Sandy was given command of his own
Flight. In 101 Squadron initially, there were 'A' Flight and
'B' Flight, with 10 bombers in each Flight. They added a
third flight called 'C' Flight and Sandy was put in charge
of 'C' Flight. Most of the group were Australians, whom
Sandy had a high level of respect for as airmen. He thought
they were the most courageous men you could put on
an aeroplane, but on the ground they caused him great
anguish as they were uncontrollable and sometimes a law
unto themselves.

Sandy was a superb squadron leader. He just had an
innate ability to lead others. The safety of his men was

always to be put ahead of his own. When he was shot down over the North Sea, he was burnt as he attempted to rescue the pilot from the plane. In another crash, Sandy lost feeling in the lower part of one side of his face, which stayed with him for the rest of his life.

On 20 August 1943, as squadron leader with Squadron 101, he was given the Distinguished Service Order. The citation read:

> This officer, who has completed many sorties since
> being awarded the Distinguished Flying Cross,
> is a fearless and courageous captain. His great
> navigational ability and fine fighting qualities have
> inspired all with whom he has flown and have played
> a large part in the many successes obtained. His
> record of achievement is worthy of the highest praise.

After substantial research, the medicos advised Bomber Command that aircrew were likely to develop psychiatric illnesses after 30 sorties. Having completing 54 sorties, therefore, Sandy was told he was being transferred to Empire Air Navigation School in South Africa to train more young men to risk their lives for the RAF, King and Country. Sandy was not overly excited about the transfer. Given the choice, he would have remained operational, but the RAF saw his value as an instructor and his destiny was decided for him. He arrived in South Africa in September 1943, and it wasn't long before it was obvious that his war service had taken a toll on him. Within weeks of his transfer, Sandy was taken to hospital with what was diagnosed as post-catarrhal jaundice. This was no doubt related to Sandy's heavy drinking during the war. It wasn't until mid-January 1944 that Sandy's health was cleared and he could report for duty.

We first met when my hockey team was asked to play a game against the officers. After the game, we were all invited to the Officers' Mess. A South African officer I knew told me that 'the Skipper' would like to meet me. I asked who this 'Skipper' was and he said 'Sandy Greig'. I told him I wasn't interested because I was married. When we left, Sandy Greig was standing at the door and I just walked straight past him. He found out I was working at the Standard Bank and phoned me there and asked me to have lunch with him at the Grand Hotel the following Sunday. I sarcastically said: 'Oh yes, I will meet you.' I didn't think it was right for me to go and I had no intention of meeting him. Instead, I went to church and then played squash.

After I came home, the phone rang. It was Sandy. He said: 'I waited for you for over an hour.' When I told him I was married and only went out with friends, he immediately asked me to go to the pictures with him. I declined. He then phoned a few more times and, on further thought, I agreed as I felt that no harm would come from going to the pictures. However, I insisted Sandy came and fetched me.

Although I was married to Charles Barry, I started meeting Sandy on a more regular basis. I was becoming torn. I was extremely depressed about the fact that my husband was a prisoner of war in Germany, maybe even dead. How did I know? Here was a handsome man called Sandy Greig making a great fuss over me and in so doing throwing a little light into my life. Paradoxically, because I was married, this little bit of light increased my anguish.

Sandy came to our home and my parents couldn't stand him. They felt it was wrong for me to be seeing him because I was a married woman and my husband was a prisoner of war. They were right. But something was happening to me, something I couldn't stop.

Other family members got on well with Sandy. Toland's wife, Elsie, had come to stay at Livingstone Road because she was pregnant; Mildred and Corrie were also pregnant and staying with us. So one day Sandy walked into our lounge room with three pregnant women sitting there and every one of them thought he was a lovely chap. When Toland came home on leave, Mum told him how concerned she was about my relationship with this Sandy Greig. She knew what was happening: I was falling in love. She asked Toland to go out to the camp, see Sandy and ask him to stay away from me but when he went there and met Sandy, they hit it off straight away and he forgot everything Mum had asked him to say.

Eventually, I could deny it no more. I was in love with Sandy, the Skipper, this strapping, tall, handsome, glorious man who had arrived in my life out of the blue. It was something I had tried to stop happening. I knew exactly what love was, because I had loved Charles so deeply. But even with the guilt, I felt that love slipping away, being replaced by this new one for Sandy.

Alone at night, I questioned myself over and over again. I said my prayers. Some nights I would fall asleep thinking of Charles and what he might be suffering – or whether he was even alive. Other nights, my last thoughts would be of Sandy. It was about this time that my letters to Charles stopped. Charles and I talked about it later, and it was painful for both of us. 'You couldn't even find the time to write to me,' he said. I said to him as honestly as I could, 'Sandy had lifted me out of a very dark place and I was in love.' There are some things in life that are hard to fight.

I was 26 when the war ended and the time came for those prisoners of war who had somehow survived to come home. I received a telegram saying that Mrs Charles Barry should meet her husband at the wharves in Cape Town. It had the details of the boat and the date but the thing that stood out were the words 'Mrs Charles Barry'. That's who I was, not Joyce Taylor.

It was all such a shock. Charles was alive, he was coming home, and I was in love with another man. My hands trembled as I read that telegram. I put it under my pillow, knelt down beside my bed and began to pray: 'God, will you take over this situation, please, and help me to do it your way, not my way.' And I left it like that. I didn't tell a single soul that day about the telegram.

The next day I took the cable down to Mr Bennett, the manager at the Standard Bank, and asked for permission to go to Cape Town to meet Charles. He said I couldn't go; I was doing a man's job at the bank and he needed me there. Then he asked if there were anyone else who could go and I said: 'No, I am his wife and I must go.' Still Mr Bennett wouldn't let me go.

Instead of being able to meet Charles off the boat, I had to phone his parents and ask if they would do it. But I told Mr Bennett that as soon as I could train someone to do my job, I would be leaving. Two weeks later, Mum and Dad took me to the station and I set off by train for Cape Town. I had already told Sandy I was going back to Charles. I asked him not to contact me. It was a tricky situation, but I was going to be honest with everyone. I didn't want to see Sandy and I didn't want him to phone.

It took two days to get to Cape Town by train and by the time I got there I was a nervous wreck. Charles was at the station to meet me. The sight of him was another shock: he was as thin as a stick and covered in boils. He just looked completely tired out, almost completely unrecognisable as the young, fit man I had last seen in Pietermaritzburg in 1940.

He had beautiful flowers for me hidden behind his back and when he presented them to me we hugged each other. But there was none of the laughter, none of the magic. I was harbouring a guilty secret, and I think he knew it. He said to me in a quiet voice: 'I don't want to drive straight home, let's go and sit at the Rhodes Memorial under the Lion's Head.' The Lion's Head is a mountain in Cape Town, a place where people go to sit and talk. His very first question was: 'Have you met anybody else?' I looked him straight in the face and stayed true to my pledge to be honest to everyone. 'Yes I have,' I said. Straight back at me, he said: 'Do you love him?' I said: 'I do, Charles, and I'd like a divorce.'

In the Taylor family, in any family at that time, divorce was seen as a disgraceful thing. But over that two-day journey to Cape Town, as thousands of thoughts whirled around in my head, I had made up my mind that I wanted a divorce. I just knew by now that I loved Sandy Greig that much.

We went to Charles's parents' home, and he could not have been a more perfect gentleman. He showed no anger towards me. We were sitting in their parlour and just as Charles was pouring the drinks Dad Barry said:

'Oh Charles, there's a message for you, your friend phoned you this afternoon; his name was Greig, somebody Greig. I've written down the phone number. Please phone him.' I blushed and began to tremble. Charles saw me. He turned and said: 'Look here, Joycie, what sort of sherry would you like?' He was changing the conversation to protect me. We drank to Charles's homecoming.

After Mum and Dad Barry had gone to bed, we went for a walk to get some sea air. Charles said: 'Joyce, I would like to go and phone this number at the ticky box.' I went with him. He rang the number and asked if he could speak to Squadron Leader Greig. They put him through and he said: 'This is Sergeant Barry speaking.' Sandy's response was, 'Oh, I wanted to speak to Joyce.' I spoke to him, but my mind was in such turmoil I have no idea what I said.

Charles then took over again: 'I would like to meet you; can you come to Cape Town?' Sandy said he could, he had a plane at his disposal. Charles said: 'Right, let's make it tomorrow or the next day.' They made it the next day.

We arranged to meet at the Waldorf Tea Rooms. Charles made other arrangements, too. He told me that when we met at the Waldorf, I was to pour the tea, and then leave. I told him I would do anything he asked because I knew I was the one at fault. I had betrayed him. At the Waldorf Tea Rooms, Charles and I sat down in silence. I put the cups out. I poured the tea, but to this day I don't know how I managed not to spill it into the saucers. I was shaking that much. Then in walked Sandy, this big, fine-looking, healthy man in his RAF uniform. They introduced themselves and sat down for tea. With my hands still shaking, I drank my tea. Then I left.

I found out later from both of them that Charles spoke to Sandy as though he was my father. He asked Sandy if he could support me. He told Sandy that I had been a very spoilt girl since I was young – spoilt by my parents, my sisters and my brothers – and that I had come from a home of nurture and love. Sandy would have to be able to provide that, too.

I walked around Cape Town for an hour then returned. What would happen next, I wondered? Well, of all things, Sandy invited us, both Charles and me, to the Officers' Mess in Cape Town to have lunch. We went, but I think I played with my food. I couldn't eat, I was still shaking. Then the three of us caught the train to Wynberg. There we had to change for Charles and me to travel to Kalk Bay. As we waited on the station for our next train, Charles said: 'I am just going over the road to the hotel. I will leave you and Sandy to have a chat.' He went over there and he met up with two sailors and got as drunk as a coot.

It was the first time Sandy and I had had a chance to speak privately. I made it very clear to him I was not happy that he had contacted me and that he was not to do it again. Not until I had sorted things out. He said: 'It is very hard for me, I love you.' I rebuked him. I said: 'I am with my husband, the man I have betrayed.'

Sandy's train came and he set off to the railway station closest to where he had landed his plane. Our train arrived just as Charles came staggering out of the hotel and we went back to his parents' house in Kalk Bay. Nothing was said on the train, given the state Charles was in.

As if all this wasn't enough to have my head spinning, we received a call from my father in Queenstown. Cecil King, my sister Dorothy's husband, was no longer missing in action. It was now confirmed. He had been killed by the Germans.

My mother and father went over to Cecil's farm and brought Dorothy back to their home in Queenstown. There was Dorothy with her two young children, Rodney and Joan. She had lost her husband, and they had lost their father, and there was me with my husband whom I didn't want. How could I possibly tell my family now about my intentions to leave Charles for Sandy?

Charles and I drove to Queenstown to see Dorothy; Charles had been one of the last people to see Cecil alive and he wanted to grieve with Dorothy. Charles then went to see Mr Rose, the attorney in Queenstown, and told him we would like to get a divorce. His exact words to Mr Rose were: 'We want a quiet divorce.'

There was nothing quiet about my parents' reaction. Mum and Dad became absolutely frantic. They made such a fuss of Charles and ignored me completely. Dorothy then said, and I remember the words and the hurt they caused so clearly even now, 'If Mummy dies, you are going to be the cause of it because you are making her heart bleed because of the divorce.'

I could hardly blame my sister, she was such a wreck. She just sat in our house. Cecil's picture was on the mantelpiece and she stared at it all day. After she said that to me about Mummy, she didn't speak, she just sat there staring at the picture of Cecil for weeks.

They were the first harsh words I had ever had with my family and the first time in my whole life that my mother and father wouldn't speak to me. It was all Charles this and

Charles that; they were making so much of a fuss of him and making it so difficult for me that after a while I decided I'd had enough, I had to go. I phoned Adelaide, my sister who lived in Durban. I told her I wanted to come to stay with her. I informed my parents I was leaving, and again Dorothy looked at me and spoke those awful words, telling me I was breaking Mummy's heart.

Mum and Charles saw me off at the station. Our goodbyes were very sad. From the way they looked at me, I don't think they believed I was going to Adelaide. They thought I was going to meet Sandy, but I wasn't and it hurt that they didn't believe me. On the train, I suddenly got so desperate I felt like taking my life.

I don't know if I really had the courage to jump. It was a terrible sin to take your own life. Whatever the reason, in the end I didn't do it. Another woman came into the carriage and for a while I had something to take my mind off my problems. She was very strange. She was going to a wedding. It was an overnight train and the seats in the car had to be converted to beds. This lady did not lie down to sleep, but instead she slept sitting upright in her bed so as not to mess up her hair. As strange as she was, I was grateful for her presence. It was something else to think about other than my own turmoil.

I arrived at Adelaide's place a total wreck. I was just so miserable about everything and at one stage I even said to her, 'I am going back to Charles.' She said, 'You are not doing anything of the kind; you are going to get well first.' I must just have looked that bad.

She was so kind. She would run down to the corner shop and buy fresh eggs and make me a boiled egg for breakfast.

She fed me with those eggs and with her kindness and she helped clear the confusion out of my mind. I took up squash, which also helped a great deal.

Back in Queenstown, Mr Rose was working on our 'quiet divorce'. I received an affidavit. I had ten days to respond; if I didn't the divorce would be final. I made no response. I was ready to let go.

We were now able to go our separate ways. I had given all the wedding presents to Charles, except for my bridesmaid's present. I also had the money the army had paid me while Charles was a prisoner of war, which I had put it into post office bonds. When the divorce was finalised, I told Charles we were going to share it and that's what we did. He accepted the money, all the wedding presents, and the love of my family.

The moment those ten days were up, something else happened. The phone rang. It was Sandy. 'You're free,' he said. I told him I was. We planned to marry and move to Pretoria, where Sandy was stationed. He had been offered a full-time commission in the RAF, a job for the rest of his life, and everyone was telling him what a fool he would be if he didn't take it.

On 8 December 1945 we were married in Durban in a nice little church. Adelaide was my maid of honour. My mother and father didn't come, but they said they would come to see us in Pretoria after our honeymoon. It was a small wedding, and I was wearing a short dress, not a long flowing one as before. It was a simple outfit with a little hat to match, and then we had the reception at the Playhouse before setting off on our honeymoon to Karridene, a seaside resort near Durban. There, we slept together for the first time. It was wonderful. The burden of guilt was gone. I could now enjoy my Sandy as man and wife.

At the end of our honeymoon, I remember we had just four shillings and a ticky left until he got his next pay cheque. We were broke, but we were rich because we now had each other. We went from Karridene back to Pretoria and stayed in a hotel. The hotel manager was happy for us to settle our account later when Sandy's pay came in. Soon afterwards, my mother and father arrived. I remember that moment clearly, too, as I was so anxious about their reaction. My father got out of the taxi and went straight to Sandy, put his arm around him and said, 'Welcome to the family, son.' My mother did the same. At last, it was over. My parents were talking to me again.

Toland was also in Pretoria. Still in the Army, he too had been offered a full-time commission but his wife Elsie said if he took it, she would leave him. Eventually I followed Toland and my mother and father back to Queenstown while Sandy attended to his duties in Pretoria. It was great to be home at Livingstone Road and to again feel the love of my whole family.

In Pretoria, Sandy received a telegram confirming his full-time commission in the RAF. They wanted him to decommission all the RAF bases that were no longer needed now that the war was over. But his orders were to travel back to Britain alone and that I was to follow later. He said if I could not travel with him, he would resign. Some of the big noises in the RAF told him he would be a fool if he refused this offer. But he didn't change his mind, and they didn't change theirs either. That's how Sandy Greig came to stay in South Africa and thank God for that!

My faith in the Lord had helped me through the most difficult of times. All those prayers I had said when I first got the telegram that told me Charles was coming home had been answered and in a way that was beyond my wildest dreams.

> I believe, I believe, I believe
> I place this day, my life, my loved ones, my work in
>   the Lord's hands.
> There's no harm in the Lord's hands, only good
> Whatever happens, whatever results, if it is in the
>   Lord's hands
> It is the Lord's will
> And it is good.

4

The Greig Clan

ANTHONY WILLIAM GREIG, SANDY'S AND MY FIRST CHILD, was born on 6 October 1946 at St Catherine's Nursing Home in Queenstown. We were living with my parents in Livingstone Road at the time and Sandy had been well and truly accepted into my family, particularly by my brother Dummy. They loved talking about rugby. On Sundays we went to church and then all the husbands and wives of my brothers and sisters came back to Livingstone Road, where my mother had made lots and lots of sandwiches and we sat around laughing and talking – one big happy family again.

When I fell pregnant with Tony, Sandy still didn't have a job. My family, especially my mother and my sisters, rallied around us to provide us with all the things we needed for this precious baby.

Tony's birth was a long one. Sandy took me to the nursing home on the Friday, when I first began having mild contractions. He then he set off to the Grand Hotel to wait for the baby's arrival, leaving me in the hands of Dr Sandy Voortman. He had quite a wait, as Tony was not born until Sunday. Despite the drawn-out birth it was beautiful, and this gorgeous little boy was put into my arms. He had a mop of black hair, not blond at all!

Our spirits lifted again when Sandy was offered a job in insurance. He then accepted a position in East London, about 180 kilometres from Queenstown, with the Liverpool, London and Globe Insurance Company as a salesman. While I wasn't happy about our little family being apart so soon after Tony's birth, we decided that Sandy should go ahead while Tony and I stayed in Queenstown. On 14 December 1946, we joined Sandy in East London. He had found a house and when he explained that it was in a relatively poor suburb called Quigney, I said, 'Never mind, I just want to be with you, so we're coming.' This was the start of a nomadic time for the Greigs, the first of four homes we lived in over the next three years as Sandy's employment took us between East London, south-west to Port Elizabeth, back to East London, then eventually back to Queenstown.

When Tony and I moved into the house in Quigney, I could feel the fleas jumping all over me and my baby boy and I burst into tears. I tried not to let Sandy see me crying because I knew he thought he had done the right thing, bringing his family together.

The carpet was filthy and the house was a complete mess. I rang my mother and asked her if she could spare me Sophie, one of our family maids, to come down and help me clean the house. Sophie had been with us for a long time, much loved by me and the rest of my family in the way that many white South African families in those days formed incredibly close bonds with their maids. They were family.

It was no surprise then that Sophie immediately got on the train and came to East London. She was just marvellous. One of the first things she did was to pick up the carpet and carry it outside. Then together we made that house shine.

It was a difficult time to be in East London because of a serious drought: the water was turned on in the morning and you could fill just three buckets, then it was turned off again until the next morning. It didn't matter if you had one child, or eight children, that was all the water you were allowed and you had to use it for your drinking and your washing, for everything. It wasn't easy with a baby, having to wash nappies every day.

Because we were in a new town, not many people came to visit us, so I spent much of my time there doing a lot of walking with my little baby boy. Everywhere I walked it seemed to be uphill. With the water restrictions and the loneliness, it was a real treat for all of us to return to Queenstown to be with family and friends for a summer holiday.

In 1948, Sandy was promoted and transferred to Port Elizabeth, but the offer did not include the transfer of his family. I gave notice on the house in East London and Tony and I moved in with my sister Corrie and her husband, Rob, on their farm, about an hour's drive from Queenstown. We lived there for six months while Sandy lived in a hotel in Port Elizabeth, the three of us getting together when we could.

One day Sandy called me to say he had found a house to rent in Walmer, a lovely, leafy suburb of Port Elizabeth. We moved there for about six months before I noticed in the paper that there was another house for rent, fully furnished, in Waverley Drive, Mill Park. I loved that house at first sight. It had a beautiful garden, was tastefully furnished and would be a perfect place for our little family. A lot of other people wanted this house, too, but the owner seemed to take a liking to me, so we got it. I was overjoyed. At that stage we had a nanny called Minnie-Mabel, whom I promoted to house girl, and then a young woman called Elizabeth started working for us as Tony's nanny. Regrettably she had to leave. She was of the Xhosa tribe and a marriage had been arranged for her.

Then Sandy was transferred again to East London. Shortly after we arrived we saw a house under construction in Surrey Road in the suburb of Vincent. When Sandy asked if it were for sale the answer was yes and he offered to buy it. We stayed in the Gonubie Hotel while we were waiting for it to be finished. I even got to choose the colours for the house. What a thrill. This was our first real home and I loved it so much. It was where Grandpa Greig, Sandy's father, William, came out from Scotland to see his son, and his new grandson, who was by now around eighteen months old, walking and full of life. One day, Grandpa Greig got all his letters out and spread them on the floor. Tony picked them up and ran off with them, with Grandpa Greig chasing. They hit it off right away.

Grandpa Greig owned a retail department store business in Scotland called Greig Bros and was very wealthy. He said he wanted to buy me an expensive present and, looking back now, he was probably prepared to carpet our new home for us, but instead I asked for a Mason and Pearson hairbrush, a gift that Tony was to learn all about a few years later.

Soon, we were on the move again, back to Queenstown, where at St Catherine's Nursing Home Tony's sister Molly Joy was born, on 14 October 1949. Dr Voortman told me she would be a beauty because her eyes were wide apart and she had high cheekbones. He later said the same about Sally Ann and he wasn't wrong on either count. By the time of Molly Joy's birth, Sandy had been promoted to manager, so he had a car to go with the job. The four of us were living in a very small rented house in Berry Street and had only been there about a week when, on the first Sunday we thought we had to ourselves after moving all the furniture in, there was a knock on the door. It was the owners; they had been transferred back from Namibia (then called Southwest Africa) and they wanted their house back. So, by the time Sally Ann was born on 12 November 1953, we were living in another house in Berry Street. Tony had just turned seven and said he had a clear memory of the day I brought little Sally Ann home from hospital.

Tony was an active little boy, a natural ball player, and he seemed to really enjoy his early years at school. Queenstown local lore has it that in his first year, Sub A, he appealed to his teacher, Miss Audrey Walden-Smith, that their usual playground games be abandoned in favour of a game of cricket. Miss Waldy (as they called her) appreciated Tony's enthusiasm and arranged for the first-ever game of cricket to be played against the 'big school', as Tony and his young friends referred to it. So the England Captain's first cricket coach was a woman. Miss Waldy said that Tony was one of the littlest lads in the class, only three foot six inches.

Tony rode to school and back on his bicycle – even during the winter months when it was bitterly cold.

He would get up early and, after a bowl of hot porridge, set off with his little skinny legs pedalling away like crazy. On arrival at school he would park his bike in the shed, and then go searching for a ball, and other boys, to play with. It was always a disappointment for him when Miss Waldy rang the morning bell calling the children into class, and putting an end to any ball games.

This was about the same time we nearly lost our home in a fire started by little Tony. Sandy and I had gone out to a cocktail party. It was only for an hour and I left our two maids in charge. Tony decided to light a fire, something he had seen a young African boy doing. The problem was Tony didn't try to light the fire outside: he lit it under his bed.

When we arrived home, the maids couldn't wait to tell us what Tony had been up to and greeted us in a very excitable manner. We had a look in Tony's room and to our dismay noticed the fire was still smouldering, and it had made its way into Tony's mattress! I made him a new bed while Sandy carried the burnt mattress to the bathroom. He threw a few buckets of water over it, then joined me in bed. Two hours later I woke up, breathless. I roused Sandy, saying, 'I can't breathe!' He told me I was having a dream and to go back to sleep. I woke again, however, an hour later. Sandy made some noises about me always complaining, but I insisted.

'Something's wrong, Sandy, I can't breathe!' Frustrated, I jumped out of bed and nearly fell. I couldn't see where I was going. It was as though I was in dense fog, but it was in fact thick smoke. Sandy hadn't extinguished the mattress properly and it had ignited, burning the towels above the bath. Flames were jumping around all over the place. Sandy ran next door and asked if he could use the phone to ring the fire brigade. The neighbour, Mr Chilcott, was so alarmed by this late knock on his door, he answered it with his shotgun in his hands. The fire brigade soon came down the street with all its bells ringing.

We moved the car from the garage and I made beds in it for Tony and Molly Joy, so at least they were safe. It was blowing a gale and after the firemen had removed the mattress from the house, bits of it were falling off and were being blown down the street on fire. If it hadn't been so serious, it could have looked quite funny, really, all these bits of mattress on fire disappearing down the street. Eventually the fire was brought under control and everyone was safe, which was all that really mattered.

The next morning, though, Sandy said to me, 'I have to do something about Tony; this is very serious and he needs to learn a lesson.' I never liked being around when Sandy disciplined Tony, so I went next door and apologised once more to the Chilcotts. When I came back, if I had been furious with the maids for letting Tony light the fire, I was absolutely fuming at Sandy. He had taken my Mason and Pearson brush to Tony's bottom and broken it. I didn't care about the brush. I just cared about Tony's bottom. It was black and blue. I didn't agree that Tony needed to be taught a lesson that way, but whatever the rights and wrongs of Sandy's punishment, I don't think Tony ever misused matches again.

After Berry Street, Sandy and I purchased a Tudor-style house with a lovely garden in Foch Avenue, which is where we were living when our youngest child, Ian, was born on 8 December 1955.

Shortly after buying the house in Foch Avenue, a young Xhosa boy named Teki Manzi, whom our family came to love dearly, entered our life. He met me at the gate one day and said he was looking for work. He was young, about fourteen years old. When I said he should be at school, he replied that he had been at school but now he wanted to work so he could help his mother. I didn't know it at the time, but he turned out to have a green thumb; everything he planted grew. Anyway, we took him on. The next day when he turned up at our house, he was wearing just a pair of old tattered shorts and plimsolls. In South Africa, these style of shoes were known as 'tackies', so we called him Tackies.

Tackies had asked me if he could live in our house, but I'd had to tell him there was no room as we already had two maids living with us. He and little Tony, who was nine years old, made a place for him in the garage. We had two garages at that house, one of which was long and roomy, so that is where Tackies made his bedroom.

Tackies often babysat the children when Sandy and I went out. He was very strict and didn't take any nonsense from them. On one occasion when he was in charge, the kids threw plums over the fence at our neighbour, who was reading his newspaper in his garden. The neighbour came over to the house and spoke to Tackies, telling him what his charges were doing, and said he would be talking to their parents. He didn't report them because Tackies made them go and apologise, individually. I later learnt that they spent ages practising their apologies in Afrikaans, as the neighbour was the headmaster of the local Afrikaans School, Hangklip.

Despite living with us, Tackies still took part in the Xhosa initiation ceremonies for young boys entering manhood at eighteen, which meant having their heads shaved, eating plain foods, undergoing circumcision by a spear blade, then living in a sutu (thatched hut) for up to three months. When he returned to us, he was wrapped in a pink rug. Underneath, his body was covered in white clay, part of the healing process after being circumcised. This custom is widely practised to this day in South Africa, but the authorities are trying to encourage attendance at clinics for the actual operation to minimise the many deaths and maiming which occur all too frequently.

On 9 December 1956, the day after Ian's first birthday, we went for a family holiday at a place called Kei Mouth, where we rented a cottage called Malvern. Kei Mouth is a resort town on the south-east coast of South Africa, just north of East London, where the Great Kei River runs into the Indian Ocean. Everyone came with us, including the maids and Tackies. It was the first time Tackies had seen the sea and when we were leaving we found he had filled the boot of the car with bottles of sea water. He believed it had magic properties and drinking it was good for your health!

During that holiday we went to the beach almost every morning, where we would meet with other family members and friends. We'd pack a picnic basket with homemade ginger beer and biscuits for the children, who were always hungry.

One particular day began as perfectly as any of the others. The only problem was that the sea water was muddy as there had been heavy rainfall inland and the Great Kei River was spewing mud into the sea. The waves were chocolate-coloured, but that didn't stop the holidaymakers from enjoying the water. With the children and Tackies in tow, we set off for a day in the sun. I settled the family at the Cwili lagoon, a few minutes' walk from the beach where the little ones, Sally Ann and Ian, could play happily and safely in the shallow water under the watchful eye of Tackies while I sunbathed just next to them on a comfortable cluster of flat rocks. Then my sister Corrie asked me to come for a swim in the sea but I didn't really feel like it, so I made the excuse that I had left my bathing cap back at the lagoon. Corrie wouldn't take no for an answer and Molly Joy ran back to fetch my cap.

Tony and the other older children were swimming in front of Corrie and me and at some stage I insisted they move behind us. Thank goodness they did. Adelaide, who was terrified of the sea, was lying on her back in the shallow waters and kept on calling to Corrie and me to come back because she thought we were going out too deep. The water was only waist deep and there were other swimmers ahead of us – I could see their bathing caps bobbing up and down, so I wasn't too worried about where Corrie and I were. Adelaide gave us another 'warning call'. Corrie and I had been diving under the breakers and I turned to Adelaide and jokingly shouted: 'Just one more wave, Addie, then we'll swim out to the sharks!'

Famous last words: As Corrie and I dived over the next wave, I felt the most excruciating pain. The only way I can describe it is to say that it felt as though two rocks had closed over my leg. Molly Joy and Tony said they saw me rise up high out of the ocean, turn around towards the beach and scream in pain. They had never heard me scream before, so they were both frightened and knew immediately that something horrendous had happened to me. It had – I had been attacked by a six-foot ragged-tooth shark.

Tony ran to get help and to find Sandy. Molly Joy ran wildly along the beach towards the Kei River and hid away in fright. It was my sister Corrie who saved my life. She stayed in the water as I fought the shark that first took hold of my leg then returned for more, snatching at my hand with its razor-sharp teeth. I fainted and Corrie held me up so I wouldn't drown. She went through the trauma with me, my precious sister. Then, for some reason, the shark let me go.

A fisherman on the rocks adjacent to the beach had seen the drama and ran to our rescue, carrying me out of the water and onto the beach. Coming in and out of consciousness, I remember very little of what happened next. Others have filled in the story for me. Sandy arrived. He told me he loved me, telling me desperately, 'Please Joycie, please don't die.' I had no idea where the children were and said I was not to be taken anywhere until I had seen them. My request was honoured and I apparently waved goodbye to all of them outside Malvern Cottage as I lay on the back seat of a motorcar ready to take me to Frere Hospital in East London. Tony and Molly Joy told me that the sight was traumatic – hand and leg bound in blood-soaked towels and their precious mother in a terrible state. Thankfully, my nephew Rodney King and his wife, Angela, were there to look after my children as I was rushed to hospital.

Someone had made up a concoction of brandy for the drive and they would give me a sip. My eyes rolled around in my head each time. At the hospital I was placed in a bath of antiseptic to try to kill the germs from the shark's teeth.

It was a trying twelve months for the family following the attack. There were times when the doctors thought they would have to amputate my leg but I was incredibly lucky that was avoided. Battling through months of pain, I had to go to hospital frequently, initially just to change my dressings, and then for rehabilitation on both my leg and hand. It was so exhausting, not just physically, but mentally. I struggled to stay on top of it all. Feelings that had been suppressed for months would come to the surface whenever I heard the news that someone else in the world had been attacked: I instantly thought of them and their families. Thereafter, I was always extremely nervous when my children went to the beach. In the end, as horrified as they had been by what they'd seen that day, it didn't stop them swimming. Years later, when Sandy and I came to live in Australia, Tony would swim out beyond the waves, right out of view, and he just rolled his eyes at me when I asked him not to do it.

Not long after the shark attack, Tony went to a fancy-dress party dressed as a shark-attack victim. Tony's cousin Rodney and his wife, Angela, helped him with the costume: he had his right leg and arm bandaged in the same way I did when I came out of hospital.

In 1958, Sandy was again transferred to East London and we moved into rented accommodation in Plymouth Drive. In 1960 Sandy had another transfer which brought us back to Queenstown. I didn't mind moving around so much. I loved Sandy and our family and I was happy to go along with whatever came our way. I got a job as secretary to Dr HQ Davies, the headmaster at Tony's school, Queen's College, where I worked for the next six years.

I was in the office the day Tony, who was now fourteen, received six of the best in HQ's office. Whenever a boy was sick, he had to report to the secretary. One particular boy had his face rubbed with chilli in the playground, to which he was allergic. He didn't come to the secretary to 'split' (report) on the boy who had done this to him, but rather to get relief. Dr Davies was in my office when this boy walked in and he asked the boy what he wanted. He replied that he wanted to see Mrs Greig. 'Well, there she is,' said Dr Davies. The boy proceeded to tell me his face was itchy and before I could reply, Dr Davies asked him, 'And why is your face itchy?' The boy looked at me, then at Dr Davies, then back at me again.

'Someone rubbed chilli on my face, sir,' he said. 'And who is this someone?' asked Dr Davies. Again the boy looked at me, then the headmaster, then me and on it went. He really did not want to split on Tony. Finally, when Dr Davies repeated the question rather loudly, the boy replied, 'Greig, sir.'

'When Mrs Greig has seen to your face, send Greig to me immediately,' Dr Davies demanded. He then said in a softer voice as he walked past me, 'Sorry, Joycie.' Tony duly arrived and went into the headmaster's office. Dr Davies said I could leave if I wanted to, but I stayed seated at my desk and from the other side of the door I heard every stroke of the cane as it landed on my darling boy.

That moment was nothing compared to the next crisis in Tony's life, his first epileptic seizure at the age of fourteen. During one winter holiday Tony stayed at the farm of a school friend, Richard Sugden. After attending a party, Richard and Tony were given a lift home in a truck by the manager of another farm, Denzyl Price. Driving rain made the road treacherous and the truck careered off the road on a bend and rolled down a steep hill into a gorge. Tony bumped his head on the way down but other than that he and Richard were okay. Denzyl wasn't quite as lucky and needed Richard's and Tony's help to get out.

Once they were back at the farm, Tony began to feel very dizzy, the same sort of dizziness he again experienced when he suffered his first epileptic seizure. This became the warning sign for epileptic seizures for the rest of his life, an aura that he referred to as 'feeling giddy'. So Tony always thought his epilepsy was related to the knock on the head from that crash on the farm.

That first epileptic fit was quite dramatic, coming as it did while he was playing in a tennis tournament between his school, Queen's College, and Dale College. His opponent was Charles Pope. In the fifth set, Tony began to feel giddy.

As he threw the ball up to serve, the world went black and he fell to the ground. He was brought home in a dazed state and we immediately took him to see Dr Voortman. Dr Voortman sent Tony off to Groote Schuur Hospital in Cape Town for tests.

There we met a specialist by the name of Alexander Gonski, a world-famous neurologist who had also served in World War Two and who eventually moved to Australia, where he received an Order of Australia for his services to medicine. After he did all his tests, he told us that Tony had epilepsy. Tony was also put on medication and Sandy and I were diligent in reminding him every day to take it. He hated those reminders, just as he hated it when people came to our house and we talked about his 'condition'.

As well as taking the pills, Tony was also given a list of things he mustn't do. Tony took his pills, but there was no way he was going to stop living the life he enjoyed. He kept riding his bike, and he kept swimming.

Tony learnt to deal with his epilepsy. He came to realise that the best protection against it was plenty of sleep. The business of always getting plenty of sleep, however, became a problem when, some years later in 1970, he was playing in a Currie Cup match in Johannesburg at the Wanderers. It was his first game for Eastern Province, against Transvaal. Instead of going straight back to his hotel room after dinner for a good night's sleep, he went out socialising.

When he returned to his hotel, he was already starting to feel giddy, that warning sign again. He collapsed the next morning and a doctor told him he could not play. Not for the first time, Tony's stubbornness won out. He played, but suffered a blackout and had a violent fit in the middle of the ground. The team formed a circle around him so no one could see what was happening. Tony was given an injection by Dr Ali Bacher, who was playing for Transvaal. It still took a while for the fit to pass while his teammates held him down.

The tennis match against Charles Pope and the cricket match at the Wanderers were the only times I can recall Tony having an epileptic seizure while playing sport.

I had enjoyed a childhood full of love and Sandy and I aimed to provide the same thing for our children. Listening to Tony, Molly Joy, Sally Ann and Ian talk about their childhoods whenever they got together, I believe that most of the time, Sandy and I achieved this. We had great holidays. The children played endless games in the garden. The maids and Tackies were well looked after and felt part of the family. Though initially he didn't know a lot about the game, Tackies eventually took part in the backyard cricket matches. So, in addition to his duties in the garden, he became Tony's personal net bowler. The fact that he threw the ball, instead of bowling it, didn't worry Tony. The faster they came, the better he liked it. Here he was, unknowingly being prepared for the day he would have to stand up to Dennis Lillee and Jeff Thomson, and then the West Indian fast bowlers.

Tony was not being selfish when he had Tackies bowling to him for hours on end. Tackies just didn't like batting that much; I think he found the ball was pretty hard. Another person who wasn't keen on the hard ball was Tony's great childhood friend, Paul Ensor. Paul was a year younger than Tony, at thirteen, and one day he complained that Tony was bowling too quick. Tony declared that he wasn't and that his young brother Ian, then aged five, could do better than Paul. To prove it, Tony strapped Ian into a pair of pads then whispered in his ear the words that were to become a code between the two of them: 'Trust me!'

Ian took his stance at the wicket and Tony, again being Tony, measured out his longest run-up and in he came to bowl at his little brother, who was hardly taller than the pads. Ian stood his ground. While the ball was fast, Tony had made sure that he pitched the ball up so that Ian was able to play it straight back down the wicket. They would trust each other for the rest of Tony's life. Tony spent a lot of time teaching his little brother the game of cricket and was always proud of his achievements.

As well as tennis and cricket, Tony loved playing golf and rugby, his father's game. He used the homemade bamboo goalposts in the back garden to turn himself into a pretty good goal-kicker. Out in that garden there always seemed to be laughter, the sound of fun and of games, mixed in with more than the occasional argument. It was always competitive. Every one of my children wanted to be a winner.

5

Hard Times

LIKE SO MANY MEN OF HIS GENERATION, SANDY NEVER really wanted to be reminded about the war, so we didn't press him to talk about it. We knew he had been in Bomber Command and was honoured as a war hero. In 1984, he and I attended a function in England, a reunion of Bomber Command. We were on the top table and when I asked why, the answer was that he was one of the guests of honour.

After all those missions, there had to be so many memories but most he kept to himself, while others would suddenly explode to the surface. When we were living in Scotland in 1967 there was one such explosive reminder. We were watching *Mrs Miniver*, a wartime movie made in 1942 featuring Greer Garson and Walter Pidgeon. All of a sudden Sandy leapt from his chair and ran out of the room with tears streaming down his face. The scene on the television was one of horror, German women and children running for cover as Bomber Command bombs rained down on them.

Sandy had seen it for real and didn't want to see it again. I recall explaining to young Sally Ann the reason behind her father's emotions.

Sandy had other dark memories. On one occasion during the war he was called to go to Beverley in Yorkshire to identify the bodies of his whole crew, after their plane crashed on return from a mission. Sandy hadn't flown with them that day because of sinus congestion. I can't even start to imagine how he felt about having to do that. He told me he never wanted to set foot in Beverley again.

He also told his nephew, Rodney King, about a recurring nightmare – a crashed plane that was on fire. No one could get near enough to rescue the crew because of the heat and flames. The crew burned to death, the pilot screaming his last words, 'You're all cowards!'

Sandy never spent Guy Fawkes Night letting off firecrackers with his children. He said he'd seen and heard enough explosions during the war and didn't want to be reminded of those days.

In 1984, while we were in England, his painful memories came flooding back. By now Sally Ann was married to a lovely Yorkshireman, Phillip Hodson. Phillip was also a fine cricketer and lover of all sports, so he fitted into our family perfectly. While staying with them in Yorkshire, Sally Ann took Sandy and me out for lunch to a teahouse in York called Bettys. As we turned the corner, Sandy realised Bettys was the old Red Lion, a pub where he and his fellow airmen had drunk in York on return from their sorties. He told us that those who did not return from a bombing raid had their glasses turned over on the bar out of respect. Sandy got up to go to the toilet, and when he returned he was ashen-faced.

The new owners of the Red Lion had kept all the mirrors on which the aircrew had written their names, and Sandy recognised a lot of the names. He also spotted part of his own service number. It was a moving experience which helped him open up a little, telling us that most of the RAF bomber bases were along the east coast of Lincolnshire and Yorkshire. He'd spent time at Holme-on-Spalding Moor, the closest airfield to York, Ludford Magna and Scampton.

Sandy fought the demons from his first flight into Germany until his death in 1990. During the war, those demons were fed daily on a number of fronts. Although he never let it distract him from his navigational role, he feared death on every one of his missions. He also carried the burden for his entire crew, many of whom were married despite their tender age. Once, in an aberrant moment, he likened his navigator's role to sitting for a five-hour mathematics exam on 54 occasions, when you knew you had to get 100 per cent or you and your crew would die. On very rare occasions he discussed the war with me, describing the pressure as excruciating. The situation was exacerbated when he became squadron leader. All the men under his command became like family and he said every death was like losing a sibling or parent. Every letter he had to write to the next of kin about the death of a loved one got harder and harder. Although the memory of these issues never disappeared completely, he said that over time they did dissipate ever so slowly. However, the guilt he felt over killing women and children never left him.

Sandy had been a teetotaller before the war; after all, he was only seventeen when he joined up. His drinking began during the war. When he first came to South Africa in 1943, he was diagnosed with something called post-catarrhal jaundice, and looking back perhaps that may have been caused by heavy drinking. I did not find out for a long time that Sandy was an alcoholic. I had never really heard of the word until one day, in 1964, many years into our marriage, long after all our children were born, Dr John Leslie came to see Sally Ann who was ill with a high temperature and flu.

When Sandy came home from work he said to me, 'When Dr Leslie is finished with Sally Ann, can you ask him to come into our bedroom because I'm not feeling very well.' Dr Leslie saw Sandy, then he came out of our bedroom. He spoke to me about Sally Ann as he walked to the gate with me. I then said, 'What about Sandy?' He replied, 'Joyce, Sandy is an alcoholic!' I was so naïve I said, 'What is an alcoholic?' Dr Leslie explained that an alcoholic is a man who can't stop drinking. I said, 'John, don't talk rubbish to me, I have never ever seen Sandy drunk. When he comes home from work he goes straight to his chair and goes to sleep. I have never seen him fall over, I have never seen him drunk. I can smell that he had a drink because he had been to the club but he has never been a drunk man, ever. So how can that be true?' Dr Leslie reaffirmed Sandy was definitely an alcoholic.

A few years earlier, in 1961, there had already been a crisis that made it clear all was not well with Sandy. I was in bed and so were the children, except for Tony who was still up doing his homework. He came to me and told me he had seen his father 'mixing some pink stuff in a glass'. As I was getting out of bed to see what was happening, Sandy came in and fell onto the bed. He had already drunk the contents of the glass. I jumped up and went to the bathroom to find an empty bottle lying on the floor. I asked Tony to call the hospital. The ambulance arrived and they quickly put Sandy on a stretcher. Molly Joy recalls being horrified by seeing her dad's hand fall over the side of the stretcher and drag along the ground as he was being carried out of the house.

'I saw the hand dragging on the grass and I tucked it up,' she says. 'I was utterly devastated. My dad was dying. I said to myself, please God, don't let my dad die. My dad was everything, he taught me to love reading, he bought me magazines every week rather than children's comics. I loved him so much and to see him laid out on a stretcher was the saddest thing, so white, so motionless. Then Mum and Tony were gone with him, leaving me at home with our maid. I cannot explain how sad that night was.'

Tony and I went with Sandy to the hospital. Tony, who was fifteen years old at the time, had to stay in the waiting room alone as the doctors asked me to come into the area where they were treating Sandy. I had never seen such a sight in my life. He had tubes everywhere and they were washing him out, trying to make him vomit up the poison. Dr Papilsky told me he didn't know if Sandy was going to live and that I should also make sure my young family was all right. I quickly took Tony home so he could look after the rest of the family. As I rushed back to the hospital, I stopped at Adelaide's house and asked her to come with me.

Back at the hospital, Dr Papilsky met us in the corridor and he told us it was very bad. He then asked if I had the bottle. I did and when I showed it to him he said he could have the chemist struck off for giving so many pills to Sandy. I recall him telling me that they were sleeping pills, often used to help with anxiety and insomnia.

My thoughts turned quickly to other things. If Sandy died, I would have to tell his father, and other family members, how he had died. I didn't think I had the strength to tell anyone that Sandy had taken his own life, so I asked Dr Papilsky what I should say. He replied: 'Joyce, just tell everyone it is a heart attack and if anybody questions you, you tell them to go and ask Dr Papilsky.'

I waited and waited with Adelaide at the hospital. It was an awful time, but it was a great comfort having my sister there to support me. Eventually, Dr Papilsky came out and said, 'I think he's made it.' He then told me to go home to my children. The feeling of relief was so great. I could go home to my children and tell them their father would be all right. When I arrived I found Tony comforting Molly Joy, sitting in the kitchen near the AGA stove, my big boy and his sister, just hugging each other. Tony took a big step towards becoming a man that night. By this time he could see there were many sides to his father, some wonderfully good, some not so good. Sandy had missed out on so much love because his mother had died when he was only eight years old. He had then lost whatever chance to fulfil ambitions he might have had to be a champion sportsman himself due to the war. In that war, he had to do things that bordered on suicidal. He saw friends crash out of the sky to fiery deaths. Many times he felt his own life threatened. It was said of people in Bomber Command that after 30 sorties, they were either in a coffin or a mental institution. Sandy did 54.

He had us, his new family in South Africa, but after what he had gone through, perhaps that wasn't enough. Otherwise, why would he want to take his own life? It was a lot for us all to deal with. Molly Joy thinks he might have felt that because of his drinking he was letting his family down. To this day, she also asks those questions about the impact of losing his mother so early, and the war.

That night, after I had comforted my children with the news their father had survived, I arranged to put a call through to Scotland to tell Sandy's father his son had had a heart attack but that 'he looks to have made it'. Then when my sister Dorothy arrived at my house, I told her Sandy had had a heart attack. She didn't believe me, telling me her husband, Vic, had seen Sandy swallowing some pills recently at the Gardens Hotel. I replied, 'I don't care what pills he was swallowing, he's had a heart attack and he's just made the grade.' And I kept that lie up. Tony knew, Molly Joy knew, but I don't think I even told Sally Ann or Ian, though they of course know now. Sally Ann and Tony talked about it last year when they were in Sri Lanka together. They wondered how different their lives would have been had their father died back then.

The following year was an extremely sad one for my family. My much loved father died from a heart attack, aged 80. It was such a shock to all of us, particularly our mother, as he seemed to be in such good health for his age. Adelaide called me at work to say that Dad had apparently been outside that morning admiring the first flower that had appeared on our Japonica tree. He was excited to share this news with my mother, Flossie, when he came inside from the garden to join her for breakfast. He then had a turn at the table.

I rushed home quickly to be at Dad's bedside. I could see he was not in a good way and the doctors asked me to hold up his shirt so they could give him a needle into his chest. With tears running down my face I said, 'C'mon Dad'. He struggled to keep his eyes open and managed to look over to my sister Blanche and say his last words, 'Look after Mum'. And with that he was gone.

My mother Flossie died 17 years later on 20 February 1979. She had a very peaceful death – just closed her eyes one evening. She was 89 and her 90th birthday cake had already been baked. Mum always waited at home (a three-bedroom flat in Queenstown) for me to come to visit her after I finished work. I would usually help her into bed before going home to Sandy. Everyone was coming to spend her 90th birthday with her on the Friday. On the Tuesday prior as I helped Mum into bed, we reminisced about Scotland.

'It is getting late, Joycie, and you must get home in time for dinner with Sandy,' she said. I promised to drop over later that evening to see her during my walk and give her a kiss goodnight. I'd only just got out of the shower at home when the phone rang. Sandy answered and yelled out to me, 'Joycie, it's your mum and you must go quick.' Mum had had a bad turn after visiting the washroom and said to my sisters Blanche, Corrie and Dorothy, who were staying with her as they'd lost their husbands, that she felt she was going to die. I arrived and Corrie took me in to see Mum.

I said, 'Mum, it's me.'

She whispered, 'Oh, my darling.' Then she was gone of a suspected heart attack. It was terribly sad. I made a little posy of frangipanis and Corrie and I went to the morgue to say goodbye to her. Mum looked so beautiful and at peace. She was buried on her birthday Friday, 23 February 1979.

Sandy's problems with alcohol were to continue long after that night in 1964 when Dr Leslie shocked me with the news that my husband was an alcoholic. It's not something that just takes hold of a family overnight. With the knowledge came awareness, though. Over the following years I was much more alert to Sandy's problem and the effect it was having on our lives, but I couldn't stop the path we were on.

In February 1967 I visited a fortune-teller called Mrs Smith. She told me I would be going overseas shortly through the death of another woman and that I would have another child. I was 47 at the time, so thought it most unlikely. Shortly thereafter, Sandy's stepmother, Bunty Greig, who ran Greig Bros Ltd in Bathgate, Scotland, took an accidental overdose of barbiturates and died. She was survived by her thirteen-year-old son, Kenneth, and Sandy's very sick father, William, or Bill as he was known. Bill had a severe heart condition and couldn't cope with running the business and looking after his young son, he persuaded Sandy to move to Scotland to help him run the family business. Within weeks, we shifted to Edinburgh. It was an extremely hard decision to move and undoubtedly affected Molly Joy more than the others, as she was doing extremely well at Clarendon Girls' High in East London and had to leave before her matric year.

The fortune-teller had been correct, I had another child to look after. Kenneth was still grieving for his mother, which was exacerbated when he couldn't handle Sandy's heavy drinking soon after our arrival. I managed to help him through his grieving and his disdain for Sandy's drinking. I tried to make him a priority; I wanted to build love and trust with him. We really did establish a wonderful bond and I became extremely fond of him.

Ian attended Sandy's old school, George Watson's Boys' College, and Sally Ann went to Saint Serf's Ladies' College. Molly Joy worked with Sandy at Greig Bros. Tony had also worked for the family business for a short stint the previous winter, 1966, having been required to live in the United Kingdom to satisfy the 'residential qualification' should he be selected to play cricket for England. His job had been to collect rents for television sets and repossess televisions from people who defaulted on their payments. However, he was too kind-hearted to do either. He would turn up to homes where young families would be sitting around watching TV. His job was to tell them, in front of their children, that he had to take back their TV if they couldn't pay. Invariably he went back to Greig Bros and paid their outstanding rent from his own pocket.

While in Scotland we lived in the affluent Edinburgh suburb of Barnton. It was luxury we had not experienced before. After about eight months settling into our comfortable new home, we were joined by Tony for a brief visit; with his family now living in Scotland, he took the opportunity to visit; it was wonderful to see him and hear all his stories from England. He was encouraged by how his summer of cricket had gone, but, typically, he wanted to find out about us and asked lots of questions about how we were getting on after such a big move. He also enjoyed driving over to Glasgow to watch our football team, Glasgow Rangers, play Celtic at Ibrox Park. At the time, Rangers were captained by the legendary John Greig (no relation), who played 755 games for them. Without thinking of the consequences, Tony took the little Greig Bros panel van to Glasgow. When he got into the van after the match a bunch of Celtic supporters, believing it belonged to a John Greig relative, picked the van up. Tony was going nowhere. He hit the accelerator, the mob dropped it, and Tony took off, grateful that they hadn't dumped him in a place he couldn't leave.

In 1968, almost a year after we moved to Scotland, Sandy's dad, Bill, was hospitalised. He had an ongoing heart condition and suffered from increasingly debilitating angina. I thought it was amazing that he had previously survived three heart attacks. Sandy's sister Isobel's husband, George Carlaw, and his stepmother's brother, Eric McArthur, resented Sandy's involvement in the firm and his heavy drinking and made life extremely difficult for him. When Bill died from complications related to kidney disease, aged seventy, Sandy tried for months to make things work in Scotland. By the end of the year he had had enough. His involvement in the family business was being met with resistance, so he decided to abandon Scotland. We returned to East London in December 1968. I was heartbroken when it was decided Kenneth should remain in Scotland.

Upon our return to South Africa, it was clear that something had to be done about Sandy's drinking. We had all had enough. Once Sandy had one drink, he couldn't stop, but he couldn't even stop himself from having that first drink. As much as it would break my heart, he had to get away from all of us. The doctors advised us the best way was to go through the courts, to have Sandy committed to an institution for treatment. Can you imagine that, agreeing to have your husband, the father of your children, committed to an institution? But I did agree. At the courthouse, we were taken into a quiet back room where an order was made. Alexander Broom Greig was committed to a place called Magaliesoord Rehabilitation Centre, in Northern Transvaal. The period of the commitment was three years.

Tony was playing cricket in England, Molly Joy was pursuing her career in Johannesburg and now Sandy was also away from the family. I've had so many sad goodbyes in my life but this one was made even harder because it involved our young children, who were still in my care at home. I took Sandy to the station and when I returned home, grief overwhelmed me. Sally Ann, who was sixteen at the time, opened the front door when she heard me approach the house. I collapsed at her feet. She immediately sent Ian, who was fourteen years old, to fetch the doctor who lived across the street, then phoned my brother Dummy, who came at once from King William's Town, about thirty minutes' drive by car. Dummy got straight on the phone to try to track down Tony in England, who was with his South African girlfriend, Donna Reed. Dummy suggested to Tony that the children could come and live with him in King William's Town, at least until I sorted myself out and got back on my feet. However, Tony thought they should move to Queenstown, where they would be closer to the larger family, and he knew that this would also be where I would end up. He also wanted Ian to start at Queen's College the following year, 1970. So he told Dummy that Donna was going to phone her parents, Jean and Gordon, and ask them to look after the two children until I had properly recovered and was settled back into Queenstown. To Tony, the Reeds must have seemed the best option at the time. I didn't know them very well, but I had also never thought to put out a call for help to any of my friends or family in Queenstown. I had always considered what Sandy was going through to be a private matter.

Gordon Reed and Donna's little sister, Eleanor, pitched up the next weekend in his truck and took Sally Ann and Ian home to their farm, 'Adjanya', which was just outside of Queenstown. They packed my belongings and put everything we had into storage. It all happened so quickly. My children were gone. I faced a dilemma because I couldn't leave my secretarial job at a dental practice in East London – my employment agreement required that I give one month's notice. I so badly wanted to go back to Queenstown and be with my family, but I had no option but to honour my period of notice. I stayed in East London with our family friends, Chum and Glad Hillhouse, to serve out the notice. After four weeks I was able to join Sally Ann and Ian at the Reeds' farm. I was grateful that they offered us temporary board, but insisted they take some rent money, which I paid as soon as my next pay packet came in.

Meanwhile, I could at least smile at one thing when I received Sandy's first letter. He had wanted to take his golf clubs to Magaliesoord Rehabilitation Centre but he had no idea what he was in for. When he arrived there, he quickly discovered it was no holiday camp and there was certainly no opportunity to play golf. There were, however, plans for a swimming pool, but he had to help dig the hole for it. He didn't last long in that job, his health wasn't up to it, so they put him in the library and soon all those wonderful characteristics that made him a squadron leader rose to the fore. He took control.

As Sally Ann puts it: 'Dad got an early release from Magaliesoord because he was brilliant. He worked in the library and gave talks to the patients there. One was about Robert Burns, who is widely regarded as the national poet of Scotland. Dad catalogued the whole library, ordered new books and set up a proper borrowing system. This way he got the paper first in the morning and did the crossword before anybody else could make a mess of it! He did the crossword every day of his life and always insisted we read the leader, the editorial, in the daily paper. He was a brilliant bridge player, too.'

After four months with the Reeds, I eventually found a flat, part of a divided house, in Queenstown for which I paid 10 rand a month. I really had to watch the pennies because at that time I was earning only 100 rand a month working as a legal secretary for a local firm, Elliot Brothers. Out of that I had to pay for the kids' clothing and school fees. As Sandy was not there to help me, I had to find a way to provide for my children.

Things moved along and Sally Ann became a boarder at Cathcart High School, where she was later to become the Head Girl. Ian was at Queen's but only as a day student. He was starting to show some real sporting talent, a level of talent that would develop to one day earn him the honour of playing cricket for England, just like his older brother. However, he was being 'distracted' by other boys in the neighbourhood, and we were advised by the school that he should also become a boarder, to 'get him off the streets'. I was reluctant for him to become a boarder because I couldn't afford the extra sets of uniforms he needed. As a day student I could get him by with just one set of school clothes because I could wash them every night. As a boarder, he was required to have six sets of school clothes.

During this period, Molly Joy was now twenty years old and had left home to pursue a marketing career, initially in Cape Town, and then in Johannesburg. She made a trip to see Sandy at Magaliesoord, telling her work colleagues she was going to visit a friend as she didn't want them to know she was really going to visit her father in a facility. She got such a shock when she got there. Sandy greeted her and the first thing he said was, 'Have you got some cigarettes?' She only had one pack and he all but snatched it from her. They weren't allowed cigarettes. Molly Joy was also quite upset by the sight of her father in a T-shirt and work overalls. She had never seen him dressed that way before.

About eight months into Sandy's time at Magaliesoord, I received a call from the psychiatrist. He told me Sandy knew more about the *Twelve Steps*, the world-acclaimed bible for recovering alcoholics, than he did, and that he should come home. I agreed, but only on the condition that if he had a drink, he had to go straight back. So in early 1970 he came home on that condition. Tony, who had been playing county cricket for the previous three summers and was pushing for selection in the England team, was home in South Africa on holidays. One night soon after his return, Sandy said he wanted to go down to the club. When he came home I could smell drink. I was furious and ready to order him out of the house and back to the rehabilitation centre.

Tony, ever the peacemaker, said, 'Shall we give Dad another chance?'

I told Tony his father knew that the moment he took his first drink he had to go back into rehabilitation. Sandy protested that he had had just one beer. He appeared absolutely normal. Because Tony asked me to, I gave Sandy one more chance, but I said it had to be his last one, otherwise Sandy would die.

Tony told me not to worry, 'Trust me,' he said, and he bought Ian the extra school clothes. So in January, 1970, Ian started as a boarder at Connaught House. But there were still money problems. Once Ian phoned from boarding school asking if he could bring two friends home for a Sunday roast. I said yes, but wondered from where I could produce a piece of beef to feed these boys. Tony took his brother aside and suggested that in the future he only bring one friend home at a time.

At one stage, I had to tell Sophie, my loyal maid of many years, that she would have to find another job. Bless her, she offered me her life savings. I told her I couldn't take the money and somehow I managed to find the money to pay her next month's wages.

Eventually, in 1974, Sandy got a job as editor of *The Daily Representative*. Queenstown was the only place of its size in South Africa to have a daily newspaper and Sandy had the job of writing most of it. He became friends with a number of other South African journalists of the time, including Donald Woods (of *Cry Freedom* fame), editor of the *Daily Dispatch* in East London; and Allister Sparks, who began his career on *The Daily Representative*. Both men were prominent in the emerging anti-apartheid movement in South Africa and Sandy shared many of their views. Sandy and Donald also served on many rugby and cricket committees together. Through Donald Woods, he came to know of Steve Biko's fight, whose subsequent death at the hands of the security forces was one of the darkest moments in the history of South Africa. Because Donald Woods had been particularly close to Biko, and because of what he was writing, he was banned by the South African Government. Woods exposed the government's role in, and cover-up, of Biko's death while in custody on 12 September 1977. He was banned for five years and subsequently escaped into Lesotho and then England. The banning system was put in place by the South African government to deal with resistance against the apartheid movement. A banned person was restricted to his or her home and could not be seen with more than one person at a time. Living under banning orders also meant that one could not be quoted, and therefore could neither speak publicly nor write for an audience. On one occasion, Woods had written an article accusing Prime Minister Verwoerd of embodying Hitler's master-race theories in his apartheid policies. As a threat to his family, Donald believed a police officer sent T-shirts to his children which had been treated with the Mace-like substance, Ninhydrin. The acid burned the skin of his six-year-old daughter. Sandy urged him to stay and keep fighting the system from the inside but in the end, for the sake of his family, he felt he had to get out of South Africa.

Sandy wrote many articles about the wrongs of apartheid. He helped expose the evils of the system, including the mass resettlement of thousands of political refugees from Herschell to Thornhill, just outside Queenstown. The South African Government had done nothing to prepare for the arrival of these refugees. There were no houses, no roads, no schools, no clinics, and there was little water and hardly any food. The people had just been dumped in the middle of nowhere. Sandy had to be very careful about what he wrote, though, running most of his editorials past a lawyer in Queenstown called Cedric Fiveash.

Years later in 1992, when Donald Woods was living in England, he was a significant contributor to Ian's benefit brochure at the end of his playing career at Surrey. This brochure was promoted during Ian's benefit season. It was a way for county players to raise funds to financially reward them for the long service to their club as a professional cricketer. Fundraising functions were held throughout the benefit year, and this brochure outlined the player's achievements and also included various tributes. Companies were also approached to make a donation and have their brands included in the brochure. From outside South Africa Woods was still heavily involved in the global fight against apartheid. He said that he knew when Ian became captain of Surrey, the county would flourish, and believed that it was a genetic trait for the Greig boys to go at things full tilt and succeed. He wrote in Ian's brochure:

> Their father was the inimitable Sandy Greig, a
> colleague on my newspaper group and a wonderful
> companion in the press box, whether at cricket or
> rugby. An outspoken individualist, Sandy never
> left anyone in doubt about his views and when as
> a newspaper editor I came under governmental
> pressure from time-to-time Sandy was usually the
> first to phone his support with disdainful disregard of
> the fact that the telephones were tapped by the state

security police. To his proud Scots blood such matters
were a provocation rather than a threat.

I last saw Sandy in Sydney in 1990, and his
pride in his sons was higher than ever. He rejoiced at
Surrey's resurgence under Ian's captaincy and spoke
nostalgically of the old days from which Ian had
gone steadily on to greater things, including a law
degree from Cambridge with cricket and rugby Blues,
followed by two Tests against Pakistan and then the
Surrey captaincy.

Donald Woods concluded his contribution to Ian's brochure
by saying he would happily volunteer to help rattle the
collections cans at The Oval during any of his benefit
matches.

Sandy never saw people as black or white or coloured.
He just saw people. I think this is what helped win him a lot
of respect as editor of *The Daily Representative*. In addition
to his brilliant command of the English language, he was
hard but fair in what he wrote.

As well as giving Sandy new direction in his life, as
editor he was able to give direction to other people, including
one of his employees, Chux Fourie.

She wrote to me recently about her experience of
working with Sandy:

Dear Joycie
My memories of Sandy are indelibly etched in my
memory. In 1975, when he heard I was coming to live
in Queenstown, he phoned and said, 'I want you to
work for me.'

There was no argument and I started work as a proofreader at the then *Daily Representative* on 1 January 1976, later becoming a journalist, sub-editor and acting editor. My abiding memories are the following, although it is impossible to decide on their order:

His immense intelligence. I believe I have never met anyone greater in this regard.

Probably as a result of the above, he did not suffer fools gladly. Many were the days when he yelled at someone, 'Have you no bloody brains in your bloody head?' And he yelled often – sometimes in peppery language!

His absolute fearlessness/courage. He was never afraid of taking on the government, with whom he radically disagreed. At that time they did not take kindly to criticism and inexplicable things happened to some journalists who spoke out. I also remember him taking on one of the leading local businessmen, in defence of something I had written, without any consideration for his own social standing in the community. This I would also describe as absolute loyalty to his staff, irrespective of possible consequences.

His resoluteness, which some might describe as stubbornness. Once he had made up his mind, not much could change it.

His humility. He once picked me out about something I had not done. He apologised so humbly and repeatedly that I had to ask him to stop.

His oft-repeated saying, 'A boss must never expect other people to work harder than he does.' He lived by this at all times.

His wonderful sense of humour. His brilliant knowledge of the English language enabled him to create puns and make clever, pithy remarks that kept us amused in spite of the pressure of work on a daily paper. (When my young sons once walked into the office he said, 'Here comes the demolition squad.')

His caring. If staff members or their families had problems he was the epitome of compassion.

His honesty and openness. He never hid his problems with alcohol, but spoke openly about what he had been through. Yet he never 'preached', criticised or disapproved of others having a drink.

He was a perfectionist. Not a comma could be overlooked without raising his ire.

To quote Kipling, he truly could 'Walk with kings, nor lose the common touch'.

I admired him immensely, learnt so much from him and (thanks to him) entered a new career path that I still love.

Despite the leadership and the courage he was showing as editor of *The Daily Representative*, Sandy had started drinking heavily again and it was hard for me to deal with. I never thought of leaving him because I loved him too much. I found solace in my Christian faith. I also became involved in Al Anon, a support group for the families of alcoholics.

Looking back, this was really the first proper help that Sandy and I had been given since the war. Some of the problems facing today's returning veterans are reasonably well known: alcoholism, depression, unemployment, homelessness, divorce and post-traumatic stress disorder. But those challenges were hidden for Sandy's generation, the servicemen who fought in World War Two. Unlike today, there were no counsellors or psychologists to deal with Sandy's battle stress. These days it is commonplace for people who work in stressful roles to be offered counselling. Police officers, firefighters and paramedics are all offered support. But Sandy was largely left to deal with the trauma himself as best he could. I have no doubt about the link between Sandy's dark experiences in war and his alcoholism. Bomber Command's blanket bombing of Germany meant that many civilians paid a terrible toll. Between 1939 and 1945, 61 German cities were attacked by air, and those cities had a combined population of 25 million inhabitants; 3.6 million homes were destroyed (20 per cent of the total) and 7.5 million people were made homeless. Three hundred thousand Germans are thought to have been killed as a result of the raids, and 800,000 were wounded.

Sandy was deeply aware of the impact his campaign had on Germany, and even though he and his squadron were under orders from the RAF hierarchy, he still had to live with the fact that he had played a role in killing thousands of innocent people. Those demons stayed with him until his death. How he remained sane and so inspirational to his family, despite major traumas after the war, is beyond my comprehension.

In 1973, I was in England visiting Tony. Sandy had been in Queenstown's Komani Hospital trying to dry out and when he was discharged he checked into the Gardens Hotel. He called Sally Ann at work, as drunk as a skunk. Sally Ann's boss knew our family history and let her leave work early. When she went to see her father, he asked her to book him into a clinic in Boksburg, which was hundreds of kilometres away. He'd had enough, he wanted to give up drinking. She packed him up, put him on the 5pm train and gave the guard twenty rand to watch over him.

After Sandy's time in Boksburg, he came back home and started drinking again, but only briefly. He went to see the Presbyterian minister, who like Sandy, was Scottish through and through, telling him he wanted to be cured of his alcoholism. He realised that rehabilitation centres couldn't cure him, he had to do it himself. He joined Alcoholics Anonymous and with the help of Dr Cliff Dent he began to help not only himself but many others who suffered from the same condition. He knew he wasn't cured of alcoholism. He always talked in terms of 'since I've had my most recent drink'. He knew he was always at risk of having his next drink and if he started again, even just one drink, he wouldn't be able to stop. Even more so now than during his service in Bomber Command, Sandy needed to find mental strength and live by the motto of RAF 101 Squadron: *Mens agitat molem* – 'Mind over matter'.

Sandy became a great servant of Alcoholics Anonymous, giving back to the organisation what it gave him. It gave him extra strength not to take that first drink. While he was not overtly religious, the combination of his wartime experiences and his subsequent alcoholism led him to place prominence on the Serenity Prayer.

SERENITY PRAYER

God grant me the serenity
To accept the things I cannot change;
Courage to change the things I can;
And wisdom to know the difference.

6

Born to Bat and Bowl

Sport has always been a huge part of my life. It was squash that helped me through the dark days after my break-up with Charles Barry. It was while playing hockey that I first caught the eye of Sandy Greig. I developed my golf and became part of the Queenstown Golf Club, where I was Lady Captain. Sandy also loved sport. He started playing golf as a boy in Scotland and got his handicap as low as four. In South Africa he didn't play enough golf to keep his handicap that low, but he did remain a keen golfer. His whole family were soccer fanatics, and supported Glasgow Rangers Football Club. Sandy also loved rugby; his school had produced a number of rugby internationals, and though cricket is not a traditionally strong game in Scotland he took quite an interest in that game, too. Because he lost so many years to the war, we will never know just how good a sportsman he might have become.

Interestingly, Tony attributed some of his success as a player and a captain to the fagging system at Queen's. First-year boarders in the junior school were called 'skunks' and had to fag for one senior boy to whom they were assigned. Tasks included cleaning shoes for the senior boy; doing his laundry; allowing him to eat whatever he wanted off your plate; and, worst of all, having to eat all the food the senior boy didn't want. Tony spent his year as a skunk eating beetroot and handing over his roast potatoes. The process was repeated when the boy entered the senior school boarding hostel. Tony fagged for an out-of-control fast bowler who insisted on standing him up against a wall and bowling bouncers to him. Little did that boy know that he was preparing Tony to face short-pitched bowling in later life.

As Tony was a prefect and captain of the cricket and rugby teams, he was assigned three skunks in his final two years at school. They did everything for him, including putting the toothpaste on his toothbrush and warming his toilet seat in winter before he used it. Although the system was obviously subject to abuse, bullies were quickly sorted out. Apparently most boys agreed with Tony's assessment that it gave him a good grounding in how to deal with people, which subsequently helped him when he was in a position of power in later life.

We gave our children every opportunity to succeed in sport. From the moment they were out of nappies we were always keen on them being active, whether it was the endless games in the garden with Tony, Molly Joy, Sally Ann, Ian and all their friends, or the formal sport at school.

However, Sandy and I had a different approach in the way we supported them. I gave them the encouragement to enjoy their sport and have fun. I was extremely outgoing, whether it was on the hockey field or the dance floor, and Sandy was typically very reserved. There is no doubt Tony inherited his showmanship from me.

Sandy was always much sterner than me. Molly Joy once asked him to watch her play at Queenstown Golf Club. She really wanted to impress him but she duffed her opening tee shot and it landed on the practice putting green in front of the clubhouse. Sandy yelled out: 'For Christ's sake, Molly Joy, ask me to come and watch you play once you can hit the ball!'

Ian fared no better in the judgement stakes. He was playing cricket for Selborne College Under 11As against Dale in King William's Town. He had taken 8–19 when his dad arrived at the ground. All he had to do to get all ten wickets was bowl the ball straight, but for whatever reason he just couldn't put it on the spot! This voice with an unmistakable Scottish accent boomed across the ground: 'Bowl at the bloody wicket!'

Sandy was hard on Tony, too. I remember going to Queen's to watch Tony score a century. He got into the car to go home and said something to Sandy about his century, no doubt expecting some words of praise. Sandy said, 'Yes, you did, but you were bloody nearly out at 48.'

Sandy's obsessive attitude to sport had a huge impact on Tony. From his early days, he would have been keenly aware of the special place sport had in the Greig household.

The BBC World Service played a major role in our lives for the international news and sport. Every Sunday we listened to Alistair Cooke's *Letter from America* and *Call My Bluff*. Sandy never missed the evening BBC sports round-up at 7.45pm. When it came on the radio, everyone had to be quiet and listen. Hearing the scores coming in from Test cricket matches and county matches, Tony no doubt began to dream of horizons far beyond Queenstown.

I have often wondered why Sandy was so hard on the children with their sport, and Tony in particular. Perhaps he was just trying to toughen them up, or perhaps there was envy because the war had hindered any sporting career Sandy might have pursued. Perhaps too, for Sandy, it was a need for perfection that had been drilled into him as a navigator, where it was a life-or-death matter. Whatever the reasons, Sandy's attitude also affected Tony's development as a sportsman in another way. It taught him to handle pressure. He knew that if Sandy were watching, he had to perform at his best, eliminating any mistakes because they would be brought home to him no matter how well he had done.

Right throughout his playing days, Tony was able to cope with pressure. If anything, it brought out the best in him. When he first went to Sussex in England to play county cricket on trial in his first year, he knew that just one or two mistakes could have put him on the boat back to South Africa. The pressure only got greater from there as he went on to play for England.

Although Sandy rarely talked about the war, Tony was well aware of his father's heroics, too. He felt he had to be as fearless as his father. From an early age, he taught himself to shut out fear, whether it was of fast bowlers or sharks.

This trait stayed with him all his life. He loved fast cars. He tried parasailing, went on the scariest rollercoasters and he even tried flying an ultralight without any training. Tony was never frightened to have a go at anything.

There were others who influenced Tony, too. His uncles all loved sport, as did his cousin Rodney King. So it was not surprising that Tony immersed himself in sport when at home and among the extended family – it was everywhere. When he started school, it was there too. Queenstown might be in a relatively isolated part of South Africa, but the sporting facilities at Queen's were first class, particularly the access to quality cricket coaching. Each summer, and usually from Sussex, a top English coach would come to the school.

Tony didn't always need someone to play with. He practised kicking his rugby ball over homemade goalposts he erected himself in the garden. Often Tackies was busy gardening and wasn't available to bowl to him, so Tony would spend hours throwing a cricket ball against the wall and catching it on the rebound. But when there were other people around, Tony was the organiser – backyard matches that involved his sisters and brother as well as his friends. He once constructed an athletics course round our house at Berry Street and organised the races. I recall little Sally Ann and Ian being so small that they just ran under the hurdles. Leadership came easily to Tony.

He first began to make a noise as a cricketer when he graduated from the Prep College at Queen's to the junior school. In a game against the school from Cathcart, a small town nearby, Tony scored 130. Sandy had promised Tony that when he made his first hundred he would buy him a bat, so he made good on that promise, taking him to the local department store and buying him a bat.

Tony saw going to school as the price he had to pay for all the wonderful sporting opportunities Queen's offered. The name, Queen's College, and the use of terms like boarders, professional coaches and first-class sporting facilities, might make people think this was a prestigious school full of the indulged offspring of the wealthy people of Queenstown. It was not. A lot of the boarders were simply the sons of the farming families in the region who lived too far away to travel to and from school every day. The boarders were the backbone of the school. As well as being from the local region they came from Johannesburg (often the sons of Old Boys), South West Africa and Rhodesia. But Queen's was also the local government-funded school for all the young boys of Queenstown.

Queen's had very high standards, something I witnessed from up close when I was working at the school in the office of the headmaster, Dr Howard Quail Davies. Dr Davies served as headmaster from 1940 until 1964 and he was very strong on looking after the Old Boys. Around 1500 Old Queenians had served in World War Two, 105 of them being killed in action. Their names are engraved in white marble in the Memorial Hall. Today, there are Old Boy networks throughout South Africa.

During the war years, Dr Davies and his staff worked hard to maintain both scholastic and sporting standards, a tradition he kept going right up until his retirement. Most of the teachers loved cricket and if one of the teams under their charge had a good game, or a good season, they let their colleagues know. Tony thrived in this competitive cricket environment. Undoubtedly, as well as having Tackies hurling the ball at him in the garden, his experience at Queen's helped turn him into the player he became.

With his schoolboy teammates, he often travelled up to 300 kilometres to play games, staying overnight in the homes of the opposition families. When he qualified for the famous Nuffield Cricket Week, which has produced so many fine South African cricketers, travelling all over the country would have helped prepare him for the travel that was part of county and Test cricket in England. And though that was still a long way off, it seems it was not completely out of his mind. When his friends came around to play in the backyard Test matches Tony organised, they wanted to be South Africa or Australia, and Tony was happy about that because it allowed him to be the West Indies or England. Under the rules Tony devised, each team was to have three batsmen, all with famous names. Each side batted until these three Batsmen were dismissed.

Tony's three West Indian batsmen were Garry Sobers, Frank Worrell and Everton Weekes. His English batsmen were Peter May, Ted Dexter and Colin Cowdrey. The games were very competitive and usually involved Paul Ensor on the opposing side. The last thought on Paul's mind when he was in a winning position was returning home for supper. On one occasion the match extended into twilight and eventually had to be abandoned as a draw because it was so dark that they had lost the ball. I called out to Paul to tell him that his mum had just been on the phone. She had no idea where Paul was, and had become extremely anxious which had manifested into anger because he had not let her know where he was. With a sense of urgency, Paul bid farewell, jumped on his bike and headed home. Because it was so dark he did not notice that someone had closed the back gate, the top rung of which hit his head just under his nose. He suffered a very swollen lip, blood nose and a deviated septum, which he has to this day.

Tony knew all about the overseas stars from the newspapers and listening to broadcasts of the Tests on the radio. Cowdrey, in particular, was a hero to Tony. In the 1964–65 South African cricket season, Sandy took Tony to see the MCC play Border at East London. From that moment, he was starstruck. It was a great honour for Tony when he later got to play with Colin Cowdrey in Test matches for England.

By the time he left Queen's in 1965, Tony had captained the tennis, rugby and cricket teams. He was particularly proud of his efforts with the rugby team because he was able to turn a poor side into a successful side by improving their spirit and attitude. That experience stayed with Tony for the rest of his sporting career.

Many other experiences stayed with Tony all his life, too. Some came from the time he spent on the farm of his cousin Rodney King, Dorothy's son. Born before World War Two, Rodney was fifteen years older than Tony. Rodney's farm, Newtondale, was in a region of the Eastern Cape of South Africa near the small town of Tarkastad. Tony would visit the farm three or four times a year, usually during school holidays. He adored Rodney, even though Rodney teased him and played pranks on him. This included sending Tony on all sorts of wild goose chases and giving him challenges that Rodney knew Tony would not be able to complete. I remember Tony getting very upset with Rodney when he had sent Tony on a job to count some sheep on the other side of the property. Tony had to make sure that all the sheep were accounted for and report back to Rodney with his findings at dinner that evening. Tony found himself riding his horse all over the farm looking for a few missing sheep, which he never found. The reason for this was because Rodney had been having some fun and told his little cousin to look for more sheep than there actually were. It was another one of Rodney's character tests.

Tony was often joined at the farm by his cousin Roy Taylor and friend Paul Ensor. Once, when Rodney offered the three boys money if they would spend a night in his shed which was about 100 metres from the homestead, all three eagerly accepted the challenge. With the help of his farmhands who made noises like ghosts, Rodney terrorised the three boys. Soon they turned up in the homestead as white as ghosts themselves. No money changed hands.

Rodney's constant teasing was so bad that he and Tony often came close to blows. This would also have had a positive impact: it taught Tony how to develop a thick skin and cope with sledging. He learnt to treat it like 'water off a duck's back' as he would often say. Tony always believed the time he spent at Rodney's farm, getting up at dawn to milk cows, doing the other farm jobs and all the pranks, was character-building. It instilled in him a discipline and a toughness that lasted all his life.

He learnt to drive when he was twelve and was also taught the dos and don'ts of firearms. Once, following a heated argument with his cousin Roy, he fired a .22 bullet into a tree above Roy's head. When Rodney heard about the incident he was furious. In fear of a thrashing, Tony and Roy were nowhere to be found until Rodney's staff 'captured' them and put each boy in a wool bale bag which they hung from the rafters. They were left there long enough for Tony to have time to think about how stupid he had been. He became a very responsible person after that episode.

Tony loved his time on the farm, and though Rodney often showed it in strange ways, he loved him, as did his wife Angela. Tony was godfather to their first son, Martin, who tragically died at the age of one due to a hole in the heart. Rodney and Angela also asked Tony to be the godfather of their second son, Ashley.

Tony's success as a schoolboy sportsman was not mirrored as a scholar. He had ambitions to become a history teacher and had been offered a place at Rhodes University in Grahamstown, after which he would have a post at Queen's College. First, though, he had to pass his final exams but when he got pneumonia, he missed the last two. The school said he could come back at the start of the next year and sit those two exams, but they were wrong. To gain admission to the university, he had to pass all the exams in one sitting. On the second attempt, he failed Afrikaans. So after turning eighteen he had to return to Queen's, in 1965, and do another whole year of school.

By that time he was an automatic selection for Border Schools in the Nuffield Week, where his performance with bat and ball secured him a spot in South African Schools Nuffield XI. In the game against Griqualand West he batted at number six and scored 23. He also made his first-class debut for Border against Transvaal B. In that game he scored 37 and took two wickets.

By the end of that extra school year he had qualified for university, but first he was required to do a year of National

Service, which at the time was compulsory for all young South African men. University was to be put off for twelve months. However, he failed the National Service medical test. We never knew the reason, but we assumed it was because of his epilepsy. So Tony had to find something else to do for twelve months, which was when he had the idea of playing a season of cricket in England. With its strong connection to Queen's, Sussex CCC was a good place to start. In Tony's last year at school the Sussex player who spent the English winter there was Mike Buss. Tony asked him what the chances might be of him playing some matches with Sussex. Mike had seen something he liked in Tony's cricket, so he urged Sussex to give him a chance. The club agreed and made a deal for a small wage of about £20 a week, but Tony had to pay his own fare to England.

Having been accepted by Sussex, Tony still had one more hurdle to overcome: gaining Sandy's approval. While his father didn't think the salary was high enough, or that cricket was a proper career, they talked about it at length and Sandy eventually agreed to Tony going to England. We were not in a great financial position at the time, so a family friend lent Tony the money to cover the fare, on a ship called the *Pendennis Castle*. To pay off the loan, he got a job as a deliveryman with the South African Railways, delivering parcels all over East London.

When the time came to leave in March 1966, fortunately Mike Buss was also on the *Pendennis Castle*, so he could teach Tony the ways of international travel. The journey was not without incident: all the passengers were at one point put on emergency alert when someone fell overboard and drowned. When the ship finally made it safely to England,

Tony quickly settled in, helped by Mike and his brother Tony, another Sussex player. Soon we had reports that Tony's dedication had greatly impressed the Buss brothers. It had been snowing, but Tony would still go out and practise his bowling.

In addition to what he considered to be a small salary, something else annoyed Sandy – the fact that Tony had to get residential status to be regarded as an English cricketer. Until that happened, he had to be registered as an 'overseas player'. Sandy felt that since he had risked his life many times for Great Britain, it was something his son should have been offered automatically.

Due to the residential qualification laws, Tony couldn't leave the United Kingdom for more than eight weeks, therefore he had to cut short his holiday in South Africa at the end of his first summer with Sussex. So instead he first went to Scotland to work in the electrical department in his grandfather's business, Greig Bros.

Eventually, when he did get home to South Africa for the Christmas holidays, we all listened eagerly to the stories of his first year at Sussex, the famous cricketers he had played against and what he hoped to achieve in his second season. It was obvious to Sandy and me that he was more interested in playing cricket than going to university. He was no longer a boy playing in the backyard pretending to be one of his heroes, or a schoolboy champion; our boy had become a man. At the end of the Christmas holidays, he began preparing himself for another season in England. Then, as the train pulled out of Queenstown station, bound for East London, with Tony waving out of the window, I thought to myself, 'He is on his way.' I said a little prayer and hoped that the Lord would help him fulfil his ambitions to become a respected cricketer in England. That he did so in a way that would exceed even the expectations of his greatest supporter, his mother, is an amazing story. It is one I am going to let my grandson Mark, who has heard much of it since the days he first sat on Tony's knee, tell from here.

7

County Apprenticeship

MY DAD WAS NOT THE GREATEST BATSMAN. NOR WAS HE ONE of the great bowlers. However, I would argue that he was one of the great all-rounders of the game. In my opinion, if a team possesses a genuine all-rounder, and their opponents don't, they have a decided advantage. It is almost like twelve playing against eleven. History suggests that if a cricketer averages 40 over his career, he is a genuine batsman. For a bowler, the ability to take a wicket at a cost of around 30 runs would be the equivalent. Dad achieved both in his 58 Tests for England, though he was always very modest about his record and his ability as an all-rounder. In his mind, a great all-rounder was someone such as Sir Garfield Sobers, for whom he had the greatest respect. In Sobers' 93 Test matches, he achieved a batting average of 57.78 and a bowling average of 34.03. What is undeniable, however, and I hear this from just about anyone I talk to who played with or against Dad, is that Dad's true greatness lay in getting the absolute best out of himself, and out of the teams he captained.

Dad saw the value of team spirit when he took over the captaincy of his schoolboy rugby team at Queen's College. As my grandmother Joycie noted, the team had not been successful under his predecessor and Dad realised quickly that the talent was there, but not the team spirit. So he set about creating a bunch of happy teammates who would play for each other.

Much of the inspiration for the way Dad went about his cricket came from the disciplines he learnt at Queen's College, and also those he learnt during the time he spent working at Newtondale, his older cousin Rodney King's farm. While Rodney teased Dad a lot, he instilled in him the need to work hard and to do things properly, no matter what the conditions. Joycie has mentioned that when Dad got to Sussex for the first year, he was out practising his bowling in the snow while the rest of his county colleagues sought the warmth of the changing room, nodding their heads at this South African and saying they thought he was mad.

Dad thought about it differently. He was at Sussex on trial, and only because people such as Sussex players Mike and Tony Buss had shown faith in him. He felt he owed it to them to deliver, and in Dad's mind this meant he should be working harder than the next bloke. Still only a young player himself at Sussex, Mike Buss really went out on a limb to recommend Dad. Tony Buss also became a big supporter. It was in Dad's nature to go over and above to repay that sort of faith and trust. We were to see this trait many years later in the relationship he had with Kerry Packer.

Another source of inspiration for the way Dad played cricket was his father. Sandy had given Dad his blessing to go to England and try to make a career in county cricket, but there was one condition: he had to do it in four years or return to South Africa and go to university, then teach at Queen's College.

The fearless way Dad went about his cricket was no doubt linked to Sandy's war record. After all, what was facing a piece of leather coming at you at 150 kilometres per hour compared with being shot at by German fighters and artillery?

Dad did pretty well in his trial year with Sussex in 1966 in a difficult environment. While some Sussex players didn't like him and even resented the presence of this gangling South African, the Buss brothers continued to give him solid support.

Being away from Joycie's motherly attention was not an issue for Dad, as this was taken care of when he moved in with the woman who was a surrogate mother to many a Sussex player, Mrs Flo Cooper. She was originally from Yorkshire, but became a great servant of Sussex cricket by providing board and lodgings for young cricketers trying to make a go of it in the county, which included my uncle Ian years later.

Most of Dad's time that first summer was spent with the Second XI, the perennial home of both young dreamers and mature cricketing fringe-dwellers and hard-heads. Dad scored 362 runs at an average of 22.62 and took 42 wickets at 21.24. They were not the greatest of statistics, but the people at Sussex liked the way he played his cricket. There was a certain swagger to it. *Wisden*, the famous cricketing reference book, would later describe Dad as having 'what Noel Coward described simply as star quality'.

When he returned to Sussex from his Queenstown Christmas holiday in 1967, it was for the first year of a three-year contract. Again he was not universally welcomed. There were some older players who felt threatened by him, as were a number of young players, so Dad knew he needed to prove himself fairly quickly. At the start of the season, former England wicketkeeper Jim Parks, the county captain, took Dad aside and told him he would be picked in the First XI, would bat at number five, and would be given the time to settle into the team. His County Championship debut was a home game at Hove against the might of Lancashire, over a scheduled three days starting on 3 May 1967.

Sussex batted first and were in trouble early against the All-England pace attack of Brian Statham, Ken Higgs, Peter Lever and Ken Shuttleworth. The Hove cricket ground is on the Sussex coast and over the years a mystique has built up around the sea fret, or misty haze, and the help it gives to fast bowlers. Brian Statham never needed any help at the best of times. He played 70 Tests for England, in which he took 252 wickets. In partnership with Freddie Trueman, he formed one of the fiercest fast bowling combinations in the history of English Test cricket.

Sussex was soon 3–34 – Statham two wickets, Higgs one – then Dad came to the wicket. What happened next is now the stuff of legend in the Greig household, as it is one of the big breaks in life that Dad was lucky to get. If Statham and a few of the others involved had received royalties every time Dad had told the story, they would all be very wealthy people.

The story goes back to when Sandy decided to stay in South Africa after the war. In the late 1940s he befriended a man by the name of Harold 'Dusty' Rhodes, an English cricketer from Derbyshire who was coaching cricket in Queenstown when my dad was a young boy. For a few years Dusty and Sandy, fellow ex-pats, used to meet regularly for an evening drink at Barwin's Grand Hotel in Queenstown. Eventually, Dusty returned to England and inadvertently didn't settle his final bar bill. Sandy kindly took care of it for him, as any good drinking mate would have done.

Some twenty years later, Dad was playing his first game for Sussex 1st XI, against Lancashire. Sussex had won the toss, batted first, and were 3 for 34 by the time it was Dad's turn to bat. He walked out to the middle knowing how important it was for him to get some runs on debut. What he didn't know was that the umpire was Dusty Rhodes, Sandy's old drinking buddy. Brian Statham, who had already taken two of the wickets, walked back past the umpire to get set to fire one in at the young debutant standing in front of the stumps he intended to knock over. Dusty asked Statham, 'Who's this kid?' Statham didn't know, but the Lancashire captain, Jackie Bond, had been on the ship that brought Dad over from South Africa. He recognised him from the fancy dress party when Dad had dressed up as Snow White and all the other cricketers on board had been the Seven Dwarfs. So he knew who Dad was, and informed Rhodes, 'He's a South African lad called Greig.'

Dad took guard from the umpire, and then settled into his stance at the crease as Statham came thundering in off his long run-up. His first ball to Dad was a screamer and pitched right up in the block hole. It cannoned into Dad's foot, right in front of middle stump. The entire Lancashire team went up for the appeal. Dad thought he was a gone for sure, out plumb lbw for a duck. He sheepishly looked down the pitch at the umpire, who looked back at him and just shook his head and said, 'Not out.'

Dad thought he must have got extremely lucky. Statham's next ball was much the same as the first one, lightning fast. It found an inside edge and took off down to fine leg for an easy single. When he arrived at the other end of the wicket, he received a curious look from the umpire. 'Your name's Greig, is it lad?'

Dad replied, 'Yes it is.'

'Are you related to Sandy Greig from Queenstown by any chance?'

Dad was taken back. He said, 'Sandy's my dad.'

Dusty Rhodes turned his head back down the wicket and Dad thought he heard him mumble to himself, 'That was a good decision, then.'

Dad went on to make 156 runs that day, one of his highest scores ever in county cricket. Sussex made 324, and the next highest score after Dad's 156, which for the statistically minded contained 22 fours, was 32. John Snow reduced Lancashire to 4–21 before the rain intervened. Dad told me that many of the other county games had been washed out, which meant that he had the headlines to himself for a few days, all these reports about this strapping big South African batsman with a shock of blond hair. It was heady stuff, but Earth and Dad were to collide pretty heavily in the next game. It was at the famous Fenner's Ground in Cambridge against the university.

Before he began a highly successful career at Essex, David Acfield, an off-spinner, played for Cambridge

University. He was also a champion fencer, winning a Commonwealth Games gold medal in 1970 and twice representing Great Britain at the Olympic Games. Dad was lucky on this occasion that David was using a cricket ball and not an épée as he put his first ball right through Dad: out for a duck.

After that setback, he took a more sensible approach to the rest of the summer. He gave himself the goal of scoring 1000 runs, which he knew from his schoolboy days of reading the English cricket reports was a decent mark to aim for, that and 100 wickets for the season. He scored the 1000 runs he wanted so dearly, 1299 in fact, and he had a decent crack at the famous double of also taking 100 wickets – he took 67 scalps. The cricket writers who had so revelled in Dad's innings against Lancashire also honoured him by naming him their Young Cricketer of the Year.

By the winter of 1967, Sandy and Joycie, along with Molly Joy, Sally Ann and Ian, were living in Scotland, helping run the Greig family business. After taking a holiday and joining them in Edinburgh, it was time for Dad to play some more cricket. Joe Lister, a former first-class cricketer turned administrator, invited him to be part of a three-month international tour of Asia and Africa. His teammates included people he was to one day play alongside in the English Test team – Mike Denness, Keith Fletcher and Derek Underwood. Not unexpectedly, Dad's bowling proved a bit too good for the batsmen of Sierra Leone, hardly the fiercest cricket rival in the game.

Travelling on a South African passport on that tour became problematic because of the growing political objections to apartheid. Dad sought permission to apply for a British passport, but the South African Embassy in London said this was not possible. Later, while back in South Africa for a short holiday, he approached the Minister of Home Affairs and was given permission. Sussex thought this a great opportunity to have him classified as an English cricketer, rather than an overseas player, but the Registration Committee didn't agree. That committee was to have trouble with Dad's status for quite some time. In 1973, he was still regarded as an overseas player with Sussex, even though by then he had played nineteen games for England.

Playing as an overseas player in 1968, Dad had a decent season with bat and ball, 1305 runs and 55 wickets, but Sussex had a dreadful year, finishing bottom of the County Championship. In that competition there was only one real highlight for Sussex, the return of former England captain Ted Dexter to the team three years after his retirement. I heard Dad talk about this moment many times because it did two things. It allowed him to see first-hand what a brilliant batsman Ted Dexter was when he scored a double century against Kent. It also had a huge impact on team spirit at Sussex, something Dad always emphasised.

In 1970, Sussex had a disappointing County Championship season but made the final of the Gillette Cup. Dad was particularly impressive in the quarter-final against Kent, scoring 54 and then taking 7–42. When he came on to bowl, Kent was 1–88, chasing 199. These were the sorts of performances that led to Dad being picked for the England team that played the Rest of the World in 1970. South Africa had been due to tour that summer but because of the sporting boycotts over its apartheid policies, the tour was abandoned.

Instead, five Tests were to be played against a 'Rest of the World' team that included five South Africans – Graeme and Peter Pollock, Barry Richards, Eddie Barlow and Mike Procter. At that time *Wisden* gave the games Test status and Dad was picked for the second Test at Trent Bridge in Nottingham, where he featured as a bowler. His selection was big news in South Africa, and in particular in Queenstown. Needless to say, it was the page one lead in *The Daily Representative*, even before Sandy had become editor.

On the night Tony's selection was announced, Sandy and Joycie were both in bed early suffering from a heavy cold. No matter how sick he was, though, Sandy wouldn't miss the BBC radio sports round-up, which gave great coverage of English cricket, and his elder son's name was being mentioned with increasing regularity. When the BBC announced Tony's selection, Sandy and Joyce made miraculous recoveries from their colds. Sandy had a huge grin and Joycie let out a huge whoopee, saying, 'It's wonderful, it's wonderful!' over and over again. Sally Ann, who was sixteen at the time, was overjoyed by the news and in the celebration that followed there might have been a few tears of happiness. Sally Ann even remembers the exact time Tony rang home that night: it was 8.52pm. Sandy answered and shouted, 'Joyce, it's Brighton, Anthony's on the line!' They told Dad they'd already heard the news and the excitement was shared at both ends of the line.

In the Rest of the World's first innings, Dad took the wickets of Barry Richards, Rohan Kanhai, Sir Garfield Sobers and Farokh Engineer. In the second, he dismissed Eddie Barlow, Richards and Sobers. Anyone would take those as their first seven wickets in Test cricket, anytime. At that stage Richards and Sobers were the best batsmen in the world, along with Graeme Pollock. England, having lost the first Test at Lord's, won this second Test at Trent Bridge by eight wickets.

England was then defeated in the third Test at Edgbaston in Birmingham, with Sandy's good friend Dusty Rhodes umpiring. Dad contributed with the bat, scoring 55 in the first innings, but was not successful in taking a wicket in the sixteen overs he bowled in the match.

In the fourth Test at Headingley in Leeds, Dad was again taking the wickets of the big names – Barlow again, Graeme Pollock, Mushtaq Mohammad and Intikhab Alam. Dad played three of the five Tests and wasn't picked for the last match, which was a surprise to the cricket writers, given the success he was having as a bowler. They were to be further surprised when he was left out of the team to tour Australia under Ray Illingworth. He told me many times how disappointed he was to miss that tour. Later, the decision to give those Rest of the World games Test-match status was overturned, but Dad still had his England cap and he wasn't about to give it back.

In 1971, Dad had to content himself with playing county cricket and do the best he could with bat and ball. In September that year Dad returned to South Africa to get himself ready for the next English summer. He knew that when he got back to England he would need to impress the selectors enough to lay claim to the all-rounder's spot in the England side. Being in South Africa also gave Dad a chance to catch up with the woman who was to become my mother, Donna Reed, whom he had been fond of for a long time.

Mum lived in Queenstown and was a friend of Dad's sister Molly Joy. Mum and Dad met when Mum was at Queenstown Girls High School, one of the most prestigious schools for girls in South Africa. Dad was a boarder at Queens at the time.

In the early days, Mum and Dad's relationship could never really progress, as Dad would go off to England to play cricket and Mum went to a finishing school in Switzerland. Dad was impressed by this, and it wasn't long before he tracked her down, wanting to see what impact a finishing school might have had on the young girl he knew in Queenstown.

The romance continued when Mum attended an exclusive modelling school in London. Dad thought he had made arrangements for Donna to rendezvous with him on his return to England from the Joe Lister-led tour. He got a shock when he arrived at Heathrow Airport, and Donna wasn't there waiting for him. Instead, she was working as a fashion designer in Switzerland.

It was to be a crucial test for Dad, not one with bat and ball, but one to see just how strongly he felt for Mum. Fortunately he didn't have to wait long for a connecting flight to Geneva. Ever resourceful, he had managed to find out where Mum was staying, and he phoned her when his plane landed in Geneva.

Mum, who found Dad's spontaneity a touch romantic, gave him directions on which train to catch to get to the town to meet her. She told me years later that when Dad arrived at the train station that day, and saw her standing there waiting for him, he ran to her with open arms. Unfortunately he didn't realise that the ice was slippery under foot, and apparently slid the last few metres on his bottom. His legs were everywhere, knocking Mum down on top of him as he came flying in. They gathered themselves and just lay on the platform in each other's arms, laughing and kissing.

They both accepted their relationship was the real deal, so Donna threw in her job and they returned to England together just in time for the 1970 cricket season.

At the completion of the season, they headed back to South Africa. Mum had been offered a job in Cape Town, but this meant she would be about 1200 kilometres away from Dad, who had arranged to be in Grahamstown as a coach at St Andrew's College during their cricket season. He hated being apart from Mum, as they had always been within dating distance of one another. He was missing her and decided he wanted her around more permanently. He called her in Cape Town, asking her when she would be going back to Queenstown, so he would make sure he was there at the same time to see her. Her response was that she had only intended to return to Queenstown as Mrs Greig. Dad responded that he would like nothing more, and explained he had been building up the courage to ask her to come and live with him in England. Being a man of tradition, he knew he had to first ask Mum's father, Gordon Reed, for her hand, as they say. He met Mum at her parents' home and they all enjoyed a cup of tea together. Mum took her mother, Jean, into another room, leaving Tony to chat with Gordon alone. While Dad was struggling to get the words out, Donna and her mother were listening in the next room.

Dad and Mum were officially engaged shortly afterwards, in fact on the day of Mum's 21st birthday while they were holidaying at Kei Mouth. Dad had been carrying the engagement ring around in the same tin as his pipe tobacco, and in his mind there was no better place to propose to her. Dad told me that he never understood why people have long engagements; he knew what he wanted and nobody was going to keep him waiting. He had known Donna for a long time. She was beautiful, smart and an absolute catch.

Tony and Donna were married on 20 March 1971, only five months after their engagement. It was a huge wedding with most of Queenstown in attendance, as well as many others who had come from all over South Africa. The weather was glorious and the sun was streaming through the stained glass windows of the Queenstown Methodist church. Donna wore a beautiful, traditional long white wedding dress. Tony and his groomsmen were in morning suits with top hats and gloves. The bridal party included Tony's sisters Molly Joy and Sally Ann, and also Donna's sister Eleanor Reed. Tony's best man was Paul Ensor and groomsmen were cousins Roy Taylor and Rory Taylor. Rodney King's son, Ashley, was the pageboy. As a surprise for his big brother and new sister-in-law, Ian arranged an impressive cricket bat guard of honour outside the church. Keeping with the cricket theme, former South African fast bowler Peter Pollock made a speech at the wedding reception. Hundreds of telegrams arrived from all over the world, including one from Sandy's close friend and newspaper colleague, Donald Woods and his wife Wendy.

After the wedding celebrations had come to an end, Mum and Dad immediately moved to England so Dad could continue playing cricket. Mum was extremely supportive and encouraging of Dad's cricket ambitions and in England she was able to adapt quickly to new surroundings. It didn't take long for Mr and Mrs Greig to make some great and lifelong friends and enjoy every opportunity to travel the world together.

Not long after settling into England with his new wife, Dad received a phone call from Donald Carr, the secretary of the English Test and County Cricket Board (TCCB), advising him that he had been selected in the Rest of the World team to tour Australia in place of the planned tour by South Africa.

The Australian Cricket Board had asked Sir Donald Bradman and Sir Garfield Sobers if they would pick the players for the touring squad. Fortunately for Dad, he was selected, along with another young South African cricketer, Hylton Ackerman. Hylton went to a rival school to Queen's called Dale College, and Dad had played cricket against him for years.

Sandy drove Dad to the airport in East London and gave him some fatherly advice. He wanted to make sure he knew what a great opportunity this was. Sandy encouraged Dad to make the most of the tour and to soak up everything he could while in Australia, including the wisdom of Sir Donald Bradman, whom Dad would most likely have the honour of meeting.

After flying across the Indian Ocean, Dad and Hylton landed in Perth, where while in transit they were approached by members of the local Cricket Lovers' Society. Three elderly gentlemen came up to them and suggested that they may like to join them in the airport coffee shop to chinwag about all things cricket. It was soon clear to Dad that they were very passionate cricket lovers and he humoured them with some polite chat. The conversation was draining after a long flight and Dad was somewhat excited to get back on the plane.

Touching down in Adelaide, they were greeted by another old bloke, a little man in glasses wearing a woollen cardigan. Automatically Dad thought this man was a member of another local Cricket Lovers' Society. Dad didn't catch the little man's name, but was happy to give him their bags to hold while they visited the bathroom to freshen up. Fifteen minutes later they eventually made their way to the coffee shop. The man who had greeted them was with a another guy called Phil Ridings, who unbeknownst to Dad was a former South Australian cricket captain and also a cricket administrator with Sir Donald Bradman. They started to talk about cricket and the little bloke (Bradman) seemed to be a bit of an expert on the subject. Eventually, Dad had to ask him: 'Tell me, do you actually have anything to do with cricket around here?' At the time, Sir Donald had retired from the Australian Cricket Board, though he was still running South Australian Cricket. His response to Dad was: 'Yes, Phil and I run things locally'. Dad had absolutely no idea who he was talking to. At this point in the conversation Garry Sobers came bounding over. Dad thought Sobers had come to meet him, so he stood up to shake his hand. Sobers walked straight past Dad and over to the little man he had been chatting with and reached out his hand and said, 'Good morning, Sir Donald. I'm so sorry I'm a little late, I was held up by traffic.'

Well Dad nearly died when he realised the faux pas he had just made. He told me that Sir Donald thought the incident was hilarious, and he never let him forget it either. Every time Dad saw him years after, he would come up to Dad and say, 'Have you got anything to do with cricket around here?'

At the start of that tour, Australia's batsmen were still shell-shocked from the previous Ashes tour, in which John Snow had bowled not just fast, but dangerously so. There was a hope that the Aussie batsmen would regain their confidence against the pop-gun attack comprising Dad, Asif Masood, an ageing 31-year-old Peter Pollock, Bob Cunis, Richard Hutton and Sobers. Dad decided he would be the enforcer. His appeals were over the top: if the batsmen got an edge, or played and missed, he would put on a mighty performance, holding his hands to his head, or shaking it in disbelief. His height just exaggerated the whole thing. However, rather than intimidated, the Australians were at first amused, and then slightly irritated because I don't think they rated him as a cricketer. To them, he was just a teddy bear, and they often told him so.

At the end of that World XI Tour of Australia in 1971–72 Dad had scored 525 runs at an average of 37, and he'd taken 26 wickets at an average of 26. These were the top batting and bowling figures. He played with world-class players, including the great Sir Garfield Sobers, who scored 254 runs in one innings which was been recognised in *Wisden* as one of the greatest innings seen by Bradman in Australia:

> Watching him in Melbourne, Bradman saw him
> play a straight drive against Dennis Lillee which
> smashed into the sightscreen almost before Lillee
> had straightened up from his follow-through. Sobers
> scored 254 (after a first-innings duck). Bradman,

no soft touch when it came to criticism, rated it the greatest innings he had ever seen on Australian soil.

Dad reckons he returned from that tour to Australia technically and mentally attuned to the demands of Test cricket. Marrying Donna and settling down must have had an extremely positive impact on his confidence. He was at a very happy stage of his life and had big ambitions for his cricket, and for his family.

8

The Crown and Lions

DAD PLAYED HIS FIRST 'REAL' TEST FOR ENGLAND IN JUNE 1972, when Australia toured England. It was at Old Trafford under the captaincy of Ray Illingworth. He loved it. He scored half-centuries, top-scoring for England in both innings on a treacherous wicket. What made it even more pleasing for him was that England won, and he got yet another story to talk about.

The Manchester wicket was seaming all over the place and soon the nicks were coming to the slip cordon, particularly off the bowling of Geoff Arnold. One flew towards Snow, who took some of the pace off it, but not enough to stop it going to the third man boundary. Dad dropped the next one, a sitter. The next one hit Snow on the foot. By now the captain, for whom they probably invented the phrase 'a canny Yorkshireman', had smoke coming out of his ears. Snow was sent to fine leg and Brian Luckhurst called into the slips. Dad could not believe it when a second catch went through his hands. By this time, Illingworth was the only slip fielder not to drop a catch; they knew a dressing-down was coming their way once back in the changing rooms. Close on stumps, the ball was nicked to Illingworth at third slip, and he dropped it. After stumps, Illingworth did an interview with the BBC in which he said: 'Old Trafford is a terrible seeing ground for slip fielders, the worst I've ever played on.'

Not only did Dad bat pretty well in that game, but he also featured in a partnership with another South African Englishman, Basil (Dolly) D'Oliveira. As a man of colour, Dolly was not qualified for selection in the South African side because of apartheid. The great English cricket broadcaster John Arlott had heard about D'Oliveira's plight and, in 1960, with the help of other cricket lovers in England and South Africa, arranged for him to come to England to play with the English club Middleton in the Central Lancashire Cricket League. From there, he had worked his way up to county level at Worcestershire, and was then picked for England. They might have come from different backgrounds in South Africa, and taken different paths to get there, but each man was now prepared to fight, and fight hard, for England. Dad scored 62 and 57, Dolly 37 and 23. With the ball, Dad claimed five wickets and Dolly two. They were substantial contributors to England's victory.

Dad also scored a half-century in a beaten side in the next Test at Lord's, when Australian swing bowler Bob Massie took sixteen wickets on debut. In the third Test, Keith Stackpole scored an excellent hundred for Australia in a drawn game. During that innings, he and Dad clashed a number of times, particularly over my father's loud 'oohs' and 'aahs' when he beat the bat. Not showing a great knowledge of zoology, Stackpole called Dad a typical South African teddy bear. No doubt Dad would have enjoyed telling Stackie there are no bears in Africa, just roaring lions that bite.

Headingley was the venue for the fourth Test. Derek Underwood bowled England to victory in three days, thus ensuring the English retained the Ashes won by Illingworth's tourists on the 1970–71 tour. Australia's consolation was that it won the fifth Test, leaving the series drawn at two–all.

Dad was by now thriving in Test cricket. He loved everything about it, most notably the passion he felt playing for England, a passion that reached exhilarating heights when they beat Australia. He was also about to discover another enduring passion – the Indian subcontinent.

During the tour of India in 1972–73, Dad fell in love with that country, a love that eventually extended to Sri Lanka. He also made it his business to have India fall in love with him. Because of his height and blond hair he stood out wherever he was in the world, which was magnified in India, where he began playing up to the crowds.

England won the first Test in New Delhi. Dad and his recently installed captain, Tony Lewis, were involved in the winning partnership. India won the second Test at Calcutta, or Kolkata as it is now known. The heat of Madras (now Chennai) proved too much for the English and they were smashed. In a drawn match at Bombay (now Mumbai) Dad had further reason to love India: it was the place where he scored his first Test century. For a cricketer raised on the hard wickets of South Africa and then the soft pitches of England, the Indian wickets presented a different range of issues, particularly against the spinners.

To score a hundred in these conditions was another sign of how his game had developed. Dad was awarded man of the match and the whole English team got to do something you don't see a lot of at a cricket match – an encore. After they left the field at the end of the game, they realised the crowd at Brabourne Stadium was cheering for them to come back, so Dad led them out to do a lap of honour. Tony Lewis probably should have been the person to do this, but he was doing media interviews. Afterwards he said he wasn't bothered that Tony had taken the initiative. Looking back, it again showed Dad's natural leadership qualities.

Things weren't all sweetness and light in India. Dad returned to England to face a disciplinary hearing. In the Kolkata Test, he had caught the Indian captain, Ajit Wadekar, in the slips. It was clearly out to everyone but the umpire. Dad lost his patience, big time. He ran down the pitch yelling and screaming at the umpire. It worked – Wadekar was eventually given out, but, as Dad agreed afterwards, it just wasn't cricket. He accepted an official reprimand.

As it transpired, April 1973 delivered Dad a double dose of responsibility: Sussex appointed him captain of the county and his first child, a daughter, Samantha, was born. Her birth was an exciting time for both families, as this gorgeous little baby girl was the first grandchild. Mum was very organised, so it went like clockwork. Dad was present at the birth and said that he had a tear in his eye at the first sight of his baby daughter entering the world. Granny Jean (Reed) and Granny Joycie both stayed with Mum and Dad.

Sam's birth created another subject for Dad and the authorities to squabble over. Mum and Dad took her everywhere; unfortunately frequent flyer programs weren't available to one year olds. The nomadic lifestyle of a cricketer became a challenge. Dad said he didn't just leave home reluctantly, he hated being apart from his family.

Cricket authorities originally forbade wives from travelling with their husbands. Dad was part of the vanguard that changed this archaic thinking. There was a softening of that rule over the years Dad played for England, but accompanying wives were tolerated rather than encouraged. For instance, on the 1974–75 tour of Australia, the wives were allowed to be with their husbands, but only for 21 days. Once that time was up, the wives either had to stay in another hotel or go home. After their 21 days were up, Dad put Mum up in another hotel. He said he felt like a criminal escaping from prison because of the secretive way he had to leave the team hotel to go and spend the night with Mum.

For Dad, who was big on team spirit, having lonely husbands separated from their wives always seemed a strange rule. It made it hard for him to get the best out of his team when it was obvious that some players were unhappy about being away from their wives for extended periods. One of the things Dad later insisted on in the negotiations for World Series Cricket was that wives be allowed to accompany their husbands. No wonder Kerry Parker had little trouble recruiting the cream of world cricket.

Meanwhile, despite that marvellous effort by Ted Dexter at Hastings a few years earlier, Sussex was pretty much a spiritless place when Dad took over as captain in 1973. One thing he did make clear was that there would be no quick fix. It would require time and patience, almost the type of patience needed to win in India, before the county would be a recognised force again.

Drawing on his experience with captaining the Queen's College rugby team, Dad set about making Sussex a better place to play cricket. Again he received great support from Mike and Tony Buss. As well as captaining Sussex, Dad played in the Test series against New Zealand and the West Indies. During that time he got a first-hand view of just how fragile a cricket career can be, even when you are captain of England. Illingworth was summarily dumped and replaced by Mike Denness.

Denness was on a hiding to nothing when he led England to the Caribbean for a return series against the West Indies in early 1974 with Dad as his vice-captain, albeit a temporary appointment. In the first Test at Port of Spain in Trinidad, which England lost, Dad had been involved in an incident with Alvin Kallicharran. It was the last over of day two and Bernard Julien, the West Indian all-rounder, was on strike. Derek Underwood was bowling and Julien kept just offering a dead bat to each ball. Dad went in as close as he could on the off side to Julien. Come the last ball, instead of playing a dead bat, Julien pushed it defensively on to the offside. Julien then turned on his heels and headed towards the pavilion behind him. Kallicharran, who had backed up, kept walking down the wicket to follow him, rather than first returning to place his bat in the crease at the bowling end. To Dad, who was chasing the ball, it just seemed that Kallicharran was setting off for a run, so he threw the ball at the stumps at the non-striker's end, hitting them. The umpire, the highly respected Douglas Sang Hue, who was later to be part of World Series Cricket, gave Kallicharran out because he had not yet called 'over' or 'end of play'. Kallicharran was so angry that he broke his bat on the steps of the changing rooms. The crowd were also angry; an international incident was brewing. Garry Sobers, who drove Dad back to the hotel, already knew instinctively that to avoid an ugly crowd incident the next morning, Kallicharran would have to resume his innings.

At the hotel, there were long discussions between England's management and West Indian officials. Eventually it was agreed that England would withdraw the appeal, even though what Dad had done was within the laws of the game, something umpire Sang Hue had verified. He said if the ball had missed the stumps it would have carried through to the boundary and Julien would have been given four runs. But the mood had moved angrily against England at both the crowd and official level. Before the agreement was reached to withdraw the appeal, there had been suggestions by some West Indian officials that Dad should fly home. The next morning, Kallicharran resumed his innings, Dad welcoming him to the wicket with a handshake, something he didn't have to do because he had done nothing wrong. The crowd was happy and the incident forgotten, except perhaps in official quarters in England. Many people felt that when Dad was passed over as vice-captain of the tour to Australia in 1974–75, this incident might have been the reason.

In the West Indies, it was the English captaincy that was proving the problem. A lot of the senior players, particularly Yorkshireman Geoff Boycott, resented Mike Denness being made captain over Illingworth. Denness wasn't an established Test player. Illingworth was old, but the players thought he had done a great job in Australia in 1970–71, and in England in 1972. Most thought he should not have been dropped for the tour of the West Indies. As vice captain, Dad felt it was his job to do everything he could to win them over, again on the basis of his credo that a happy team was a successful one. Part of that meant dealing with Boycott, whom he confronted about his behaviour and attitude. Being Geoffrey Boycott, he came back with a few confrontational remarks of his own, the result being that neither man spoke to each other for a week.

By the final Test in Port of Spain, the team had achieved a level of harmony that had them only one–nil down in the series. Dad thought this was a miracle, because the West Indies were by now growing into the formidable side that would dominate the game for the following two decades.

Then came another miracle. They won the final Test in Trinidad to square the series. Boycott scored 99 and 11. The biggest surprise, however, would have been Dad's bowling. He took thirteen wickets, not with his customary medium pace, but with off spin. He revelled in taking the ball away from the left-handers in the West Indian batting line-up. These included the great Clive Lloyd. Dad got him cheaply in both innings in this match. The series tied, Denness held on to the captaincy, while Boycott went into a self-imposed exile from international cricket for three years.

Back in England, Denness captained England against Pakistan and India and was then picked as captain for the 1974–75 tour of Australia. Dad was in the team, but disappointed not to be vice-captain; the position was given to John Edrich, a man of great experience who would, literally, bleed for England. So would a few of his teammates.

After winning the final Test against England at The Oval in 1972, the Australian team under Ian Chappell had really begun to grow into a tight unit. By the time

Mike Denness's side arrived in Australia in 1974 replete with a battery of fast bowlers of its own, Lillee was in the early stages of a comeback after a back operation, the success of which was still uncertain. As for Jeff Thomson, he was known for being smacked all over the ground by Pakistan when he made his Test debut in 1972. Before playing in that Test he had broken a bone in his foot, but hadn't told the selectors. The selectors were angry with him for not disclosing his injury, as he shouldn't have played. Over in England, the British press also mistook him for another fast bowler, Alan Thomson. This other Thomson had played four Tests against Ray Illingworth's side in 1970–71 and while he had bowled plenty of bouncers at both the English captain and John Snow and managed to get twelve wickets, he had done so very expensively at an average of 54.50 runs per wicket.

Alan Thomson's career was pretty much over by 1974–75 and, for a time, it looked like Jeff Thomson's career might go the same way after his unhappy Test debut. His career had drifted for a while, but playing for New South Wales in the final Sheffield Shield match of the 1973–74 season, he bowled pretty quickly against Queensland, at that time captained by Greg Chappell. Over the winter, Greg managed to convince Jeff to move to Queensland.

England played against Thomson in a tour game versus Queensland, but Greg Chappell told him to bowl within himself, which led the English press to believe that his claim that he loved hitting batsmen and seeing their blood on the pitch was no more than typical Aussie boasting.

Lillee and Thomson were picked for the first Test on Queensland's home ground, the 'Gabba. Australia batted first. When Lillee came in to bat, the adherents of the 'fast bowlers' union' in the English side declined to bounce him, as fast bowlers were generally thought to be incompetent batsmen and so agreed not to bowl bouncers at each other. Thinking that was a load of rubbish, Dad went to Mike Denness and asked to bowl. He bounced Lillee with his first ball, hitting his glove out in front of his face and knocking him off his feet. Alan Knott took an easy caught behind.

Dad got a short, sharp lesson in Australian expletives as Dennis walked down the pitch back towards the pavilion. Long after the tour ended, Dad denied this was the start of the bouncer war that was the central theme of that series. He reckoned the Australians were ready to serve them up anyway. He was just getting his retaliation in first.

England was soon in trouble in its first innings, courtesy of that well-known Australian sheila, 'Lillian Thomson'. When Dad came in, it was to the sight of Lillee far off in the distance. Dad reckoned the first ball was so short and fast that wicketkeeper Rod Marsh had no chance of reaching it, even with a stepladder.

It was about now that the spirit and genes of Sandy Greig took hold. Rather than being subdued by the attack, Dad began to goad Lillee. When he hit a four, he signalled it before the umpire. The angrier Lillee got, the shorter he bowled. The 'Gabba wicket was more suited to well-pitched-up balls. Dad readily admits there was a lot of luck in his innings, but he scored a century, and that was to remain one of his favourite memories. London *Sun* newspaper cricket writer, Clive Taylor, wrote: 'In five hours in which he might well have won a medal for valour, the Queen's Award to Industry, and an Oscar for acting, Greig dragged England from 4–57, to 9–248 when he made the return journey to a reception that was tumultuous. What we have here is vintage Greig – handsome, arrogant, mocking, bloody-minded, brave and talented beyond the ordinary. Greig's performance will have legend-makers speaking of him in the same awesome company as Hammond, Compton and the golden names of the game.'

Unfortunately, Thomson broke Edrich's arm during that match, the first of many injuries the English were to suffer at the hands of Thomson and Lillee. After the departure of Edrich and a few others, Dad was joined at the wicket by Derek Underwood, the spinner.

Dad told me Derek was one of the bravest tail-end batsmen in the game and had no idea what to say to him when Derek nervously came out to bat. I recently asked Derek about that first Test at the 'Gabba in 1974, and what it was like facing that deadly Australian pace attack. He told me that Dad had the Aussie bowlers very hot under the collar. Apparently when he arrived at the wicket he asked Dad if he had any advice. Dad's response was: 'Yes, fight for your life.' Thomson let it fly at him, and his second ball missed his head by only a fraction. He told me he was as white as a ghost. Somehow he managed to survive until the end of the over and he strolled down to meet Dad mid-wicket and said, 'I see what you mean.'

Derek told me that Dad was seeing the ball very well that day and was dispatching Lillee and Thomson to the boundary with ease, giving the 4 run signal back at them. Derek watched as Lillee got wilder and wilder. He went down the wicket and said to Dad: 'All right for you, mate, but give me a thought will you?' Dad's response was a huge smile.

There's no doubt Dad relished this fight in the same way he did many other times in his sporting life, and beyond, when he found himself in a tough situation. In recent years he has been quoted by many a past Sussex player who had played under Dad's captaincy in the 1970s. 'You have to stand up in order to be counted.' he would say to them before big matches. While writing this book I found another quote of Dad's which we've also included at the beginning of the book. It's worth repeating it here, as it sums him up so well:

> You need talent, but you need more than that. You need this special thing that some people have which makes them play above themselves; a little better than you perceive they should be, based on talent alone. You need to relish confrontation. I adored backs-to-the-wall situations.

No mention of that first Test at the 'Gabba can be made without telling the sandshoe crusher story, well at least in Australia. Dad was always dismissive of the story, saying it was beaten up by the Australian press. For a start, he wasn't wearing sandshoes, he was wearing a brand of cricket boots called Nike Astro Grabbers. They looked like sandshoes and were different from the traditional cricket boot. The pitch had been very muddy when the English side inspected it two days before the start of the Test, so no doubt he wore boots that would give him the best possible grip.

Since Lillee had bowled too short to Dad in the first innings, the Australian captain, Ian Chappell, demanded that in the second innings both Lillee and Thomson pitch the ball up. Thomson bowled Dad with a big in-swinging yorker for two. The Australian players and the media claimed the ball, which they dubbed the sandshoe crusher, had been specifically designed to dismiss Dad because of his exaggerated backlift.

Dad said it was the only time he was bowled out in the series and the use of the expression 'sandshoe crusher' was just a conspiracy between the Australian team and Australian media to try to psyche him out in future matches. In later years he claimed it was typical Australian bulldust in the same way Shane Warne claimed he had developed a new mystery ball before every series and the Australian media would whip it up into a big story.

In 1974–75, with limbs being broken and blokes leaping and falling about all over the place, England needed reinforcements. The tour selection panel got together and it was decided to send for Dad's schoolboy hero, Colin Cowdrey, who was now in his forties. Emerging from the English winter to the heat of an Australian summer, convivial as ever, he must have had some idea of what lay before him because when he opened his kit bag, it was full of foam rubber, most of which he wrapped around himself before he went in to bat. Dad said no one in the English team laughed when they saw what he was doing. They knew immediately their revered new teammate, one of England's finest ever players, a man who had gone out to face fierce West Indian paceman Wes Hall with his arm in a plaster cast, was well aware of what they were all up against.

Perth's WACA is the fastest and bounciest wicket in Australia, probably in the world. In the second Test, Colin Cowdrey batted at number three for England in the first innings and opened in the second. When he first arrived at the crease, the famously polite Colin actually walked up to Jeff Thomson and said, 'Mr Thomson, it is so good to meet you.' Thommo's reply was apparently something along the lines of, 'Well that's not going to f****** help you, so get up there and bat!' In both innings, Cowdrey stayed at the wicket for a long while, taking blow after blow to his body. Dad felt he had done the job the selectors had asked of him, though he was out to Jeff Thomson in both innings.

The Australians won handsomely – by nine wickets – and had much to celebrate in addition to a 2–nil advantage in the fight for the Ashes. A highlight of Australia's first innings was when Doug Walters hooked the last ball of the day from England fast bowler Bob Willis for six to not only bring up his century, but to score 100 runs in a session.

The third Test was drawn, but Denness failed in both innings, so he dropped himself for the fourth, with Edrich, now fit again, taking over as captain. The change in captaincy had little impact on England's fortunes. Australia won by 171, Dad top-scoring in England's second innings with 54. Australia won the fifth Test and then, without Thomson due to injury and Lillee breaking down after just six overs, lost the sixth Test. Denness made 188. Dad made 89 in England's only innings and took five wickets, four in the second innings, as Australia was dismissed for 373, four runs shy of making the English bat again. It was some compensation for what had been a difficult tour.

Dad had been building himself a following in Australia as a sort of anti-hero. The Australian players admired his courage and grit but thought he behaved as though he were a superstar. To their mind, he was an average player rather than a great one. As for the crowds, Dad gave them a lot of stick – and got a lot back. He kept his collar turned up and tied a white handkerchief around his neck. When things were quiet, he would ask Mike Denness to send him down to third man where he could engage in a bit of polite conversation. Whether or not Australians liked Tony Greig, they couldn't avoid him. He became an indelible part of that summer, along with the little ditty that summed up the series: 'Ashes to Ashes, dust to dust, if Lillee don't get you, Thommo must!'

9

Captain of England

In 1975, cricket's first World Cup was held in England. 'Fortunately' for Dad, Australia defeated England in the semi-finals. I was born on 20 June 1975, the day before the West Indies beat Australia in the final at Lord's. I don't think Mum would have been too impressed with Dad heading off to play cricket a few hours after I was born. Sally Ann came to England to help with Sam and be with Mum. British car dealers Leyland had given Dad a mini clubman for Mum to drive, and her tummy was so big she couldn't fit behind the steering wheel. Sally Ann had to drive everywhere. Dad had two weeks with no cricket that season. The first was the week I was due and the other was the week we moved to Dyke Close.

On the eve of the first week I showed no signs of appearing so Mum decided to take matters into her own hands. She ran a very hot bath, took a huge dose of castor oil (first sucking on ice to kill the foul taste) and then poured a strong gin and tonic, which she drank lying in the hot bath. Sally Ann insisted she leave the door open and checked on her every few minutes. They laughed their heads off. Dad got in at midnight and at 2.00am he woke Sally Ann to say that Donna was in a terribly sick state with an upset tummy and that the ambulance was on the way. He was furious with Sally Ann for allowing Mum to do what she did. But it worked – I came that day. I weighed a whopping 12lbs 15oz. Believe it or not, when my own daughter Jessica was born in Sydney nearly 30 years later, the midwife recognised the name Greig and said she had delivered Tony Greig's son in England and to this day he was the heaviest baby born at Brighton Hospital. She said Tony's son 'came out looking three months old'. She almost fell over when we worked out that I was that baby.

After the World Cup, Australia stayed on for a four-Test series. Denness, who was captain for the first Test at Edgbaston, won the toss and asked Australia to bat. Even Jeff Thomson got runs as Australia reached 359. Lillee, Thomson and Max Walker then combined to bowl England out twice on a rain-affected pitch. The English cricket press had been hounding Denness for some time, which hadn't gone unnoticed by the selectors – they had only appointed him for the first Test.

After such a heavy loss, his sacking appeared inevitable. Dad, however, said it was not until the rest day, a Sunday as it turned out, at Edgbaston that it dawned on him he might be the next England captain. Having already been dismissed in England's second innings, he could relax a bit, so he met up with some of his teammates at a pub in the country where the Sunday papers were laid out for the customers. The columnists had it in for Mike Denness, with some suggesting Dad was the man to take over.

He wondered whether the Wadekar and Kallicharran incidents were being discussed again at Lord's. He reflected on the way previous captains had been dealt with, including Ray Illingworth whom Dad always felt had been unfairly treated. Like Ian Chappell, who had witnessed how Bill Lawry had been dealt with when he was stripped of the Australian captaincy, Dad vowed that if he became England captain he would never allow himself to be treated in the way Denness was at that moment. He also said to himself that if he were offered the job, he would take it. Soon after, he was asked by Alec Bedser, chairman of selectors, if he would accept the captaincy. Dad said 'yes' without any hesitation. He was humbled by the appointment, and although there was no higher honour in English sport, Dad wanted the job not for the kudos, but because he thought he could make a difference in the selection room and inspire the team to reach greater heights.

One of the first changes Dad made as captain, after all the rounds of media interviews, was to literally put a bit of Steele into England's batting. David Steele was 33, prematurely grey, and with his spectacles he looked more like a librarian than an opening batsman capable of repelling Lillee and Thomson, but Dad had a high opinion of the Northamptonshire batsman and thought he could make a much-needed positive contribution. In fact, Dad approached all the England bowlers, plus a few others, and asked them one simple question: 'Who is the hardest, most qualified English batsman to get out in county cricket?' Almost to a man, they came back with the same name, David Steele.

In the changing rooms before the second Test at Lord's when Dad presented Steele with his England cap, Steele was clearly moved. Steele was to repay Dad's faith enormously. He made 50 and 45 in that Test, which was drawn. David and Dad featured in a long partnership, and Dad went very close to scoring a century in his first Test as captain, reaching 96.

Dad's joy at the team's improvement and his own success was heightened when his father, Sandy, accepted his offer to fly him to England for the Test. Sandy's trip was not without its problems. Having taken out South African citizenship after he married Joycie, he didn't realise he now needed a visa to get into England. When he arrived at Heathrow Airport, he was put in a special room for deportation. During a heated exchange with the immigration officer, he declared that during the war he had flown into England 54 times without a visa. That argument held no weight, so he insisted on seeing a supervisor. That brought no joy. Sandy then insisted on seeing the supervisor's supervisor, who turned out to be a man of Indian descent. Sandy played the 'I'm here for a week to see my son Tony captain England' card, and the supervisor, a cricket fanatic, let Sandy in. Tony's match was made even more memorable as his sister Sally Ann attended, as well as his South African cousin Rodney King and his wife, Angela. Rodney had honoured a commitment made many years before to attend Dad's first Test as captain.

At Leeds in the third Test, David Steele made 73 and 92. During this match protestors dug up the wicket and the players arrived for day five to discover the disaster. The vandalism to the Headingley pitch was done by supporters of George Davis, an ex-armed robber who was serving a twenty-year prison sentence for the London Electricity Board robbery. England was pretty certain to win that game and if Dad had made an issue of it, he could have pressed for the game to be completed. Instead, in a display of great sportsmanship, he agreed with Ian Chappell to call the game off. Ian has always said this was a fine gesture, and one that took a lot of pressure off him at the time. It used to amuse, if not bemuse, Dad that the press, the self-appointed moral guardians of society, wrote about his indiscretions hundreds, if not thousands, of times, but never referred to his decision to agree to call off the Leeds Test when in a winning position.

In the fourth Test, Steele scored 39 in the first innings and 66 in the second, part of a brave rearguard action to stave off an innings defeat. He frustrated the hell out of the Australian bowlers, who struggled to find ways to dismiss him. Nevertheless, Australia won the series 1–nil.

Dad was to discover quickly how fickle the English cricket media could be. Hailed as the saviour when first appointed, he was now being criticised for not delivering a victory. His initial aim when he took over the side had been to improve team spirit and performance. He thought it was harsh considering England could so easily have won the Test at Leeds and thus drawn the series. The media's unfair treatment of him reinforced Dad's promise to himself that he would eventually get out before the media and selectors got him.

With no Tests scheduled for England in the winter of 1975–76, Dad returned to the grassroots and played club cricket in Australia. Before he was appointed captain of England, he had negotiated a deal to play in Sydney with Waverley Cricket Club. Dad's future long-time friend and manager Bruce Francis had played for the club, which was looking to sign a top player. Initially the push had been for Dennis Lillee, but when he successfully overcame his back injury and resumed his career for Australia, he was unavailable.

Bruce had then approached Dad. They had known each other since the Rest of the World tour days, roomed together on an International Wanderers tour of Rhodesia, and played against each other at county and international level in England. Their friendship was even strong enough to survive a potentially embarrassing moment during the third Test at Trent Bridge in 1972.

Bruce was playing for Australia and fielding on the third-man boundary. Outside the boundary, but inside the fence, there were a number of good-looking young women sitting in deckchairs. Bruce being Bruce smiled at the young girls and said, 'Good morning, girls.' They smiled back. As the day wore on, the conversations continued and he was even offered ice blocks and chocolates. At stumps, Bruce, again being Bruce, invited one of them out for a drink that night. As was the custom, the two teams met in the changing rooms for a beer after the day's play. Dad looked across at Bruce and said, 'What's Donna doing tonight?' Bruce didn't know what he was talking about, until Dad added, 'That was my wife you just invited out for a drink!' Shame-faced, Bruce just managed to blurt out, 'Well at least you have to admire my good taste.' He was horrified when he found out the girls were all wives of the England players and were deliberately trying to distract him. Dad, Mum and Bruce became great friends from that day on.

After Dad was appointed captain of England, Waverley grew worried he would pull out of their deal, or at least ask for more money. However, Dad believed a deal was a deal and reassured Waverley Club president Phil O'Sullivan that he was still coming when Phil phoned Dad to double-check. Dad confirmed that the arrangement would stay exactly as had been agreed.

In September 1975, the Greig family moved to Sydney's Eastern Suburbs. Mum had reservations, as she really enjoyed living in England. We had a lovely home in Hove and she had lots of friends there. Dad had decided that Sydney was the place he one day wanted to live, so he rented a house in Watsons Bay with no expense spared, almost as if he was trying to hoodwink Mum into agreeing to a permanent move. It was vital to him that Mum liked it in Australia. To Dad, Australia seemed to offer everything. It didn't take long for Mum to warm to the Sydney lifestyle and she quickly made some new friends. She found Australian people not unlike South Africans in some ways, mostly easygoing and friendly, and she saw the beach and harbour lifestyle of Sydney as a wonderful place to bring up a young family. Dad would take Sam and me down to Camp Cove beach on a regular basis, maybe a little too regularly for Mum's liking – after taking us there one day when Dad was busy, she witnessed her first topless bathers, something she had never seen before in South Africa. The penny dropped immediately for Mum. Apparently she had some fun with Dad when he arrived home that evening. She brought a smile to his face when she jokingly told him that she had done a little topless bathing herself.

Dad loved playing cricket for Waverley. He knew all about how club cricket worked, particularly how competitive it was going to be, having been brought up in the same sort of environment in South Africa. What he didn't realise was the extent to which these guys were yearning to win, and celebrate their wins. They hadn't won for some time, yet they had some pretty good cricketers, four of whom had played first-class cricket. They just couldn't put it all together.

Dad's biggest contribution wasn't with his bat; he didn't score many runs. It was getting these guys to actually believe they could win. Waverley were given a real thrashing in Dad's first match. In the second match they recovered from four wickets for one run in the first over to be 8–48 at stumps on the first day, chasing 52 – a match they went on to win outright, setting them on their way for the rest of the summer.

Waverley had as good a spinner as Dad had ever seen in David 'Cracker' Hourn. With Cracker bowling left-hand chinamans and Dad bowling off-spin, they made it very difficult for the opposing batsmen. They also had some great support from the pace bowlers: David's twin brother Dennis Hourn swung the ball in a lot and was quite quick; Dick Rowland was really fast; and David Gibson also had a nasty off-cutter and could button up one end if a bowler got really tired. Amazingly, without the use of sports scientists, Waverley only used thirteen players in first grade for the whole season.

There were lots of post-game celebrations during Dad's and Uncle Ian's years at Waverley. The players were a tight group of mates and seemed to have a great deal of fun in each other's company. I recall so many post-game sessions in the bar underneath the old stand at Waverley. This little bar, referred to as 'back rooms', was legendary in grade cricket circles. On one occasion Kerry Packer called in to take Dad and Kepler Wessels to dinner. Instead of jumping to attention and leaving straight away, Dad bought Kerry a soft drink, then took him around the room and introduced him individually to everyone – including players from the lower grades and the opposition.

Fortunately for us kids there was also a decent children's playground at the back of the club where we were required to entertain ourselves for hours. The playground had a huge, five-storey rocketship and we used to climb to the top, where you could look out over the surrounding rooftops. I remember sitting at the top of that rocket and listening to Neil Diamond blaring out of the Waverley back rooms. The music was always accompanied by rounds of cheers and fits of laughter from those enjoying themselves inside.

Neil Diamond also played a significant part in my father thanking some of the people who helped him during that first summer with Waverley. Mum and Dad hosted a party at our home, a lavish event attended by 30 people, during which he handed out tickets to a Neil Diamond concert at the Hordern Pavilion at the old Sydney Showground.

I have fond memories, too, of the many gatherings with players and their families at the home of the then club president, Phil O'Sullivan, who was a great host. He had an old Bondi tram parked in his backyard alongside his swimming pool and as a kid I thought it was like having your own real-life train to play in. Dad and his mates saw it as a place to celebrate their cricket victories – there must have been a few cans of beer drunk in the tram that year, as Waverley First Grade won the 1975–76 competition for the first time in 30 years. Phil O'Sullivan and Bob Horsell should be given credit for the fantastic morale and club spirit at Waverley, now Eastern Suburbs Cricket Club. They both put their heart and soul into the club and cricket over the years, so Dad was delighted in 2011 when he heard the new grandstand at Waverley Oval was being named in their honour. Waverley Cricket Club has a great reputation in England. It's near Bondi beach, near the beautiful harbour, it really has everything.

Dad and his Waverley clubmates had many big nights, but none as big as the night Waverley played a social game in the mid-west New South Wales town of Cowra. No one had a worse influence on Dad than his Waverley teammates Dave Gibson, Dick Rowland and Dennis and David Hourn. They poured him into bed in a 'semi-conscious state', long after Cinderella had left the pub. Dad woke up to a cow pulling his bed across the motel room. His teammates had snuck a cow in from one of the surrounding paddocks and tied it to his bed with a sign saying, 'Room service, fresh milk for your coffee'.

Dad also enjoyed the new career skills he was learning in Australia. He didn't take any money from the club itself, rather he earned a living working for a number of successful businessmen associated with the club. Australians soon had to get used to his South African accent turning up on their television on a regular basis as he did commercials for Kellogg's Nutri-Grain and numerous products for Waltons, including pantyhose.

The Kellogg's relationship turned out to be a godsend for Mum, Sam and me. Kellogg's advertising director, Gerry Brooks, went the extra mile to make Mum feel welcome and his wife, Faye, became one of her best friends in Australia. Sam and I loved their two children, Ursula and Mathew, and over the years when Dad was tied up with cricket we went on many holidays with the Brooks family to Boomerang Beach near Forster. Our holiday with them on a Halvorsen cruiser on the Hawkesbury River was like a scene out of a Chevy Chase movie, but is still recalled often with great fondness.

Ursula Brooks is now a successful actor in the US, and recently she sent me these memories from Hollywood, where she lives with her husband, Jonathan LaPaglia, star of the ABCTV series *The Slap*.

I remember Donna and Tony coming in to see me in hospital the first week after my accident. [Ursula was knocked down by a car outside Mosman police station and spent four months in hospital recovering.] Donna was so supportive – she used to visit me a lot and really helped me by encouraging me to look forward to all the things I would be able to do when I got out of hospital. It seemed like an eternity to be in that bed not able to get up for months and even though I was so young I remember being really inspired by her sense of hope and kindness. She was such a great beauty, it was always so wonderful to be around her.

I also remember going to the ballet once with Donna and my mother. We all met at the Opera House and Mum and I arrived a little earlier than Donna. I remember seeing her walk through the foyer of the Opera House and literally the whole room stopping because she was such a vision of beauty. She and Tony had just come back from a vacation and she had her hair cut and styled and she was wearing this amazing dress and she was so happy. It's weird that I remember that but it was just one of those quintessential fashion style moments that you have when you are growing up and you see someone who stops a room.

By now Dad was also falling in love with Australia. He felt it was a place where, if you were prepared to work hard, you would get the financial reward you deserved. Later, when it became obvious he would be drummed out of England because of his involvement in World Series Cricket, it was an easy decision to make the move to Australia permanently. But that was still some time away. After helping Waverley win the Sydney First Grade premiership, something he really enjoyed, particularly given the lack of success at Sussex over the years, he then had to return to England to captain the side against the West Indies. Though Mum thoroughly enjoyed the six months we lived in Sydney, the prospect of going home to England in early 1976 for an English summer excited her.

The West Indies had lost in Australia during the 1975–76 summer when Dad was playing for Waverley, mainly because they had become very undisciplined. They were a highly talented side but just needed to be galvanised. Along with Michael Holding, the young fast bowler from Jamaica, Vivian Richards was beginning to show what a great player he would become. And then there was Andy Roberts, a marvellous fast bowler who had honed his skills against the finest, playing county cricket in England. Nevertheless, the West Indians arrived in England to mixed reviews.

Dad certainly respected them, but while he was in Australia he had developed a plan he thought would cause them to lose discipline again. He talked about restricting their scoring rates and generally frustrating them.

When Dad was interviewed by the BBC on the eve of the first Test match, he'd expected a lot of questions about his team and how they would perform. Instead the interviewer only wanted to talk about the West Indians, and that is why the infamous 'grovel' interview went the way it did. Dad just wanted to talk about his team.

> I like to think that people are building these West Indians up, because I'm not really sure they're as good as everyone thinks they are. I think people tend to forget it wasn't that long ago they were beaten 5–1 by the Australians and only just managed to keep their heads above water against the Indians just a short time ago as well. Sure, they've got a couple of fast bowlers, but really I don't think we're going to run into anything more sensational than Thomson and Lillee and so really I'm not all that worried about them. You must remember that the West Indians, these guys, if they get on top are magnificent cricketers. But if they're down, they grovel, and I intend, with the help of Closey [Brian Close] and a few others, to make them grovel.

The reaction was enormous and the words were to haunt Dad for the rest of his life.

Dad explained his position when he wrote the foreword to David Tossell's book, *Grovel*.

Do I regret what I said? Of course I do. There are times you get things wrong and you have to admit it and accept the consequences.

But prior to using the word 'grovel' I tried to explain that the West Indies were, at the time, a team that could run really hot or really cold. It doesn't seem to me that around that time there was much middle ground in their cricket. I saw them really struggle against Australia the previous winter, losing the series 5-1, and I certainly went into that summer thinking that there was a chance we could beat them.

Of course there was an awareness emerging that here was a fantastic group of cricketers. Anyone who had seen Viv Richards bat or Andy Roberts and Michael Holding bowl knew they were going to be a force. We were perfectly aware that we were going to be up against it on occasions. Any team that has a combination of Roy Fredericks and Gordon Greenidge at the top end, Richards coming in soon after and Clive Lloyd to follow has a pretty potent batting line-up. But you never go into a series thinking you are going to be beaten and I felt it was simply the West Indies' strengths that the reporter was emphasising.

It is my nature that every now and again I am going to say something that is going to backfire and if I had chosen a different word to make my point my comments would have been absolutely accepted. I would also ask those who chose to judge me on that statement: If, in your work, you have a microphone picking up your every word and a camera over your shoulder, how many of you are going to stand that scrutiny? There are going to be occasions when you say or do things that are inappropriate.

Anyone who wants to suggest it was my South African background that was behind my comment and put any racist tone to this thing just doesn't know me.

Once the cricket started, history shows that the West Indies had the better of the series, but I believe that if a few things had gone our way it could have been much closer than the final score of 3–0.

Mike Brearley, who was always a big supporter of Dad's, probably said it best when he noted that it was tactless from any source, 'but in the mouth of a blond South African it carried an especially tasteless and derogatory tone'. Dad had not meant it that way, but that's how the cricket world – and beyond – came to perceive it.

Of course there was also an overtone of apartheid, with Dad being South African. It goes without saying that Dad wasn't a racist. His father had been part of the anti-apartheid movement in South Africa. Dad had played with and against cricketers from all over the world and counted people such as Garry Sobers as friends. Thankfully, as the years passed, the West Indians involved in that tour realised that what Dad said might have been tactless, but it wasn't racist. When Dad died in December 2012, *Mumbai Mirror* journalist Vijay Tagore interviewed Michael Holding, and he said:

> I'm currently in the US and got to hear about
> Tony's demise last night … I got an email from an
> Australian friend and was shattered hearing the news.
> Tony Greig was a towering figure in world cricket,
> and that is not just because of his height and build.
>
> My relationship with him was not very cordial
> initially, particularly for that comment he made
> about the West Indies team. But I got along very well
> with him later. I worked with him in Sharjah with
> Mark Mascarenhas and we spent some quality time
> together. We used to go for dinners and I got to know
> him more closely. Then we spent time in Australia
> working for Channel Nine. I went to his house
> for dinner many a time; my relationship with him
> changed for the better as my interactions increased
> over the years. He was a good man.
>
> Our rivalry on the field was always intense. It
> was particularly so during the 1976 series because of
> the comment (we will make them grovel) he made
> about the West Indies team. It did not go down well
> with us. At that time, the remark was thought to have
> racist undercurrents but actually he did not mean
> that.
>
> I've got to know the man very well in the later
> years and I can say with assurance that he was not
> a racist. He was a man always looking to make a
> headline but he was not what he was portrayed to
> be. He was just a fighting cricketer who would battle

hard on the field. I discovered that he was different from what his comments made him out to be.

As a commentator, he had very few peers. He was very good with the mic, having done the job all over the world. I do understand that he has a particularly large following in India and Sri Lanka. A lot of Indians, I know, enjoyed his commentary.

He took on the Australian commentators when he worked with Channel Nine. He always tried to add balance to the commentary when the Australians were blatantly taking sides. With the exception of Ian Chappell and Richie Benaud, the Aussies were the cheerleaders of Channel Nine. Tony was different, providing unbiased audio output.

I also shared some great moments with him in the World Series Cricket. We could see how the game benefitted from the World Series Cricket. He recruited the players for WSC from all around the world, including the West Indies. It was a great thing for the game.

Tony was huge in the cricket world. It will miss him not just for his knowledge of the game and commentary, but also for his wisdom and uprightness. My condolences to his family.

Back in 1976, as anyone who has watched the 'Fire in Babylon' documentary would know, there was a lot of animosity towards Dad in the West Indian cricket team. The grovel comment galvanised them, particularly Viv Richards. He scored 232 in the first Test, which ended in a draw. That was the game when David Steele further reinforced Dad's decision the year before to pick him. He got his first Test century. The West Indian fast bowlers also made their intentions pretty clear regarding Dad, when he came to bat. He lasted just twelve balls against some pretty sharp bowling before he was bowled by Andy Roberts for a duck.

A whole day's play was washed out in the second Test at Lord's, in which England had a handy first innings lead over the West Indies. In the third Test at Old Trafford, England was to suffer a humiliating loss by 425 runs. Gordon Greenidge scored centuries in both innings, while Viv Richards, who had missed the second Test due to an injury, scored 135 in the West Indies' second innings. England was bowled out for 71 and 126. Dad made nine and three, bowled by Michael Holding in the second innings, stumps askew, the bowler performing a celebration that said it all. Dad was highly critical of that Old Trafford pitch. In 1977, he was fined by the TCCB for writing a newspaper article saying the ground should never be used for Test cricket again. He had seen brave teammates such as John Edrich and Brian Close, who had to go out and bat late in the day, reduced to little more than targets in a shooting gallery. When he came in to bat, he said it was the only time he had ever felt truly frightened – the combined factors of a sub-standard pitch and the fast bowling might of the skilful Andy Roberts, a maturing Michael Holding and the brute force of Wayne Daniel.

As ever with Dad, there is a funny story to come out of even the toughest moments. Late on the third day of that third Test, when Brian Close and John Edrich were opening the batting, Dad looked around to see who might be a good night-watchman in case one of them was dismissed. There appeared to be a serious shortage of candidates. This was because Derek Underwood and Pat Pocock, the two spinners, were in the toilets, pretending to be dying of some dreadful affliction and thus not able to pad up. As it transpired, neither was required.

The West Indies went on to win the fourth and fifth Tests. Dad scored 116 and 76 not out at Headingley in the fourth Test and if he could have found someone to bat with him in the second innings, they might have won that game. Only Dad, Bob Woolmer (37), Peter Willey (45) and Sundries (32) made double figures as England lost by 55 runs. The West Indians also won the three one-dayers. Apart from those two scores at Headingley, Dad had only managed 51 runs in the other Tests, and was now getting from the English cricket media the same treatment they had handed out to Mike Denness. There was already talk that Mike Brearley would replace him as captain. What probably saved Dad at the time was that Brearley was yet to prove himself a Test cricketer; he'd only just made his debut in the series against the West Indies with a highest score of 40.

Instead Brearley, who was eventually to become one of the most admired English captains and write the book *The Art of Captaincy*, was appointed vice-captain for the 1976–77 tour of India. Ken Barrington, one of England's finest batsmen, was the manager.

Dad fronted up for his press conferences in India determined not to make the 'grovel' mistake again. He already knew one of the first questions would be about the umpires. The New Zealanders had just left India and had been highly critical of the umpiring. There would also be those who had not forgotten the Ajit Wadekar incident the last time Dad was in India. So the question came: 'What do you think of Indian umpires?'

Dad seized the opportunity and praised the standard of umpiring in India, hoping his kind words would lower the chances of any decisions going against his team. In the end, apart from a few moments in Bangalore, not too many did. It was Dad the diplomat at his best.

England won the first Test at New Delhi, the Essex left-arm fast bowler John 'JK' Lever taking ten wickets, three of those lbw. Dad's diplomacy was working beautifully. At one point the Essex County Cricket Club had posted this story on its website in which John remembered that Test match, and the hilarious incident that followed it:

> It was the first Test of the series and my memories of it are pretty cloudy. I got a few runs and took a few wickets when the second ball we used swung around a little bit. I do remember though that three of those wickets were lbw which was a bit surprising because it was before the independent panel of umpires had been introduced. We won the game and the lads were in the changing room and obviously quite pleased. Tony Greig, the captain, told them to get on the bus and get back to the hotel and we'd see them there later, explaining that he had some interviews with the press to carry out and that the press wanted me there as well.
>
> I wasn't really sure what all the fuss was about but anyway I went along to the press conference and we finished about three-quarters of an hour later.

We came out of the stadium and I asked Greigy how we were going to get back to the hotel, nobody had thought to lay on a car or taxi, there was nothing. So I found myself outside this stadium in Delhi with Tony Greig and all of a sudden, he waved at a guy riding a motor scooter and he pulled over. Greigy then asked him for a lift back to our hotel and the chap looked at him and obviously recognised him – he was six-foot-seven with fair hair plus we were both still in our cricket whites. Then another guy on a scooter pulls up. I got on the back of that bike, Greigy was on the first bike and off we went weaving through Delhi at a time when I thought it was rush hour, although I've since learnt the traffic is congested like that all the time. Neither of us had helmets to wear and I was thinking, 'This is a nice start to my international cricket career, it's quite likely to be the end of it as well!'

The guy riding the first scooter just couldn't believe he'd got Tony Greig, the England cricket captain, on the back of his scooter and all the time, he kept looking at him. He was driving along these congested roads, turning around and looking at his passenger and my bloke's doing the same.

Somehow, we managed to negotiate a roundabout with what seemed like hundreds of cars and eventually we arrived back at the hotel and somehow still in one piece! Somewhat relieved, we walked in and the first thing that the rest of lads asked was, 'Where have you been?' I said, 'You won't believe this.' The story became part of the entertainment for the evening.

Not just for the evening. Over the years, Dad really came to embellish that story in his own way, such that it ended like a car chase scene in a movie, a bit like the one in the James Bond movie featuring the Indian tennis player Vijay Amritraj.

For Dad, that series in India long remained one of the highlights of his cricket career. It featured an innings he reckoned was among his finest – in the second Test in Calcutta, which England won. Over the years many writers have referred to Dad's innings in that Test, some as recently as 2012.

During England's tour of India in November 2012, another South African-born England batsman, Kevin Pietersen, scored a century at the Wankhede Stadium in Mumbai. Many described it as the greatest innings ever played by an English batsman. A fortnight later, writing in *The Guardian*, former England player Mike Selvey suggested there were a few innings that could attract that title, and one in particular – Dad's 347-ball, three-day, illness-affected and match-changing 103 at Calcutta's Eden Gardens:

Bishan Bedi won an important toss, but his batsmen wasted the opportunity and were bowled out by Bob Willis for 155. Greig and England knew that a sizeable lead, achieved at any price, would win them the game and quite possibly be key to the success or otherwise in the challenge for the series. By the end of the second day, England, in reply, were 136 for four, with Greig unbeaten on 19.

The third day was scarcely one for the purist but never lacked drama. Estimates put the crowd unofficially at around 100,000. The noise was deafening: firecrackers exploded, giant catapults, made from the inner tubes of truck tyres, projected oranges from the crowd right to the centre of the field, mirrors flashed. It was an intimidating atmosphere.

Throughout the entire day, Greig played an innings of unwavering determination, self-denial and immense courage. The conditions alone – in which the ball was already spitting and turning sharply for Bedi, Erapalli Prasanna and Bhagwat Chandrasekhar – were wretched. Early on in his innings, Greig, a robust front-foot player whose game was largely dictated by his height and reach, drove Chandra uppishly and was fortunate that the ball did not go to hand. Thereafter he resolved not to play another forcing shot off the front foot, relying on defence, and scoring square of the wicket off the back foot.

Dad told me a lot about that innings, especially how each time they came off the field Bob Willis would approach him. Bob had bowled his heart out on a wicket specially prepared to help India's spinners; Dad said he never saw Bob bowl faster than he did that day. The Indian batsmen were scared of him. It took its toll, however – when he got back to the changing rooms at the close of play, he was utterly exhausted. They finished off the tail the next morning, restricting India's first innings total to 155, with Bob's figures at 5–27 from twenty overs. Dad now had to encourage the batsmen to repay Bob, so he asked each of them to try and get in, and if they got in, to stay in. When wickets fell early, Derek Randall (on debut) did his best to turn things around. Eventually, though, the burden fell on Dad. First, he had to last until tea. Then he had to last until stumps. Dad came off the field at the end of the second day nineteen not out. When he retired to his hotel room that evening, he was feeling confident about what he had to do the next day. However, he told me it was one of the worst night's sleep he ever had. He'd caught a fever and became violently ill, shivering and sweating at the same time. He had to keep ringing room service to have the sheets changed. He also called the team physiotherapist, Bernard Thomas, who took Dad's temperature and shook his head. Dad asked him what it was. Bernard said: '104, the same as the number of runs you need to make.'

The next day, Dad forced himself to eat some breakfast, then went to the ground, where he sat quietly in the changing rooms trying to re-gather what strength he could. Somehow he survived the stinging Calcutta heat, his own high temperature and the guile of the Indian spinners on a wicket that had been tailor-made for them by the Eden Gardens curator.

Again runs were not the priority. Dad went on to make 103, one run short of the score requested by Bernie Thomas, but it was more than enough for England to win the Test and eventually the series. For the first time in five ventures since World War Two, England beat India on their own soil. That innings of Dad's in Calcutta inspired his team for the rest of the tour.

Mike Selvey was later to write in *The Guardian* that my father was the most inspirational captain he had played under, and he deserved to be remembered for that rather than the unfortunate use of the word 'grovel' or his involvement in WSC:

His epitaph will be written around one single unfortunate word, and his major participation in the initiative that was to change the face of cricket forever, and not for the worse. But this is to do him a disservice for he was so much more than these things: Tony Greig was a great cricketer, a fantastic captain, a showman and salesman.

I can still see him now, standing in the middle of a heaving Indian cricket stadium, a beacon of leggy burnished blondness rising above everyone else around him, collar up, white neckerchief, directing the traffic of his England team. He had his lieutenants alongside him, lucky man that he was, some of the wisest men in the game in Mike Brearley, Keith Fletcher and Alan Knott. Any cricketer would be a fool not to draw on that well of knowledge and nous. Greig's strength as England captain was not in his tactical acumen, or even man-management skills. Instead, it was rooted deep in a charisma like none since Denis Compton was Brylcreeming two decades before, and unmatched since except by the remarkable Ian Botham. To a man, his players would do anything for him.

Other visiting captains have gained immense respect in India, but Greig achieved what none has done in managing to turn the massive crowds to his advantage and get them onside. To help win them over, the entire team would, before a match and at his behest, put on the touring blazers and walk round the ground, waving. It was a simple enough exercise but not only did the crowd respond positively towards the visitors during matches, but at times, as Greig gained a stranglehold on the series, they appeared actually to turn their support away from India. I think that was a considerable element in the success of the campaign.

Throughout he played the showman in an environment made for him. If a game started to drift and the crowd (always huge) became restless, he would encourage Derek Randall to turn some cartwheels or do some trickery in catching the ball. Once, Randall, not playing in a match, assembled a squad of police, donned one of their hats himself and marched them round the ground. If he was batting and a firecracker exploded, Greig would clutch his chest and stagger as if shot. Slapstick worked. It brought to mind the way in which he hammed up to the West Indian crowd at The Oval the previous summer, grovelling in front of them as his team were destroyed. None of this though should mask the fact that first and foremost he was a cricketer of great ability, a brilliant all-rounder whose Test match batting average of more than 40 and bowling average of around 32 fulfilled the first criterion in defining the best that the former average should exceed the latter. For England, Botham could better him, but none other, and his ability as an all-rounder, from almost the same loping run, to bowl both medium-fast swing and properly spun offbreaks (not cutters, as some inaccurately and to his lasting irritation, suggest) with equal facility to a high standard has been matched only by Garry Sobers.

Having conquered India, Dad's next big challenge was the 1977 Centenary Test in Melbourne. En route to Australia, the English tourists had a stopover in Sri Lanka. A few matches had been arranged in an effort to support cricket there, as Sri Lanka at that point had not been granted Test status. This was Dad's first visit and he instantly fell in love with the country and the hospitality of its people.

The Centenary Test was to be a celebration of the great rivalry between Australia and England that began at the Melbourne Cricket Ground in 1877, but it turned out to be more than that. Just as the first match had been 100 years before, this game became a watershed in the history of cricket.

In a memorable week, Dad's banter with David Hookes when David came in to bat lightened a very tense situation. Dad said, 'When are your balls going to drop, sonny?' David's reply was along the lines that at least he was an Australian playing for Australia, not a hairy-back playing for England. Hookesie then famously hit Dad for five fours in a row, something my father reckoned he was reminded about at least once a week after he came to live in Australia. It was a great game of cricket – without the Ashes at stake both sides played attacking cricket. In the end, Australia won by 45, exactly the same margin as in the first Test back in 1877.

Cricket was on a high, but amid all the reunions and bonhomie, many at the MCG during that match were harbouring a secret, one that would change the course of the game forever.

10

Wooing Dad

THE READER'S DIGEST VERSION OF MY DAD'S INVOLVEMENT IN World Series Cricket (WSC) has been widely covered in the media and in a number of books over the years. In some people's eyes he was a traitor, the man who betrayed not only English cricket but the fabled role of England captain. To others, admittedly a much smaller group, he was a hero, fighting for the rights of professional cricketers to earn a fair income.

In the end, I don't think Dad particularly saw himself in either camp, but he did see World Series Cricket as a chance to ensure the financial future not only of our family, but also of professional cricketers generally. He was also very excited about becoming involved with Kerry's business empire as well as some of the innovations that would come with World Series Cricket, particularly the way the game was to be televised.

It's amazing to think that after all these years, after all that has happened to cricket since 1977, the full story of

World Series Cricket has never been written from the point of view of the four people Dad believed closest to it: Kerry Packer; Lynton Taylor, the Publishing and Broadcasting Limited (PBL) Managing Director and Executive responsible for WSC; Dad; and Dad's manager, Bruce Francis. Consolidated Press Holdings owned and controlled Australian Consolidated Press (ACP), Nine Network (9 Sydney and 9 Melbourne only in those days) and Publishing and Broadcasting (PBL).

I was only a couple of years old when the World Series Cricket commotion started – obviously too young to remember – but Mum said it was mayhem for months. As I was growing up, Mum and Dad told me everything that went on at that time. They told me that it was during the overseas signings, court cases and everything else associated with World Series Cricket that Dad and Kerry went from being associates to incredibly close friends.

Dad had continued to cross paths with Bruce Francis since their first meeting in 1971 when they played each other in a county match between Sussex and Essex. Dad enjoyed Bruce's company and friendship, particularly while away on tour. In September 1972, they toured Rhodesia together with the International Wanderers, sharing a room during part of the tour. They also toured South Africa together with the Derrick Robbins XI in early 1975. Dad asked Bruce to look for some opportunities for speaking engagements in Australia during the English off-season. This was the first time Dad started considering the commercial opportunity that his growing profile in Australia afforded him.

When Bruce returned to Australia, Waverley Cricket Club was looking for a replacement for their first-choice star recruit Dennis Lillee. Bruce suggested Tony Greig to the club, and from there on Dad's destiny in Australia just seemed to come together for him. At this point Dad had asked Bruce to manage his Australian interests. Bruce negotiated Dad's contracts, ghosted his articles and helped him with speech writing. Bruce's role as Dad's Australian manager was in a non-official capacity, as Bruce never sought payment for his services. Bruce told me that he felt his association and friendship with Dad was beneficial enough.

Bruce lived 500 metres from our house in Sydney, and visited my Dad, and our family, regularly, during the late 1970s and 1980s. I recall him also spending time with my grandfather, Sandy, who moved to Australia with Joycie in 1984. I have drawn on the vast inside knowledge Bruce has of the goings on in the Greig family, and the cricketing world, during those early years of my life. Although Bruce wasn't employed by World Series Cricket, he was in a unique position during the 'Cricket War'. Not only was he speaking to Dad on an almost daily basis, but he was also asked by Kerry to coach his son, Jamie, now called James, and did so from September 1976 until November 1985. Overseas trips and James's twelve months at boarding school notwithstanding, he was at the Packer house a number of times a week during the WSC planning and playing periods. Because of Bruce's background as a Test cricketer and his role as Dad's manager, Kerry confided in him.

One of Dad's favourite stories about Bruce concerned Kerry. He said it encapsulated both their personalities perfectly. Bruce was coaching James on 17 December 1978 – Kerry's 41st birthday – and Kerry asked him to join the family and a close friend of Jack Nicklaus, Jim Montgomery, for dinner. During dinner Kerry said he intended introducing twenty-over matches in Australia and he was optimistic that it would be so revolutionary and exciting he would be able to sell it in the United States.

Bruce had been around long enough to know that you didn't burst Kerry's bubble straight away, if at all, and immediately took another mouthful so he couldn't speak. When finally forced to comment, he sheepishly said twenty overs per team was too short and it would never happen. When Kerry claimed they were already playing twenty-over cricket in the Sunday League in England, Bruce tried to think of a way to gently disagree with the big man but instead he blurted out: 'You are wrong'. Not the diplomatic words Bruce meant to use.

An agitated Kerry, who probably didn't like to be contradicted in front of a friend, then asked Bruce if he would like a little bet. When queried how little the bet was, Kerry asked Bruce how much his 'joint' at Dover Heights was worth. Four hundred thousand was Bruce's response and Kerry then offered to put up $500,000 as his side of the bet. Bruce told Kerry his mother would kill him if he took the bet because a bet had to have an element of chance and since he had played in the Sunday League for Essex he knew it was not twenty overs. Bruce was right. Kerry subsequently chided Dad that his mate blew the opportunity to make $500,000. Dad, Kerry and Bruce's father, Cass, all thought Bruce was soft for not taking the money, but they admired his integrity!

Dad expected to be involved as an adviser in the making of the 2012 TV mini-series *Howzat! Kerry Packer's War*, and to that end, asked Bruce Francis to write a draft script. Dad made only two minor corrections to it. He believed it was so comprehensive Channel Nine could have produced four two-hour episodes. He was so pleased with how thorough it was he emailed me a copy. The account that follows is Dad's story, much of which is taken from the draft script, together with information gleaned from listening in on discussions as a boy between Dad and Kerry in the hot tub at Palm Beach, and through conversations over the years with Bruce. Most of it has never before been put on the public record.

The World Series Cricket story began in the early 1970s, even before Kerry had taken over the family company following the death of his father, Sir Frank. Kerry and Lynton Taylor, who was then director of programming for the Nine Network, had long been in discussions about the new government content requirements on Australian television and the cost of televising sport compared with drama. Drama was considerably more expensive to produce.

They also discussed the likely impact the introduction of colour television in March 1975 would have on sport. As it transpired, Australia made the fastest transition from black and white television to colour in the world, which had a huge effect on viewing numbers and helped send advertising revenue soaring.

Kerry was a sporting nut. He loved all sports, but more importantly he loved sportspeople. He spent many hours of his life talking to sporting heroes, soaking up their knowledge and making suggestions as to how to improve their sport. It was therefore fundamental to him that the

Nine Network should become the home of the world's greatest sporting events.

Kerry worked under the oppression of his father until Sir Frank's death in 1974, at which point he assumed control of the media empire his father had built. His brother Clyde had always been the chosen son to lead the company, but Sir Frank and Clyde had a falling out in the early 1970s, after which Clyde left Australia and moved to Los Angeles. From there he provided one of the more memorable quotes to come out of the World Series Cricket controversy. Asked his view on Kerry Packer's new venture, he said: 'I am not my brother's wicketkeeper!'

Kerry was dyslexic, so he preferred not to use books to acquire the knowledge, he needed – in addition to his own acumen – to become a successful businessman. The only way he could absorb the information he so voraciously sought was through discussion with experts. He would sit for hours and sometimes days and even weeks talking to experts in the field in which he was interested until he felt his knowledge was the equal of those experts. In 1974 and 1975 he would call Lynton Taylor into his office to discuss the future, and particularly the programming on Channel Nine. In those meetings Lynton came to fully understand Kerry's infatuation with sport and his belief that live sport was to be his vision for Nine when he took over from his father.

Those meetings were so exhaustive they would sometimes last all day and go long into the night. After Sir Frank's death, the plans were laid for the development of the Nine Network as the leader in news, entertainment and sport. While always insisting upon financial integrity, Kerry was prepared to invest heavily in these areas of the business, sometimes to the dismay of his television executives. He was willing to listen to everyone and consider their views, but if he believed in a project, he made the decision regardless of opinion and in 99 per cent of cases he was proved right. Once a decision was made he would back it to the hilt and expect his executives to do the same. That combination made everything successful!

Could Kerry be volatile? According to my dad and quite a few others, the answer was yes. Was that his normal mode of operation? No. He hated failure and he hated lies. Dad said that if you told him the truth, however unpalatable, he would support you and then work with you to find a way out of the problem. He felt Kerry had been portrayed unfairly in the many biographies and mini-series, in which the image had been of an ogre always shouting and screaming, constantly aggressive. Nothing could be further from the truth. It was especially untrue during World Series Cricket. His love of the game and the players saw him at his most docile. His only objectives were to make World Series Cricket a success and in the process the players would be financially better off than they had been under the traditional cricket administrators.

By early 1975, Lynton Taylor and Kerry were talking frequently about the imminent arrival of colour television and the impact that it would have on sporting coverage. They also knew that the Australian Federal Government's legislation on local content needed to be met with affordable programming, and that sporting coverage could provide that facility.

Kerry was also seeking guidance from overseas. He became friends with Mark McCormack, the American owner of the International Management Group (IMG), which acted for many of the world's leading professional sportspeople. McCormack introduced Kerry to former tennis great and tennis promoter Jack Kramer. It was Kramer who had revolutionised tennis, creating a professional circuit that included many of Australia's finest players, the legendary Rod Laver foremost among them.

Kerry and Kramer had many long conversations about the professionalisation of sport. Later Kramer sent Kerry a one-hour tape detailing his experiences in tennis and made suggestions as to how to achieve the same success in cricket. Kerry passed the tape on to Lynton Taylor, who found it enlightening, literally. It recommended the playing of the game under lights, thus allowing it to be broadcast prime time on television. Dad also listened to the tape and said Lynton Taylor revisited it many times during the lead-up to the first year of World Series Cricket.

Kerry's search for knowledge continued elsewhere. He went on a fact-finding mission to the United States set up by champion golfer Jack Nicklaus. Kerry was to stay with Nicklaus at his holiday home, but at the last minute a couple of Nicklaus's sons decided to join their father, so he made arrangements for Kerry to stay with a close friend a couple of doors down. The friend was away for a short while when Nicklaus took him to the house, which was open, and told Kerry to make himself at home. Kerry surveyed the house, picked the bedroom he preferred and stripped off. When Nicklaus's mate turned up he found a naked and sound asleep Kerry Packer in his bed. Despite this little hiccup, Kerry told my dad the trip provided the key intelligence that enabled him to launch his revolutionary idea.

On 18 February 1976, the comedians Paul Hogan and John Cornell opened a nightclub in Woolloomooloo called Pips. Marjorie Wallace, a former Miss World, was brought to Australia to be part of the opening festivities. Dad and Bruce Francis were invited to the opening, and so it turned out was Kerry Packer. He was introduced to Dad by Waverley Cricket Club official Iain Macfarlane, who was also a partner of Sydney businessman John Singleton in the SPASM advertising agency. Macfarlane had been responsible for lining up Dad's original Kellogg's and Waltons contracts.

One of Kerry's magazines, *The Australian Women's Weekly*, was among the sponsors of Dad's contract with Waverley. Kerry told Dad how impressed he was with the mileage he and Dad's other sponsors, Kellogg's and Waltons, had achieved out of their involvement with him. He declared that companies had not even scratched the surface with respect to the potential returns from investing in sport and that he intended to revolutionise the use of sport as a marketing tool. He confided in Dad that he and Lynton Taylor were halfway through their plan to make Channel Nine the number-one sports television network in the world and that he wanted to get involved in cricket as a broadcaster and promoter. He slammed the ABC's coverage of Australian cricket, saying he could do a much better job if he had the exclusive rights. If he ever became involved, he said to Dad, the players' pay packets would increase substantially. Kerry's parting comment to Dad was: 'We must catch up, son, when you return to Australia in September.' After his successful stint playing club cricket in Australia, Dad returned to England in March 1976 to continue his career.

In keeping with Kerry's desire to televise the world's major sporting events, Lynton Taylor recommended that Channel Nine acquire the rights to broadcast cricket when the ABC's contract with the Australian Cricket Board (ACB) expired at the end of the 1975–76 season. Kerry agreed, and in March 1976 sent Alex Baz, a former TCN 9 Sydney station manager, to meet Alan Barnes, the secretary of the ACB. Baz told Barnes that Channel Nine would pay a healthy premium for the exclusive rights to Australian cricket. Barnes informed Baz that the decision as to who would get the rights would not be made until later in the year and he would be notified when he had to lodge a bid. Baz followed up this meeting with a call to Barnes, reiterating that Packer wanted the exclusive rights and insisted Channel Nine be informed when it came time to make an official submission.

Despite this agreement, on 11 June 1976, Barnes sent a letter on behalf of the Australian Cricket Board to Kerry informing him that the ABC had been given the non-commercial broadcasting rights for a three-year period, until the conclusion of the 1978–79 season. The letter stated that only the rights for commercial broadcast were available. Kerry was incensed, believing he had been double-crossed. He subsequently said everything that followed emanated from this instance of the Board's deceitful behaviour. It reverberated through cricket like the bullet that killed Archduke Ferdinand in 1914. Kerry immediately set up a meeting with ACB chairman Bob Parish and board member Ray Steele to see if anything could be salvaged. Parish informed Kerry that the ABC had been exceptionally good to the Board and under no circumstances would the Board break its contract with the government broadcaster.

Kerry's now famous response to this was: 'There is a little bit of whore in all of us. What's your price?' Parish restated that the exclusive rights were not for sale. Kerry grew even more livid, telling Parish he had been 'screwed'.

Kerry then proposed to Parish and Steele that the Cricket Board and Channel Nine jointly promote a series of matches over a five-year period, played in January and February each year, starting in 1978. Kerry said the matches would not clash with the Board's existing international commitments and that Channel Nine would televise them. He even offered to underwrite the costs. When Parish and Steele were dismissive of the idea, Kerry became even more attracted to the idea of organising his own matches.

In late September 1976, the Greigs – Dad, Mum, Sam and I – returned to Australia, as Dad had been booked to do some commercials for Kellogg's Nutri-Grain. It was on this trip that Dad lost all our passports in Paris – he'd been asked to do a press interview in Paris and left them on a seat in the transit lounge. We discovered we didn't have them when we landed in Bangkok and were not allowed back on the plane. So we were about three days late getting to Sydney once this problem had been sorted out.

Dad and Kerry had the catch-up they first talked about in February, during which Kerry described how he had been double-crossed by the ACB over broadcasting rights to cricket in Australia, and that his proposal to jointly promote matches in January and February each year had been rejected by Bob Parish with contempt. Kerry was incensed by the action of the ACB and said he intended to promote his own matches and wanted Dad involved. Dad was in absolute awe when Kerry outlined some of his plans and explained the structure of his business interests, and later said this conversation had a significant impact on his decision to join World Series Cricket.

Kerry's parent company was Consolidated Press Holdings (CPH), which owned and controlled Australian Consolidated Press (ACP), Nine Network (Sydney and Melbourne only) and Publishing and Broadcasting (PBL). PBL controlled PBL Productions and Nine Network International as well as a number of radio stations and other miscellaneous companies. As Managing Director of PBL, Lynton Taylor reported directly to Kerry. Also reporting directly to Kerry were Len Mauger, then Managing Director of the Nine Network; Sam Chisholm, Managing Director of TCN 9 in Sydney; and David Evans, Managing Director of GTV 9 in Melbourne. Essentially, therefore, Lynton Taylor had direct responsibility for the majority of the companies under the PBL banner.

Kerry went into great detail with Dad about how Lynton Taylor had secured the rights, or was in the advanced stages of securing the rights, to:

Tennis: Wimbledon, US Open, German Open, Italian Open, French Open and the Lipton Championship (which evolved into the 'fifth' major, the Miami Masters, now conducted in Miami each year);

Golf: US Masters, US Open, British Open, US PGA, British Women's Open;

Cricket: Ashes series from England, Australian Test series against West Indies, South Africa and India;

Formula 1 (The coverage of these races led to the event being brought to Adelaide for the Australian Grand Prix.)

Kerry could see that Dad was just blown away by these plans and decided to really excite and baffle him with science by discussing how it was done and in particular the involvement of satellites in the process. To deliver the sporting signals to Australia, Nine needed satellite circuits that were extremely expensive in those days. The uplinks in the country of origin and the downlinks in Australia were also very expensive. For instance, a signal from the UK or Europe required two satellites including a downlink and an uplink in Singapore, then a cable link from Ceduna on the South Australian coast to Sydney, another huge cost.

There was only one satellite provider in those days, Intelsat, and they provided circuits on a temporary basis at exorbitant rates. They had never agreed to a permanent lease with any broadcaster or telecommunications company or provider. Lynton Taylor and Bruce Robertson, the Nine Network chief engineer, spent many weeks convincing Intelsat that they should lease permanent circuits to Nine, and eventually their board agreed to the request. It was a world first. Nine leased two circuits: UK to Los Angeles and Los Angeles to Sydney, obviating the need for the 'two-hop' satellite circuits from the UK with signals going via Singapore and Ceduna. Nine also convinced Intelsat to allow it to set up its own satellite dish at Willoughby for both down- and uplinking, another world first. Those facilities not only supported Nine's sporting events but also became an invaluable tool for news, entertainment and *A Current Affair* producers, enabling market leadership, as well as allowing the real-time delivery of 'event' television, from royal weddings to Oscar presentations.

Now Dad was really interested. He had been seduced and admitted in hindsight he probably subconsciously committed to joining Kerry's cricket venture at that moment.

He was being exposed to a world he never knew existed. He loved learning about all this sort of stuff and was keen to be involved in it. Like Kerry, he had a thirst for knowledge, and, as this was to become, a real adventure.

Aware of my dad's rising interest in his empire, Kerry canvassed his thoughts on whether overseas stars would be interested in playing in a privately promoted cricket series in January and February 1978. Dad indicated that the players were so disenchanted with their remuneration and the dictatorial attitude of the boards – not just in Australia but around the world – that he thought most would jump at the opportunity.

Kerry completed his wooing of Dad in October 1976 by driving him to his farm at Ellerston, near Scone in New South Wales, to show him where he could spend his weekends. They drove in Kerry's Jag. Kerry's PA, Pat Wheatley, organised his Ellerston trips and often phoned some of Kerry's neighbours to ask if they would join him for drinks or dinner. As loyal as she was to Kerry, Pat Wheatley also enjoyed winding him up behind his back and one neighbour in particular was always given pre-warning of Kerry's expected arrival at the farm. He often waited beside the road in his Porsche so he could race, and beat, an infuriated Kerry over the last few kilometres. This time, with my dad in the car, the neighbour won again. Kerry told Dad that one day he would have a car that would beat his neighbour's.

In early October 1976, after swearing him to secrecy, Dad discussed Kerry's embryonic cricket ideas with Kellogg's advertising director Gerry Brooks, while they were on a flight from Melbourne to Sydney. Dad wanted to ascertain whether Kellogg's would have any objections if he were to be offered a contract from Kerry to play cricket. Dad also wanted Brooks's opinion of Kerry, how loyal he was to his staff and whether Brooks thought he was capable of pulling off such an audacious project. When Brooks told Dad the Packers had a reputation for loyalty second to none, he was hooked, even six months before he had a contract placed in front of him.

At the time, there was growing discontent among leading Australian players with their treatment by the ACB. Dennis Lillee, in particular, was concerned for the future of cricketers who were poorly paid and had nothing to fall back on once their careers were over. He wanted to play a series of matches after the regular international season with the television and gate money going to a players' retirement fund. After discussing the idea with his manager, Austin Robertson, and a number of other players, he asked Robertson to see if his close friend John Cornell, who knew Kerry well through Channel Nine's *A Current Affair* and the Paul Hogan shows, would take the idea to him.

On 14 November 1976, John Cornell, Austin Robertson, Dennis Lillee and Rod Marsh met for drinks during a Sheffield Shield match in Sydney between New South Wales and Western Australia. It turned into a real bitch session about the poor payments and belligerent attitude of administrators to players. Lillee and Robertson told Cornell they wanted to play some matches at the end of the season to raise funds for the players' retirement funds. At Robertson's request, Cornell approached Packer about backing the scheme. Packer was interested in their idea but already had well-developed plans to do his own thing on a much grander scale.

Cricket was booming in the mid-1970s courtesy of the brilliant talent pool of players such as Dennis Lillee, Jeff Thomson, Doug Walters, Ian and Greg Chappell and Rodney Marsh. They had become national heroes by beating England in the 1974–75 series, attracting huge crowds to the games in that series and the following one against the West Indies.

There was no doubt large amounts of money were being generated, even without a lucrative television rights deal. Just how much, only the ACB knew. Officials were particularly smug about how fortunate it was that, according to their constitution, annual reports and accounts were highly confidential. Because of this, resentment among Australian cricketers had been growing for years, even decades. Stories of harsh treatment by the Board were passed from generation to generation of players. Though some might have been exaggerated for effect, there was enough truth in the stories to create an underlying antagonism towards the administrators.

Nothing better represented the Board's attitude to the players than this comment by Alan Barnes, the secretary: 'If you don't like the pay and conditions, there are thousands of others waiting to take your place.'

Back in 1972 on the Ashes tour of England, a decision by assistant manager Fred Bennett truly revealed the Board's miserly attitude towards its players. After a game at Canterbury, hot finger food was served at a small celebratory function, so Bennett decided the players wouldn't be entitled to their normal meal allowance. He also added for good measure that if the touring party of seventeen didn't like it, then there would be seventeen other players out there who would play for Australia for nothing.

Another example of the cricket authorities' meanness towards the players was the allocation of tickets for Sheffield Shield games at the Sydney Cricket Ground – just two per day.

Then there was the SCG's caretaker, Stan Mealy. He would always try to shunt the players out of the changing rooms by 7pm so he could close up and go home for his evening meal. During one Shield match between New South Wales and South Australia, Greg Chappell's girlfriend – Judy Donaldson, whom he later married – went into the South Australian changing room at about 6.30pm after everybody but the players had left the ground. Mealy went berserk when he went into the room at 7pm to move the players out and reported the matter to Alan Barnes. Next morning, as punishment, the twelve bottles of beer normally put in the ice cooler for the players to drink at the end of the day's play was withheld. The New South Wales players stood around in their civvies until about fifteen minutes before the start of play, implying they were going on strike. Then another official, Bob Radford, agreed to supply the beer on the condition the players agreed to leave the changing room by 7pm.

Before the Boxing Day Test became a fixture at the MCG, New South Wales and Victoria would play each other in a Sheffield Shield match that started before Christmas Day and finished after it. Because there was no play on Christmas Day, Norm O'Neill and Barry Rothwell, two New South Wales players, flew home to have lunch with their families. Despite paying their own return fares to Sydney, they were docked the meal allowance for the day because they weren't with the team.

I know Dad heard plenty more stories like this as he got to know the Australian cricketers better, and he had plenty of his own to tell about cricket administrators in England.

Meanwhile, to complete their plans to televise all major sport on Nine, Kerry and Lynton Taylor had agreed to try to buy the exclusive rights to the 1977 Ashes tour of the UK. Lynton was talking to the Test and County Cricket Board (TCCB) and gained a favourable hearing from the marketing manager.

Kerry had also been thinking about the Lillee proposal, but wanted do something on a bigger scale to achieve something the equal of the cricket broadcasting rights he had been denied by the ACB. Lynton Taylor cautioned that his idea was fraught with complexities.

Following on from the early favourable talks with their marketing manager, the TCCB agreed to meet with Taylor to discuss the rights to the Ashes series, so he flew to London in late January 1977 to begin negotiations. He arrived on a Monday morning and arranged a cocktail party at his hotel for all members of the TCCB and executives that afternoon. The party went well but there were clearly strong reservations about awarding the rights to a commercial network, even though broadcasting back to Australia by satellite in real time in colour would be creating history.

Taylor met with the TCCB from Tuesday to Thursday and, while progress was made, he sensed they were still reluctant to grant the rights without considerably more discussion. At the Thursday meeting, they advised that they had asked the Australian Cricket Board for their view. Unsurprisingly, the ACB was emphatically opposed to granting the Nine Network the rights and wanted the TCCB to open discussions with ABCTV.

On the Thursday night, UK time, Kerry made what by then was his customary daily call for an update. He told Lynton he was to be on the plane home on Friday night come what may and that if no agreement was reached, the TCCB was to be told 'we would not be back'. He then dropped the bombshell: he had decided to proceed with his plans to form a breakaway international cricket series with the world's leading players and all he needed was the players' agreement. Lynton was dumbfounded. Here he was in the middle of negotiating rights with the governing body of the game while Kerry was hell-bent on taking them on. Dad said the conversation went along the following lines:

Lynton: 'Kerry, I don't want to know, this is highly embarrassing.'

Kerry: 'Then I'll end the call; let me know what happens tomorrow!'

CLUNK. The phone line went dead.

As Kerry instructed, Lynton rang the TCCB's marketing manager, informing him that he was flying home on Friday night and if they couldn't reach an agreement, he would not re-open discussions. They arranged a morning meeting, but there was no agreement. The TCCB wanted to discuss the matter further among themselves, and told Lynton they would advise him later. He returned to his hotel, packed his bags and waited. At 3.30pm he was called to a 4pm meeting at Lord's. He had a plane to catch at 7pm.

An hour into the meeting, the TCCB finally agreed to Channel Nine's offer and a Heads of Agreement was drafted and signed. Taylor left Lord's at 5.45pm for the 7pm flight, making it through peak-hour traffic to board the plane just as the doors were closing. As there were no mobile phones in those days, he could not tell Kerry about the deal until he arrived back in Australia.

Amid the heated negotiations, the 1977 Centenary Test was about to begin. When the ACB's Bob Parish and Ray Steele heard about the TCCB selling the television rights to Kerry, they admonished Board officials Doug Insole and Donald Carr during the Test at the MCG. In an angry exchange, they informed their English counterparts that in future they would handle all broadcasting rights negotiations for matches involving Australia and this was the first and last time Packer would broadcast any such matches.

Meanwhile Bruce Francis and Gerry Brooks took James Packer and Gerry's ten-year-old son, Mathew, to the Centenary Test in Melbourne. Despite the fact that Dad was captain of England and involved in a vital Test, Bruce, Gerry and the boys spent every night in Dad's hotel room until about 11pm, something I can't imagine Sir Donald Bradman or Sir Len Hutton allowing to happen. Dad even had to play secretary for James and ring Kerry, who was overseas, on his behalf one night because James thought Channel Seven had stolen *Hawaii Five-0* from Nine. It transpired that the channel knob on the television in Tony's hotel room was broken and he was actually watching Channel Nine although the knob said it was Seven.

Dad always discussed major decisions with Sandy, but, since he was in South Africa, Dad went to see Bruce Francis's father, Cass, on Sunday 20 March 1977. He was seeking a bit of paternal advice on what to do before meeting with Kerry at his home in Sydney's Bellevue Hill. Cass Francis advised Dad that his major responsibility in life was to his wife, children and conscience, and if he thought it was right it didn't matter what anyone else thought.

Mr Francis then recited one of his family's favourite poems, *Stanzas of Freedom* by James Russell Lowell. The essence of the poem was summed up in the lines: 'They are slaves who dare not be in the right with two or three.' Dad told him that was Sandy's attitude at his Queenstown newspaper when he took on the South African government in his editorials.

Bruce had filled Dad in on all the developments since their last meeting with Kerry in September, but Dad wanted to hear them straight from the horse's mouth. Furthermore, he didn't want Kerry to think he was a traitor for considering jumping the establishment ship and was at pains to spell out why he was interested in the project: poor pay; no retirement program; poor player food at the grounds; scandalously low car travel reimbursement; excessive and unreasonable control over books and newspaper articles; having to ask the TCCB for permission to take wives on tour; and poor ticket allocation for players. As a sign of the times, and Dad's generous nature, he had paid more money for tickets for his friends to attend the Centenary Test than he received for playing in it. A second meeting was set up for Tuesday morning at Kerry's Park Street headquarters to discuss a contract.

After the meeting with Kerry at his home, Dad went to a barbecue in Pennant Hills at the home of Arthur Jackson a hypnotherapist who was a friend of Bob Willis. Fast bowlers Bob Willis and John Lever were also there. Dad was so excited after his meeting with Kerry that he nearly spilt the beans at the barbecue. He said big things were going to happen in cricket and it was crucial that players became super-fit if they wanted to earn big money in the future.

On Tuesday 22 March 1977, Dad and Bruce met again with Kerry to discuss a formal contract. According to the transcript, part of the meeting went like this:

Kerry: 'I hope you understand you two are sworn to secrecy.'

Dad: 'Yes, Kerry.'

Kerry: 'Good. Are you ready to sign?'

Dad: 'Sign what? What are you offering me?'

Kerry: 'As captain of England I'm prepared to pay you the highest amount. I will pay you $30,000 a season for three seasons.'

Dad: 'That's a huge amount for just about every cricket player in the world but it's not a lot for me. Thanks to Kellogg, Waltons, the *Women's Weekly*, Golden Books, TAA and speaking engagements, I received more than triple that playing grade cricket for Waverley last season. I'm due for a tax-free benefit from Sussex next year and Mick Jagger has indicated he will do a benefit concert at Wembley for me. That could bring me anything up to £1 million tax-free. Although you only intend playing your cricket in Australia, and thus it won't affect English cricket, the TCCB may roll over and ban us if intimidated into doing so by the ACB.'

Kerry: 'I know you are very important to the success of the project and I know the Germans, the South Africans and the Chappell brothers thought they were the superior race, and I know this will come as a huge surprise, but you are not the best player in the world and consequently I can't pay you a lot more than the rest of your World XI teammates, or the Australian superstars for that matter. I'll tell you what I'll do. I'll give you an extra $10,000 a season for being captain.'

Dad: 'Thanks, but it's still small change. Kerry, money is not my major concern. I'm nearly 31 years old. I'm probably two or three Test failures from being dropped from the England team. Ian Botham is going to be a great player and there won't be room in the England Test side for both of us. England captains such as Tony Lewis, Brian Close, Colin Cowdrey, Ray Illingworth and Mike Denness all lost the captaincy long before they expected. Hell, Ray Illingworth ended up flogging Christmas cards for a living in the villages of Yorkshire. He did a great job, but that's not for me. I won't be treated any differently from the other England captains. I don't want to finish up in a mundane job when they drop me. I'm not trained to do anything. I went straight from school to playing for Sussex. I am at the stage in my life where my family's future is more important than anything else. If you guarantee me a job for life working for your organisation, I will sign.'

Kerry: 'No problem. You can have a job for life starting on $25,000 a year. Do we have a deal?'

Dad: 'Not so fast. My family has to be happy. It will be gut-wrenching for my family if we eventually leave England. Donna has just finished doing up our home in Hove. She did a magnificent job and will be loath to leave her home and friends. We loved living in Vaucluse last year. If we move to Australia, I want a low-interest housing loan which will enable me to buy a comparable home in Vaucluse.'

Kerry: 'No problem. You can have as much as you want at two per cent. Is that it or do you want more licks of the lolly?'

Bruce Francis: 'Who is this contract with?'

Kerry: 'JP Sport.'

Bruce Francis: 'JP Sport has a paid-up capital of $98. That won't go very far among the players if the project doesn't get off the ground.'

Kerry: 'I'll give you my personal guarantee that you'll get every penny.'

Bruce Francis: 'Can we have that in writing?'

Kerry: 'There wouldn't be a businessman in Sydney or Australia for that matter who wouldn't accept my personal guarantee. I sold the *Telegraph* to Murdoch in the back seat of a car at Canberra airport for $15 million.'

Dad: 'I have no problem with accepting your word, Kerry. But my word is as good as yours. If you want my signature on a piece of paper it should be good enough for you to give me your signature on a piece of paper. I'm happy with the terms. I'd like my solicitor to go through the contract before signing.'

Kerry: 'No, you can't take away a copy of the contract. There is no mystery to it. It's built around the 1972 ACB England tour contract which Bruce gave us. The major variation is that it's tougher on player obligations. For the first time in your lives you'll have to behave like professional sportsmen – on and off the field. Do that and you'll have no problems. If you two want to play big businessmen you can go into that room next door and pore through the contract. I promise you the room is not bugged. You can keep me waiting an hour or two and pretend that I'm in here trembling about whether you are going to sign it or not. Then come back when you have finished your silly games and sign the flaming thing.'

In early April 1977, Kerry met with Richie Benaud to discuss his plans and said he would like to retain Richie as a consultant. Kerry desperately wanted Benaud on board, not only in the interests of the game and players, or because of the invaluable advice he would give, but because it would give the whole project credibility, as he was one of the most respected figures in world cricket. One of the first things Richie did was to advise Kerry to send a letter to the ACB notifying them of his intention to organise his own matches. His advice on cricketing matters to Kerry and Lynton throughout World Series Cricket was priceless and much of the overall success was due to his involvement.

People have often made the point about how much my dad, Greg Chappell, Dennis Lillee and Rod Marsh sacrificed to join World Series Cricket, but Benaud's sacrifice was just as great. With the exception of Sir Donald Bradman, he had the most credibility in world cricket. He threw his lot in with Kerry because he believed World Series Cricket would benefit the game. Sadly, many former close cricketing friends then turned their backs on him.

With Richie's signing, the impossible had been achieved. The England captain had been won over, the entire Australian team had been seduced and even Richie Benaud had been signed. It was now time to woo the world.

11

Wooing the World

WITH DAD ON BOARD, AND AFTER DENNIS LILLEE AND Austin Robertson had tied up all the key Australian players, Kerry told Dad his first duty was to join Lynton Taylor in wooing the overseas players. When that was done, he would become one of the front men for the organisation and he then had to woo the media, the public and, if necessary, the judges. Quite a job.

Kerry wanted Dad to head to the West Indies immediately with Austin Robertson to entice the key West Indian players into the World XI team. Dad was prepared to do so but when he told his English manager, Reg Hayter, he was going to the West Indies for a holiday, Hayter was forced to reveal that *This is Your Life* in England was doing its program on Dad in a week's time. He was therefore compelled to delay his trip and returned to England.

On 30 March 1977, Dad was featured on *This is Your Life*. Sandy, Joycie, Sally Ann and Ian were all brought to

England for the show, along with his former South African gardener, Tackies, who stayed with us for a week and caused some awkward moments. On the first morning, Tackies bounced out of bed and started doing odd jobs around the house. Dad was concerned our neighbours would think he had imported cheap labour from Africa.

The night after *This is Your Life*, just as everyone was heading off to bed – Sam and I were already in bed – Dad said, 'Ian, put the kettle on – coffee all round. Please join me in the lounge room because I have a major issue to discuss with you.' He explained that an Australian television tycoon was setting up a cricket organisation in opposition to the establishment and intended to sign the best players in the world, and he himself was considering signing. He didn't tell them that he had already signed because he felt it would influence their thoughts. There is no doubt that while he was addressing everyone in the room, he was really after Sandy's opinion. Sandy was to his right and Ian was to his left, so he started with Ian and moved from one person to the next, giving Sandy time to think through his response. Eventually it was Sandy's turn and he said England had given Dad the chance to play international cricket, and he now held the most coveted job in the game. Sandy then said he believed Dad had an allegiance to England and therefore he should not sign. After Sandy was finished, Dad said, 'Thank you all for your thoughts – I have already signed and Donna and I leave for the West Indies tomorrow to sign them up.'

Besides the fact that he disagreed with Dad's decision, what hurt Sandy most was that he was asked for his opinion when in fact his opinion was irrelevant, since Dad had already signed. As they all left the room, Sandy took Ian aside, asking him what he was doing the following day as he wanted Ian to take him to the airport: he intended to cut short his stay and go home early – he was devastated and deeply hurt, an unintended consequence of Dad not being able to discuss the issue in person with my grandfather prior to the decision being made.

Under the guise of a holiday to recharge Dad's batteries after a long and arduous cricket season, Mum and Dad went to the West Indies. It was written up in the media they were on a second honeymoon, and no doubt they did have a good time in the Caribbean, in between Dad convincing the likes of Clive Lloyd, Viv Richards, Michael Holding and others to come on board. Clive was the first signing and assisted the signing of all the other players. The signing team included Austin Robertson and Kerry's legal adviser John Kitto.

Signing the English players Alan Knott, Dennis Amiss, John Snow and Derek Underwood was less exciting than contracting the West Indians but it did require a number of overnight stays at the Dorchester Hotel, which Dad said wasn't hard to endure. Having flown to London himself, Kerry's strategy in securing Knott's signature was a clear sign to the players that they were entering a totally different world, one in which their employer valued them as employees, not as mere servants. He had a suite at the Dorchester and a limousine was sent to pick up Knott, who was then told to wait in his own room at the Dorchester until Kerry was ready to see him. After all the second-rate accommodation he had experienced, not just as a first-class cricketer but as a player representing England, Knotty thought he was in heaven.

It wasn't just my father who had a big influence on the life of Alan Knott and his family. My mother did, too. Alan and his wife, Jan, stayed with us when we were living in Sydney. Alan says Jan wasn't much of a fitness buff at that time, but she went along to the gym with Mum. Jan was so inspired by what she had seen that when the Knotts returned to England, she set up her own business, running a gym on top of Alan's sports shop.

Dad influenced the decisions of the Pakistani players Imran Khan, Zaheer Abbas, Asif Iqbal, Mushtaq Mohammad, Majid Khan and Javed Miandad, as well as speaking to a number of South African players. He later said that because the South Africans had been exiled from Test cricket for a number of years he hardly needed to seduce them. He said it was more like asking them to have a cup of coffee with him. They jumped at the opportunity to play with and against the world's best cricketers.

Lynton Taylor and Austin Robertson travelled to all parts of the globe to offer contracts, using JP Sports as the signing vehicle to hide the identity of the real names behind the venture. It was a company owned by John Cornell, Austin Robertson and Paul Hogan. Through PBL, Kerry bought the majority of the company and the final shareholding was: PBL 49 per cent; Kerry 2 per cent; John Cornell 17 per cent; Paul Hogan 17 per cent; and Austin Robertson 15 per cent.

On Kerry's first visit to England in 1977 to sign players, Dad picked him up at Heathrow Airport in his brand-new top-of-the-range Jaguar and drove him to the Dorchester. Kerry expressed surprise at Dad's apparent wealth and chided that his obvious independent affluence was the reason for his indifference to his initial offer of $30,000. Dad then confessed that Alan Caffyn from Leyland car dealership lent him a new Jaguar and Donna a Mini Clubman each year!

Dad then recalled his hair-raising ride the previous October to Kerry's Ellerston farm and Kerry's obsession with finding a car to beat his neighbour. He arranged for Kerry to talk to Leyland head office about the new Jaguar XJS. Kerry was suitably impressed and said he would take one. When he was informed the car came in five different colours, he decided he would take one of each. Two were for him to drive, one based in Melbourne, one in Sydney. The other three were for his executives Sam Chisholm, Harry Chester and David Evans.

Champion racing driver Kevin Bartlett was brought in to fine-tune Kerry's Sydney car. The early testing, which could be heard at his Bellevue Hill home, was done on the very short Syd Einfeld Drive behind Bondi Junction; the big test was to be during the drive from Sydney to a WSC match in Canberra.

Kerry was followed by the Channel Nine helicopter with Bartlett on board. The plan was for Bartlett to drive the car back to Sydney after Kerry had popped into the cricket – the helicopter would return Kerry. Along the way, Kerry picked up a hitch-hiker who no doubt quickly wished he had been left by the side of the road. Kerry began thrashing the life out of the Jaguar, with his passenger sitting terrified in the seat beside him. Eventually, the car's engine blew up still some distance from Canberra. The helicopter landed, dropped off Bartlett, and took Kerry, along with the now seriously confused and shaken hitch-hiker, to Canberra. I'm not sure whether Bartlett hitched back to Sydney or climbed in with the tow-truck driver.

Not content with owning the cream of Australia's cricketers and a World team, which included five West Indians, Kerry then began talking to Lynton and Dad about signing a second Australian team and a complete West Indian team. This gave him three teams for his Super Tests. He explained that he had two reasons: first, he wanted to take cricket to the regions for the team not playing in the Super Test; second, he wanted to strengthen his hand so that cricket administrators would be forced to negotiate with him. He reasoned that the public would be the final judges, arguing they would vote with their feet if the official Australian team started losing matches. If he were able to sign a second Australian team, the establishment would be forced to pick a Third XI to play against India and England. Kerry suspected the Australian Cricket Board would then try to drag other countries into the battle at the International Cricket Council level. He believed that if he signed the full West Indian team the West Indian public would force the West Indian Board to support him.

Meanwhile, Dad's mother had become very sick on returning to South Africa after attending *This is Your Life*. Dad was worried about her health, but his cricket commitments prevented him from leaving England. Dad mentioned to Bruce Francis that his mum was struggling and his dad was still hurt, having not yet come to terms with Dad's WSC decision. Bruce offered to visit them in South Africa with the aim of cheering up Joycie and placating Sandy about Packer and WSC. On Saturday 23 April 1977, while in South Africa, Bruce attended a cricket dinner in Johannesburg at which the former South African batsman Lee Irvine was one of the guest speakers. During his speech, Irvine mentioned that an Australian television proprietor was going to run a series of matches to be broadcast on the proprietor's television station, going on to say that Graeme Pollock, Barry Richards, Eddie Barlow and Mike Procter had signed contracts to play. Bruce phoned Kerry, who immediately began preparing the announcement of his plans in his *Bulletin* magazine. The Irvine story appeared in the South African *Sunday Times* the next day, well before Peter McFarline (*The Age*), Alan Shiell (*The Australian*) and Ian Wooldridge (London *Daily Mail*) were to 'break' the story during the 1977 Ashes tour. It was amazing that no one, particularly Australian and England cricket administrators, picked up on the *Sunday Times* story. Was it arrogance, complacency, or, by now, indifference?

On 7 May 1977, during a match between Sussex and Australia, Dad hosted a party at our home in Hove for all the players and media. McFarline and Shiell had pieced together parts of the emerging WSC story, yet to break in Australia, and approached Greg Chappell for confirmation and elaboration. Chappell told them nothing. McFarline – always a forthright sort of bloke, in Dad's opinion – then tackled English fast bowler John Snow about his involvement. Snow immediately informed Dad of what McFarline and Shiell had apparently already filed for their newspapers. The following day he released a short statement saying he had signed to play for Kerry.

Back in Australia, on 9 May, Bob Parish opened his newspaper to read that a number of players had signed contracts to play cricket with Kerry. Later that day he received the letter from Kerry informing the Australian Cricket Board of his intention to run his own cricket series. That afternoon,

Kerry and John Cornell held a press conference at which Kerry said: 'We'll do all we can to cooperate with the Cricket Board and, if they cooperate with us, there is no reason why Test cricket as it is now will be affected. But if they don't cooperate they'll walk straight into a meat mangler.'

On 13 May, TCCB secretary Donald Carr called to tell Dad he was sacked as captain of England. Cricket Council Chairman Freddie Brown made the public statement, saying:

> Captaincy of England concerns involvement with
> selection and development of England players in
> the future and clearly Greig is unlikely to be able
> to do this as his stated intention is to be contracted
> elsewhere during the next three winters. His action
> has inevitably impaired the trust which existed
> between the cricket authorities and the captain of the
> England side.

Dad made a statement in reply: 'Obviously I am disappointed. The only redeeming factor is that I have sacrificed cricket's most coveted job for a cause which I believe could be in the best interests of cricket the world over.'

Although Dad was being hammered unmercifully in the media, only two articles really affected him. Henry Blofeld blamed the medication Dad was taking for his epilepsy for his treacherous decision. Dad was livid, because he believed such comments could do untold damage to epilepsy sufferers throughout the country.

And *The Times* cricket correspondent, John Woodcock, a good friend of Dad's, said: 'What has to be remembered of course is that he is an Englishman, not by birth or upbringing, but only by adoption. It is not the same thing as being an Englishman through and through.'

Dad and Kerry had an interesting phone conversation along the following lines about that comment:

Kerry: 'What have you done to John Woodcock to prompt what he wrote about you? I can't believe what I am reading.'

Dad: 'I have read Woodcock's garbage. I always thought of John as a good mate. I'd back my family's contribution to Great Britain against Woodcock's or his media mates. I was only born in South Africa because my dad was sent to South Africa during the war to train South African aircrews to help save Britain. My father was a Scot. He was a squadron leader during the war. Dad suffered dreadfully through his war experiences and at times it had a huge impact on our family. Despite that, my siblings and I were brought up on a diet of stories from my father of love for Great Britain. Don't anyone tell me I'm only an Englishman by adoption.'

Dad needed little encouragement to come out with both guns blazing, saying in a TV interview: 'They should not demand trust from me without earning it and they have not earned it. All cricketers I have spoken to have approved. They believe there is no way the average cricketer will lose out from what I am doing. I am after security for the Test player, the bread-and-butter player and the cricketer of the future. I have acted unselfishly in the interests of all cricketers.'

Kerry did an interview with David Frost and cricket writer and former Sussex player Robin Marlar, known as 'Snarler Marlar', on BBC television. Kerry emphasised he had sought a compromise but the establishment was not interested. That held no water with Snarler Marlar, who proceeded with an aggressive, indignant interrogation of the Australian. As many other would-be interrogators have found out, Kerry was a more than worthy opponent for Mr Marlar.

At around the same time, the 1977 Commonwealth Heads of Government Meeting (CHOGM) was held in London, during which an agreement was reached on the British Commonwealth response to South Africa's apartheid policies. In time, this would also have some impact on the make-up of the WSC playing list.

On 23 June, Kerry, Lynton Taylor, Richie Benaud and columnist David McNicoll met with the International Cricket Council (ICC) emergency sub-committee at Lord's. Kerry had been making noises for weeks that he was looking for a compromise, and supposedly to that end, ICC chairman 'Tadge' Webster listed five conditions he believed were the basis for a compromise. Kerry agreed in principle with the conditions and then said: 'I would want a complete and absolute guarantee of no victimisation of players. That is number one. Number two is that I will want the television rights for the series after the conclusion of the ABC's contract. I would want to buy those rights.'

Parish and Steele remained totally opposed to Kerry being given exclusive rights, irrespective of how much he offered to pay for them. Kerry held a press conference at the end of the meeting, during which he said: 'I am only in this arena because of my disagreement with the Australian Cricket Board. Had I got those television rights, I was prepared to withdraw from the scene and leave the running of cricket to the Board. I will now take no steps to help anyone, every man for himself and the devil take the hindmost.'

Kerry felt the ICC hadn't had any intention of compromising and that he had been the victim of a PR stunt. Most officials and the media believed that the battle-lines had been drawn and it would be a fight to the bitter end: nothing short of bankruptcy for one side or the other would end it.

As angry as cricket officials were, there were a few who could see the dangers of the battle ahead. Surrey officials Bernie Coleman and Raman Subba Row were concerned about the cost of fighting Kerry and asked Dad to organise a secret meeting with him, with a view to achieving a compromise. The three of them met at the Grand Hotel, Brighton, and could not find a way around Kerry's desire for exclusive television rights.

On his return to Sydney, Kerry held a press conference. He was livid about the outcome of the ICC meeting and warned that there would be 'an all-out scrap' if any of his players were victimised. The London meeting with the ICC, he said, had been 'a set-up' designed to tarnish his image.

At the time, Australia and England were engaged in a five-Test series for the Ashes and there were reports of simmering tensions within the Australian cricket team, divided between those who had signed for WSC and those who hadn't. However, relations between England Packer players and the rest appeared to be cooling down a little. Lynton Taylor and Dad, who grabbed every opportunity to woo the media and public, were invited to make a presentation to the English Cricketers' Association, which at the time was run by the former England fast bowler

Jack Bannister. It was not an easy meeting, but Dad felt that by the end they were less antagonistic and many understood that WSC would ultimately improve the financial position of cricketers worldwide.

This conciliatory tone was not widespread. A pettiness was emerging among previously close friends. It was the practice at my sister Sam's school for the teacher to hand out invitations to birthday parties of children in her class. In July 1977, when Sam's best friend had her birthday party, my sister was the only one not to receive an invitation. Dad was waiting to pick up Sam and was standing close to the party girl's mother. When asked by her daughter where Sam's invitation was, she replied that Sam wasn't invited. Dad was devastated and after a lengthy chat with Mum over dinner, they decided it was time to leave England. Mum was mortified. She had made many close friends in England and had just finished renovating our home.

Back in Australia, Kerry addressed several luncheons to sell marketing and advertising packages and pitched to individual advertising agencies. He was personally involved in convincing Peter Ritchie and Bob Mansfield (Peter's deputy) to have McDonald's sponsor both the series and the TV coverage.

Meanwhile, all sorts of battles were going on around the world. On 25 July, the Sydney Cricket Ground Trust knocked back Kerry's request to use the ground. Kerry immediately telephoned New South Wales Premier Neville Wran, who agreed that the Trust had acted irresponsibly in refusing the request. The following day, Mr Wran announced that he had sacked all the Trust members. Kerry's bid to hire the 'Gabba was also rebuffed due to threats from the Australian

Cricket Board that Queensland would lose its annual Test match.

The ICC also got in on the act on 26 July, when ICC secretary Jack Bailey read out a statement at Lord's: 'Notwithstanding anything hereinbefore contained no player who after October first, 1977, has made himself available to play in a match previously disapproved by the conference shall thereafter be eligible to play in any Test match without the express consent of the conference to be given only on the application of the governing body ...' World cricket was in turmoil and everyone involved was resigned to the fact that court action was the only way it would be settled.

In addition to banning the Packer players from Test cricket, the English authorities attempted to ban them from county cricket. WSC, John Snow, Mike Procter and Dad believed this was a restraint of trade and sought orders to prevent the ICC and TCCB from implementing such bans.

Although Dad was desperate to win the court case, scheduled to be heard towards the end of September, so that all the players could continue playing county cricket as well as for WSC, he was concerned that the English cricket authorities might go bust. His thoughts were encapsulated in a letter to Bruce Francis on 21 August 1977:

> There is so much happening behind the scenes to stop the court case. As you can imagine the Test and County Cricket Board can ill-afford to spend between £200,000 and £300,000 on an action Kerry Packer has brought only for one reason and that is because he promised to protect his players to the end. From a personal point of view I don't think Kerry

is really bothered whether he wins or loses. In fact, if he loses it will cost him less money because then he will not have to follow through right to the end. Which basically means going to the High Court of Appeal then to the House of Lords and then last of all to the Privy Council. Lord's have got to go all the way if they want to push their side through, and that is going to cost them a fortune. As I see it that is unfortunate because the game can ill-afford that sort of money. As I have said before, Kerry is prepared to drop the case relative to county cricket as long as his players are not victimised.

If Dad was showing signs of going soft, ACB chairman Bob Parish certainly wasn't. Up until early September, the ACB had kept its powder dry – preferring to let a very anti-WSC media and public do the shouting on its behalf. But on 7 September, Parish came off the Wes Hall long run, having a real whack at Kerry while reading a nine-page statement.

At this time preparations for the upcoming court case were taking place. Jock Harper, a solicitor from Kerry's Australian legal advisers, Allens, recommended English law firm Linklaters & Paines to prepare the court case in that country. When Kerry and Dad met with solicitors from the firm and enquired about the best QCs in England, they were confronted by waffling, eccentric, stuffy English solicitors not used to dealing with someone such as Kerry. When they didn't receive an acceptable answer, they said they would return the next day. They did, stopping off on their way to a game of golf with a helicopter waiting to take them to the course. Kerry ended up retaining the top six

QCs in England, although he only used two. When Dad asked him why six, Kerry said, 'If I'm trying to back the winner at Wimbledon I'd rather have my money on the first six seeds than on the seventh seed. The TCCB will have to hire the seventh-best QC in England.'

The case began on Monday 26 September 1977 in the High Court and lasted 31 days. Kerry was very confident the court would rule in favour of the players' right to ply their trade wherever they wished, and had no doubt that he, Dad and Lynton would convince the judge of their case. Initially, Kerry's confidence in Dad's ability to win over the judge with his arguments was misplaced when the judge admonished him for 'tampering' with a witness. Dad didn't think Geoff Boycott should be appearing as a witness for the other side and rang to tell him so. Boycott reported Dad and he was given a strong dressing down by the judge.

During the court case, Kerry told his legal team that since he was paying big money he owned them until the end of the case and, consequently, they had to have lunch with him, Lynton, John Cornell, Austin Robertson and Dad at the Wig and Pen Club on The Strand every day. At the end of each day, they met for drinks at his penthouse suite at the Dorchester. Kerry also told them that if they won the case he would fly them and their families to Australia and give them the best holiday they had ever had. He said that they would discuss the legal team's performance after each session and place a pin on a map of the world to plot their progress to Australia. If they had a good day the pin would be moved closer – say Paris to Rome – but if they had a bad day the pin would be moved back to London. Kerry had hired a special room for the duration of the trial where the map and pin stayed on the wall. Mr Justice Slade reserved his judgement, eventually delivering it during the trial matches for World Series Cricket in Melbourne. Kerry won on every issue and on hearing the result phoned Dad extremely early in the morning with the great news.

Kerry and Dad had returned to Australia well before the judgement came through. When Dad didn't realise he had again lost his passport until he reached the Qantas check-in desk in London, Kerry phoned the then Australian Prime Minister, Malcolm Fraser, who organised for Dad to enter Australia without a passport – a reflection of the Packer influence.

The legal battle moved to Australia. Kerry had successfully lobbied the new SCG Trust; they gave him permission to use the SCG for thirteen days at a cost of $260,000. The New South Wales Cricket Association (NSWCA) then challenged the SCG Trust's decision and won the case.

The courts were not the only battlefield. Ian Davis, one of the Australian cricketers who had signed with WSC, was employed by the Commonwealth Bank and a bank spokesman announced that Davis would not be given time off to play in the Packer matches. Kerry and Lynton Taylor discussed the bank's position and decided to 'show the bastards'. Sir Frank Packer had banked with the Commonwealth Bank for years, but Kerry closed every one of his accounts with them.

There were also housekeeping issues to attend to, like the new drop-in pitches curator John Maley was preparing for the non-traditional grounds that would host WSC. Dad and Kerry had a discussion along the following lines about their progress:

Dad: 'The pitches look great to me. Maley is an extraordinarily hard worker and is very demanding. I understand he employed 50 people and only half a dozen met his standards. He sacked the rest of them.'

Kerry: 'For Christ's sake get him into head office. We could do with a good clean-out.'

That November there was also a phone call between Malcolm Fraser and his Jamaican counterpart, Michael Manley, which threatened to undermine the project. Mr Manley told Mr Fraser that under the Gleneagles Agreement he had to refuse entry to all South African nationals contracted to play for World Series Cricket. This agreement had been made at the Commonwealth Heads of Government Meeting at Gleneagles in Scotland earlier that year. The various Commonwealth presidents and prime ministers agreed to discourage any sporting contact with South Africa, either teams or individuals, as part of the fight against apartheid.

If Mr Fraser were to be consistent, and retain any credibility in his opposition to apartheid, he had no choice but to ban the South Africans. However, after discussions with Lynton Taylor and Dad, Kerry told Mr Fraser that he must inform Mr Manley he couldn't ban any South Africans who had UK county contracts. Apparently, Mr Fraser saw Kerry as more of a threat than Mr Manley, as he capitulated, agreeing to Kerry's demand. When the visas for the South Africans weren't on his desk on the expected day, Kerry harangued the Foreign Minister, Andrew Peacock, and told him he would take the team to South Africa if the visas weren't on his desk by Friday. They arrived Thursday. The reinterpretation of the Gleneagles Agreement by Mr Fraser later reached farcical levels when South African Garth Le

Roux played some token cricket for Sussex Second XI so he could play WSC in year two.

Mr Fraser went out of his way to accommodate Kerry, even recommending that Kerry meet with Mr Manley to maintain a good relationship, particularly if WSC wanted to tour the West Indies in the future. After a series of meetings in England, Kerry and Lynton travelled to Jamaica to meet with Mr Manley. Crazily, their luggage was lost in transit so a new wardrobe had to be hastily purchased before the meeting. Kerry and Prime Minister Manley met one-on-one, after which Kerry reported that the meeting was cordial and productive. While in Jamaica, Kerry and Lynton also met with Allan Rae, Chairman of the Jamaica Cricket Board and Vice-Chairman of the West Indies Cricket Board.

Stage two had been completed. The administrative team led by Lynton and his extraordinary PA, Irene Cave, had miraculously carried out the logistical tasks – travel, accommodation, advertising, clothing and drop-in wickets at non-cricket grounds. Kerry, Lynton Taylor, Austin Robertson and Dad had wooed enough players to have a World XI and a West Indian team under contract. Although not winning media or public support at this stage, Dad had done an excellent job in getting the WSC message to the cricketing world. Kerry, Dad and the team also did a wonderful job in winning over Justice Slade, as well as destroying the credibility of the Gleneagles Agreement. All that remained was to win over the Australian public with outstanding cricket and to convince Sir Donald Bradman, so that he would pressure key ACB executives Bob Parish and Ray Steele to seek a compromise.

12

Wooing the Australian Public and Sir Donald

FINALLY, THE BIG MOMENT HAD ARRIVED. THE FIRST SUPER
Test WSC match between Australia and the West Indies
took place on 2 December 1977 at VFL Park in Melbourne's
eastern suburbs. Built for the Victorian Football League, the
ground had many critics for being so inaccessible, as it wasn't
on a public transport route or close to the city like the MCG.
In winter, it was also freezing and was dubbed by the football
fans exposed to the elements as 'Arctic Park'. Unfortunately
the match was a huge setback for Kerry and the players: just
under 14,000 spectators turned up over three days to see the
West Indies defeat Australia by three wickets.

The main grandstand did have decent hospitality rooms
and Kerry entertained a lot of dinner guests during that
first match. Unhappy with the entree on the first night,
he ordered the waiters to clear the table and take the food

back to the kitchen. He did the same with the main course. Then, at Kerry's request, the manager of the Glen Waverley McDonald's, who was a guest in the VIP room, organised for his staff to deliver hundreds of Big Macs, french fries and apple pies to the dining room. Kerry was hoping to teach the caterers a lesson to ensure that they served first-class food the next night.

If the dinner had been bad, the newspaper coverage of the first few matches was far, far worse. English television personality and former sportswriter Michael Parkinson led the charge, with this article appearing in the *Sunday Times* on 4 December 1977:

> Kerry's problems with crowds – I have seen bigger attendances at the quarter-finals of the Barnsley District Shin-Kicking Competition – is easily solved. All we have to do is look to history for the answer. Then we discover that once upon a time we dealt with a similar problem by deporting our criminals to Australasia.
>
> Thus, at one master stroke, we can rid ourselves of one problem, and solve another for our dear Aussie friends. Now … I would suggest that if we shipped over there a boatload or two of hooligans who nowadays make up soccer crowds, Kerry's problems would be at an end.
>
> To start with, the yobbos would be guaranteed to turn up, not because they like cricket, but because they had nothing else to do. Secondly, they would fulfil Kerry's declared intention to shake up cricket by bringing to the game all the elements of a soccer

match which it so far lacks. There would be running fights between overs, demonstrations of bottle-throwing and stand-demolition during the drink breaks, and gangbangs at the tea intervals.

Throughout, the game would be enhanced by the sound of well-known soccer chants echoing round the cricket stadia of Australia. Thus we would have 'F… the umpire' or 'West Indies are sh..'. None of this pleasing and refreshing wit would be lost on the television audience, who would hear it loud and clear on the special microphones installed by Kerry so that he might go down in history as the man who made the first recording of what a human being said when he had his skull cracked by a cricket ball.

Apart from the fact that the public response to his new ideas about cricket has generally been one of resounding apathy, Kerry is seen to be pressing on with selling the game like a hamburger. Which is all very well if you happen to think of cricket like you think of hamburgers, which I don't. Nor do I think of floodlights when I think of cricket. But Kerry does and his players were seen somewhat shamefacedly practising with various coloured balls under lights last week.

Meanwhile, ever avid for new ideas, Kerry remains open to suggestions as to how he might extend the boundaries of the new cricket. I have several ideas, including a plan for underwater cricket to be played in a shark infested tank at Wembley. The winners would receive their cheque from Jacques Cousteau.

Kerry knows, however, that the key to the success of his circus is not whether there should be three stumps or five, or red balls or white balls, but whether or not he can persuade the Americans that cricket is a game worth watching. Only when the Yanks have bought his ideas will the players achieve their ambition to earn as much money as Nicklaus, Borg and the like.

Recently Sir Michael told me that he was very glad that he and Dad became friends, in spite of his feelings at the time. He shared with me his reflections now on the article he wrote back in 1977: 'We are all entitled to an opinion, and similarly we are entitled to change it which is what I have done. It's a mark of the maturity and good nature of Tony Greig that we made up and became friends to the day he died. There is no doubt Tony Greig and Kerry Packer changed the game forever and for the better.' In December 1977, the second Super Test at the Sydney Showground was watched by a crowd of just more than 23,000. It also only lasted three days, the West Indies beating Australia by nine wickets. This was the match in which David Hookes had his jaw broken and was transported to hospital by Kerry in his own car, as he declared the ambulance was taking too long. The story goes that Kerry sped through the streets of Sydney to the hospital, screeching around corners as he went, while David held onto his broken jaw with one hand and to the door handles with the other, to keep his balance.

Although the crowds improved slightly from match to match, interest in the results was negligible in comparison to the highly successful cricketing establishment's India v Australia series.

Despite the enmity between WSC and the ACB, on 9 January 1978 Kerry offered to release fourteen of his players for the Australian tour of the West Indies. Lynton Taylor also contacted the Pakistan Board of Control, promising them that WSC would release its players to play in official Tests. He subsequently visited Pakistan to meet with the Board's president and the Pakistani players, and gained the Board's full support.

On 18 January, Pakistan was due to play England in the third Test at Karachi; Imran Khan, Zaheer Abbas and Mushtaq Mohammad were invited to be part of the Pakistani team. The English team was unanimously opposed to the WSC players playing in the Test, and there were threats of boycotting the match. The following day my dad put out a statement defending Mike Brearley, who had taken over from him as captain of England: 'This isn't the doing of Mike Brearley,' he said. 'It's the work of Geoff Boycott and his cronies. They put the team up to this.'

Writing in Sydney's *Sun* newspaper, Dad accused Boycott of being afraid of fast bowling. In return he again took a lot of criticism, but by now it was all water off a duck's back. Still, English officials chased him: he copped an eight-week suspension from county cricket for criticising Boycott. Being forthright people, Dad and Geoff Boycott, the archetypal dour Yorkshireman, were always going to rub up against each other. Geoff sided with the establishment when WSC broke. However, over the years the two men spent a lot of time together in commentary boxes around the world and managed to rub along pretty well. When

Dad died, Geoff wrote a tribute to him in London's *Daily Telegraph*. He said Dad was an imposing figure who played the game with a smile on his face. He also said that many people forget just what a good cricketer Dad was, because his performances are often overshadowed by his involvement in WSC.

Geoff Boycott then concluded:

You have to put that in the context of the era. There is money galore in cricket these days. Ordinary, average players can now earn a lot of money playing in different Twenty20 leagues around the world. They can pull in sums we could only have dreamed about in the 1970s.

Tony played in an era, like me, when we earned tuppence ha'penny playing for England. In the summer of 1977, when he signed for Packer, we played five Test matches in England against Australia for £400 per Test.

That was not exactly riches so when Kerry came along and offered £25,000 guaranteed each year for three winters' work you can understand why people snatched his hands off.

Tony was also looking for a job after cricket. All those people who slapped you on the back when you were playing were not there to give you a job when you finished. And Packer gave Tony a job commentating that lasted for 33 years and one he performed very well.

He was a valued friend and family man and he was a gentle giant.

In the second half of 1978, Lynton Taylor visited Bombay and New Delhi to sign five of India's top players for the 1979–80 season. They would replace either the English or Pakistani players in the World XI, subject to the make-up of the fourth team to be introduced in the third series.

The need for this trip to India came about because at the completion of the first series of WSC – which featured a World XI led by Dad and teams from Australia and the West Indies – a meeting was held to review the past year and analyse what might be done to improve things in the second and third years.

At the meeting were Kerry, Dad, John Cornell, Lynton Taylor, Austin Robertson and Richie Benaud. The major concern for the second year was that WSC would not attract the required crowds unless the Australian team started winning more matches. The major concern for the third year was to have fresh faces.

Then there was this conversation:

Kerry: 'Tony, you'll need another opener for your World team.'

Dad: 'Why? I'm quite happy with Barry Richards and Gordon Greenidge as my openers.'

Kerry: 'I'm telling you, you'll need another opener.'

Dad: 'Wait a minute. You are kidding. There is no way the Australian public will accept Barry Richards playing for Australia. I don't care that he owns a unit in Mosman and I don't care how much you need Australia to win, Richards can't play for Australia. Richards will be opening for me.'

Kerry: 'The fact that I pay the bills gives me the right to decide who plays where.'

Dad: 'Come on you guys, please tell Kerry, Richards can't play for Australia.'

Silence

Kerry: 'Next item.'

Kerry then went to the toilet.

In his absence, Dad asked the other attendees: 'Do you guys really think Richards can play for Australia?'

All: 'We agree with you.'

Kerry then returned from the toilet.

Dad: 'Kerry, while you were away we discussed the Barry Richards situation and everybody agrees with me.'

In the end, Dad got his way. Fortunately for him his subsequent recommendation to approach Kepler Wessels proved to be a good one, as Wessels ended up opening for Australia with distinction.

The World Series Cricket executive team was disappointed with the crowds and concerned about the escalating costs but were very positive about the competition between the teams and the extraordinary quality of the cricket. Just as importantly, they were elated with the television ratings, which were the best indication that, given time, the crowds would come to the games. This proved correct at the beginning of the second year. At no stage was there any negativity or suggestion that World Series Cricket would not work.

The cricketing establishment was fortunate in 1977–78 to have the Indian team touring Australia, led by the charismatic Bishan Bedi. The ACB also produced another trump of their own by persuading Bob Simpson, the former Test captain, to come out of retirement at the age of 41. Simpson by now was in the public relations and marketing business so brought a double set of skills to the job. He scored 89 in his comeback game and Australia won the first Test by sixteen runs. It was an easy story for Australians to follow, easier than the one WSC was trying to sell. The Australians won the second, India the next two, and the fifth Test, a thriller, was decided in Australia's favour.

Before the start of the second series, Kerry, Bruce Francis, James Packer, David Gyngell, and some of James's schoolmates were practising against the bowling machine in Kerry's backyard when John Cornell, his wife, Delvene Delaney, and Austin Robertson drove in with the first copy of the famous 'Come on Aussie, Come On' WSC commercial. The adults retired to Kerry's study and the following conversation took place:

Delvene Delaney: 'Kerry, I've never seen so many guns. Do you do much shooting?'

Kerry: 'A little.'

Delaney: 'Are you any good?'

Kerry: 'I get by. Delvene, pick a spot on that tree and I'll show you how good I am.'

Kerry opened the window and screamed out to the kids, 'Come inside!'

Mrs Packer then ran into the room: 'Not that tree, Kerry. It took us days to get the bullet out last time.'

Kerry: 'There will be no problems this time. This is a .450 elephant gun. This will go straight through the tree.'

Kerry hit Delvene Delaney's chosen target.

They then watched the WSC commercial and got very excited.

The first match under lights at the SCG in season two – Kerry had by then won that battle, too – was a great success. Now Kerry and the rest of the WSC team could begin to think of victory over the ACB. The full house at the SCG brought tears to Dad's eyes. He was coming back from playing in the town of Orange in the New South Wales Central West. It had been an exhausting trip, but the throng of people trying to get into the ground electrified him. For him it was one of the first clear signs it had all been worthwhile. Dad saw Kerry and walked up to him, saying, 'This is it.' Kerry replied, 'Yes, I think you're right.' Because of the unexpected crowd, people were struggling to get through the turnstiles so Kerry manned one gate himself to help ease the congestion, and then threw open the gates – much to the annoyance of the SCG Trust.

The popularity of WSC was in part due to the poor performances of the ACB's Test XI against Mike Brearley's England team in the 1978–79 season. Even without the likes of Dad and Alan Knott, England was a very strong side. For a while, Australia found a new fast bowling hero in Rodney Hogg, but as England dominated the series the crowds fell away. The consensus among Kerry, Lynton, Austin, Richie and Dad was that the Board would have to negotiate a settlement if it were to survive.

Before the last Super Test in Sydney, 2–4 February 1979, Dad asked Kerry for twenty complimentary tickets for his corporate sponsors. Kerry said there would be no problem on condition that he write Dad's next column for the *Sun-Herald*. Dad agreed. Kerry, or probably one of the respected journalists he had working for him, possibly Trevor Kennedy or David McNicoll, duly wrote the column, which upset the Australian players greatly – particularly Ian Chappell. In short, the column said the Australian WSC team was useless. It was written to motivate the public to attend and to support 'their' team.

With the World XI requiring a couple of runs to win, Ian Chappell brought himself on to bowl and deliberately, I am told, bowled four wides so no one had the honour of hitting the winning run.

The relationship between Dad and Ian Chappell had its moments in those years, often revolving around the way the rest of the Australian team, and the rest of Australia, felt about my father. Ian Chappell shook hands on the field that day with every member of the World XI, except Dad. At one point Phil Wilkins, the highly respected cricket writer, asked Ian why, and he replied that he didn't respect Dad, adding that Dad should not have been in the World XI. Once, when Chappell tried to enter the World XI changing rooms, Dad told him to come back when he had calmed down. Ian's actions devastated Dad, something that was totally out of character for him.

By this time, Dad had developed a pretty thick skin, and he had plenty of arguments with other people. He was always able to put these arguments behind him. The clash with Ian really got to him, though, and Dad's close friends reckoned there would never be a rapprochement between the two. Despite the rift, in subsequent years both men were honest in their appraisal of each other as cricketers. When asked who he would get to bat for his life, Dad always said Ian Chappell. In turn, Ian always praised Dad for his support that day when the wicket was dug up at Leeds.

When WSC ended in 1979, the two men began commentating for Channel Nine, at best merely exchanging polite hellos. Dad's closest friends in the commentary box in those early days were Bill Lawry and Keith Stackpole.

In November 1982, there was an incident that encapsulated Dad's relationship with Ian. Dad and Bruce Francis were flying from Sydney to Hobart. The flight went via Melbourne and Launceston and Ian joined the plane in Melbourne. Dad knew about the Launceston stopover, but Ian apparently didn't or had forgotten. Dad and Bruce were in row 1 in first class and Ian was in economy. When the plane landed, Ian took his bag out of the overhead locker and left with the other passengers who were disembarking in Launceston. Bruce saw Ian's mistake and said to Dad, 'Shouldn't we tell him?' Dad said, 'No, let him find out for himself.' Ian found out for himself when he asked a taxi driver to take him to the Wrest Point Casino. The taxi driver must have said something like, 'It'll be a bloody big fare!' Dad and Bruce smiled to themselves as they watched Ian emerge from the terminal at a gallop as the last passenger, climb up the stairs and take his seat for the final leg to Hobart.

Ian and Dad eventually became very good mates when they stopped behaving like petulant children. Ian said the penny dropped for him that he was going to be spending a lot of time with Dad in the commentary box, so they'd better start trying to get along with each other. Whenever I went into the commentary box with Dad, Ian was always one of the people to make a point of saying hello. If I had a guest with me who was having a look inside the box, Ian was always the first person to come and chat to us and make my guest feel welcome.

Many have taken credit for the TV sports coverage initiatives, but the major changes were driven by Kerry Packer and carried out by the highly creative and technically savvy operators at Nine.

Kerry instigated the following initiatives:

- Cameras at both ends of the ground.
- Sound from the centre of the ground, leading to microphones behind the wickets and eventually to stump cam.
- Larger lenses on cameras so close-up shots of the players could bring the viewer closer to the centre of action. One of Kerry's staff, Nine Network chief engineer Bruce Robertson, was sent overseas to investigate the best and latest lens technology to achieve this aim. Kerry nearly choked when advised of the cost, but approved the expenditure.
- Lights for the introduction of night cricket.
- New slow-motion technology.
- Coloured clothing.

Coloured clothing was not a marketing initiative or a gimmick. Once lights were available and the white ball was in play, coloured clothing became essential. It was impossible for the umpires to judge exactly where a white ball hit a white pad. The fieldsman also lost the white ball against the white clothing and it was much the same for television viewers at home.

When the then New South Wales Premier, Neville Wran, approved the building of light towers at the SCG, Lynton Taylor was in New York on business. Armed with input from some of the players, Lynton and Kerry had a phone conversation, at the end of which they reached the conclusion they needed coloured clothing. Lynton's wife, Ros, knew one of Sydney's leading designers, Mel Clifford, so Lynton rang him from New York and asked him to design a set of cricket clothing for each of Australia, the West Indies and the World XI. The colours were to represent their identity. Mel Clifford jumped at the chance.

On Lynton's return to Australia, Clifford presented his designs. Lynton suggested a few changes but eventually the Clifford designs were approved. No one involved in the running of WSC had any idea of the furore that would engulf them when the West Indians first saw their 'pink' clothing. The colour was officially coral, to represent the waters of the Caribbean. Instead, to the West Indians, it was plain old pink, a colour which in their part of the world was associated with the gay community. After some discussion, they agreed to wear the clothing, but WSC agreed that a variation would be made the following year.

Dad's World XI played in duck egg blue; Australia played in yellow, or gold. The coloured clothing gave rise to the name 'pyjama cricket', a term probably coined by Bill O'Reilly.

Overall, Kerry took a personal and hands-on approach to the TV coverage, talking to producer David Hill for hours on end, either in his office or on the phone. Kerry had a personal line from his office into the commentary box. When it rang, everyone knew it was him on the phone.

During 1978 and 1979, Lynton Taylor was in continual contact with representatives of the Test and County Cricket Board (TCCB), West Indies Cricket Board (WICB), Pakistan

Cricket Board (PCB) and the South African Cricket Board to try to coordinate the players and the schedule, and, if possible, gain their support for a compromise. The TCCB, led by Doug Insole, was implacable and, although WSC had Raman Subba Row and Bernie Coleman from the Surrey County Cricket Club trying to ameliorate things, it was mission impossible.

Lynton thought a breakthrough had been made when ICC Chairman Charles Palmer, and Secretary Jack Bailey agreed to a secret meeting with him in New York in mid-1978. The meeting was cordial and some positive suggestions were made, but after their return to London the usual rejection of any agreement between WSC and the various cricket boards of the world was received.

Following the meeting in New York, Taylor travelled to Barbados for a pre-arranged secret meeting with Jeff Stollmeyer, President of the WICB, and Vice President Allan Rae. They travelled from Barbados by boat to a remote island where Stollmeyer had a summer house. After a positive meeting, the path was cleared for WSC's proposed tour of the West Indies in March/April 1979. While in Barbados, Julian Hunte from the Saint Lucia National Cricket Association and the Windward Islands Cricket Board of Control also met with Lynton just to shore things up there.

During that tour in March/April 1979, Lynton learnt that unlike other West Indian countries, it was not possible to repatriate gate receipts and television fees from the matches to the USA or Australia from Guyana. Someone suggested WSC might be able to take silver out of the country to the value of their earnings, so Lynton set up a meeting with the Finance Minister and put the suggestion to her. He was lucky to escape without a jail sentence for even suggesting such a preposterous option. A considerable sum of money was therefore left in a bank account in Guyana, which WSC used for the benefit of cricketers there over a ten-year period.

Discussions with the ICC and international boards, including the TCCB, still did not bring peace, and PBL doubted there was ever any intention by the ICC and the TCCB to achieve it. In Australia there were a number of olive branches held out by both sides but none was ever grasped. Kerry decided Sir Donald Bradman, who had in the past worked for his father, Sir Frank, was key and he needed to be wooed. The President of the NSW Cricket Association was Tim Caldwell, whom Kerry knew through his company's bank dealings. At Caldwell's request, Sir Donald agreed to a meeting at his home. The meeting was so top secret that Kerry confided only in Lynton and Dad about it.

The meeting went well and it was agreed that a further meeting should take place between a committee of the ACB and PBL to establish a peace treaty in the interests of the game. The Board representatives were to be Bob Parish, Ray Steele, Tim Caldwell and Sir Donald; Lynton was designated as the PBL representative. Kerry gave him no instructions other than to say that fundamental to any settlement were the exclusive TV rights to all cricket under the control of the ACB and its associations, and all cricket played internationally by the Australian team. Anything else was a bonus.

During the meeting between the five nominees held at the NSW Cricket Association, a general discussion took place in which Lynton laid out the PBL requirements in principle. No roadblocks were put up. Sir Donald was committed and concluded the meeting with the following statement: 'Let's get a deal done. I do not care what we have to give up to achieve an agreement as long as the ACB has control of the game.' Lynton seized on Sir Donald's comment that control of the game was paramount like Sir Donald used to seize on a half-volley!

With those words still ringing in his ears, Lynton delivered a 'wish list' to ACB secretary Alan Barnes that was approved in principle by the Board's committee members. Barnes and Lynton, with the assistance of John Kitto from PBL, developed a long-form agreement that was approved and signed by all parties, thus bringing peace to world cricket. The essence of the agreement was:

— Ten years of exclusive broadcast rights. PBL
   wanted fifteen years but the lawyers felt that could
   be struck down for being too long, so PBL agreed
   to ten years with a watertight option for a further
   five years.
— The ACB controlled the game.
— PBL and the ACB shared the following revenue on
   a 50/50 basis:
   The gate
   The sponsorship revenue
   The merchandise revenue
— PBL was responsible for the marketing of the game.
— PBL was responsible for the merchandise.
— Ticketek was to be granted the ticketing rights at
   all grounds when they became available.

- There was no TV rights fee.
- No player would be prejudiced in future selection by having signed with WSC and this was to be agreed by all cricketing boards worldwide.
- The schedule of matches was prescribed. A five-Test series and a fifteen-match one-day triangular competition called World Series Cricket. The schedule was to be drafted with input from PBL.
- Lights were to be installed at all grounds where matches were to be played and as many one-day night games scheduled as lights allowed were to be scheduled.

Having consummated the deal with the ACB, PBL Marketing had to make sure that the cricket coverage would reach every Australian. There were two problems. First, at that time there were no facilities to deliver television signals to many parts of Australia, including Perth and the rest of Western Australia. And second, few of the regional stations initially prepared to take the cricket.

At that time, all stations including regional stations programmed their own schedules. Films or tapes were delivered to them by plane cargo and played out according to each station's schedule. The AUSSAT satellite system had not been introduced, although the need for such a system had been recognised by Kerry Packer in 1977 when considering distribution of World Series Cricket. Kerry spoke with then Prime Minister Malcolm Fraser about the necessity for a satellite system and he received a positive hearing. Kerry brought Donald Bond, a Canadian satellite consultant, to Australia, who along with Les Free, a former

Chief Engineer at Nine, and Lynton Taylor, developed what became known as the 'Bond Report' that eventually led to the creation of AUSSAT and the availability of television to all Australians.

Lynton Taylor delivered the report to Malcolm Fraser. This subsequently led to changes to the Broadcasting Act allowing aggregation of television ownership and today's networking, which occurred in 1987. Another benefit created by World Series Cricket.

The ABC had developed a network throughout Australia by relaying their service from transmitter to transmitter with the addition of microwave systems and therefore could deliver the cricket throughout Australia. Lynton Taylor approached the General Manager of the ABC, Talbot Duckmanton (later Sir Talbot), and Assistant General Manager Television Graham White, and negotiated a deal for the ABC to carry the cricket in regional Australia for $1,000,000 per year for three years. The ABC was to provide its own commentary. The deal caused much consternation in Canberra and with the *Friends of the ABC*, who saw the deal as a 'favour' to Mr Packer and a waste of ABC funds. It should be remembered that in the last year of the deal for cricket with the ABC, it paid $100,000 for Australia-wide rights.

With the deal done, the cricket was available to the whole of Australia. By the end of the three-year deal, the regional networks had realised the rating and commercial value of cricket and took over the regional coverage.

Kerry famously claimed 'you only get one Alan Bond in your lifetime' after he sold Channel Nine to his fellow Australian businessman for in excess of $1 billion in 1987. Dad often used to joke that this was not quite true. Lynton had negotiated a deal for PBL that was tantamount to a licence to print money. WSC had cost PBL $34 million but the Nine Network at this time was writing record revenue and could sustain the cost. PBL recovered the entire amount within two years. ACB officials whined for ten years that the settlement left them with the bottom out of their pants. Whether the ACB just used the terms of the peace settlement as an excuse for rejecting players' demands for more money is not known. However, a number of buildings belonging to the associations had to be sold to make ends meet and the ACB's whingeing eventually became the catalyst for a number of Australia's top players deciding to tour South Africa in 1985 in a rebel team.

The peace deal was kept secret for a period to allow PBL to talk to its players and resolve all contractual matters, and so that the ACB could seek the support of governing bodies around the world. The latter did not prove easy, due to the stubbornness of the TCCB. To them, Kerry winning probably meant my dad winning, too.

As a sign of Kerry's good faith, all contractual commitments entered into by WSC were met: the players were paid out in full. International cricketers were signed to US entity IMG, controlled by Mark McCormack and one of Mark's senior executives, Alastair Johnston.

The final matter to be tidied up was the buy-out of John Cornell, Paul Hogan and Austin Robertson from JP Sports – now World Series Cricket – so PBL could enter into the board agreement with that company, which was to be renamed PBL Marketing. Lynton sat down with John Cornell in 1979 and finally agreed to a buy-out of the three directors for a combined total of $100,000.

People often talk about the legacy of WSC. I think it is best summed up by my dad when Dad gave the Spirit of Cricket Cowdrey Lecture at Lord's in 2012:

> I have never had any doubt that I did the right thing by my family and by cricket. I have worked for Kerry Packer's organisation for 35 years and my family's future has been secured. After the initial nastiness and internal feuding, cricket and cricketers also did quite well out of World Series Cricket.
>
> WSC ensured cricket reinvented itself to survive the changing world;
>
> WSC was the jolt the administrators needed, and it flagged the message that they were substantially under-selling the sport to the television stations;
>
> Players immediately received substantially more money at both Test and first-class level, which increased the longevity of their careers;
>
> Companies saw value in using cricket as a marketing tool;
>
> TV coverage improved significantly, which increased interest in the sport;
>
> Night cricket created a new audience, both television-wise and at the ground, and generated significantly more income;
>
> WSC revolutionised cricket pitch preparation through the drop-in pitches;
>
> Cricket's success inspired other sports to imitate cricket with things such as TV coverage and sponsorships.

I only have two regrets about World Series Cricket. EW Swanton was very good to me throughout my career and I am saddened that despite numerous attempts by me, I never had a chance to make peace with him after World Series Cricket. Second, I had a wonderful relationship with the chairman of selectors, Alec Bedser, which continued through and beyond World Series Cricket. I know Alec understood why, but I dearly would like to have told him of my plans before they became public. However, I promised Kerry I wouldn't.

13

Mum and Dad

DAD WAS A BIG MAN ... TALL, WITH BIG FEET AND BIG HANDS. As a young boy I always felt safe when he was at home and scared when he wasn't. He was big on life and told big stories, regularly mesmerising me with tales of his youth. Mostly these stories were of his childhood in South Africa, including his stays at Rodney King's farm at Tarkastad, the family beach holidays at Kei Mouth and his time boarding at Queen's College. A natural storyteller, he was always able to capture my interest and create much excitement, and this talent meant he was a brilliant off-the-cuff after-dinner speaker and a great cricket commentator.

When my sister Sam and I were young, Dad would spend hours and hours telling us the most wonderful adventure tales. He would come up with all sorts of characters in his plots, and sometimes would even include my teddy bear or Sam's dolls for added effect. Some 30 years later, we witnessed Dad repeating his stories to our little brother and sister, Tom and Beau (from Dad's second marriage). We often said Dad could have been a very successful author of children's storybooks.

His passionate love for South Africa always came through in his stories. He was proud of his background, despite the fact that many South Africans were seen as pariahs by the world at the time. His South African roots certainly helped form part of his character, as did his relationship with his father, Sandy. Dad was in awe of Sandy's courage in flying all those missions over Germany as part of Bomber Command. I think one of the reasons Dad went about his life so fearlessly was because he was influenced by his father's experiences in World War Two. Sandy had also instilled in him a deep appreciation of the history of Great Britain and a love for King and Country, which shone through in his stories.

Dad had a strong sense of family and made sure Sam and I valued the importance of family from a very young age. With our relatives spread all over the world, aunts and uncles would ring us on our birthdays, there were always phones ringing at Christmas and gifts that had crossed continents and oceans sat under the tree. We were fortunate that both sets of grandparents, and also Aunty Eleanor, immigrated to Australia shortly after we arrived.

I will always remember the strong bond Dad had with both his parents, but particularly Granny Joycie. If we were going out for dinner, or for a walk to the park or to the beach for a swim, Dad would always call and ask if his mum would like to join us. She did every time. Even later in life when Joycie had moved back to South Africa, Dad was conscious that we should never forget to make her feel special. Although it wasn't necessary, he would prompt our memories: 'Don't forget we have to call Joycie on her birthday tomorrow.' Dad usually called her daily, and tried to visit her each year in South Africa.

Mum and Dad socialised a lot, and I can recall Sam and I having babysitters on a regular basis. Before we left England in late 1975, Mum's sister Eleanor flew to Brighton at the end of her nursing training to help Mum with Sam and me. Mum had huge demands on her because Dad was captain of England at the time and she was required to attend many functions and spend weekends away with him.

On the rare occasions Dad had a day off from cricket, he and Mum would take us kite flying on the dyke or for long walks along Brighton Beach promenade. Dad's sister Sally Ann, who was also living in England, provided an additional layer of support. My mum and Sally Ann were close and I know Mum greatly appreciated her help and companionship. Both Eleanor and Sally Ann were very important in Mum and Dad's life because they gave them the opportunity to have quality time off together.

Sam and I often reflect on the fun we had with Dad – he was all about excitement which, being kids, we absolutely loved. We have such fond memories of our childhood; we were always active, hardly surprising when we look at Dad's childhood. We were genetically programmed that way. We went to the beach often and played the 'under or over' game from an early age. If a big wave had broken we would all scream out 'under', dive to the bottom and grab the sea floor as the white water crashed over our heads. If a wave was small or unbroken, we would shout 'over' and toss ourselves over the crest of the wave. We did it for hours.

Mum and Dad took us fishing off Sydney's Rose Bay Wharf all the time. Dad made it a competition as to who could catch the most yellowtails and leatherjackets. Mum usually won, as she was the most patient member of the family and had secret bait of raw minced meat. Dad preferred using prawns. If you landed a tiny yellowtail, Dad would build up so much excitement you would think you had a barracuda on the end of your line. We had so much fun on that wharf. There were also frequent visits to Lyne Park on the harbour at Rose Bay, where Dad would push us for hours on the swings. I can remember going so high that our toes would nearly touch the treetops. We would ride bikes around Centennial Park while our German Shepherd, Sheba, ran on the grass alongside us.

Sheba was a remarkable dog. She joined our family as a puppy when I was six years old, and Dad put a lot of effort into training her to do some brilliant tricks. Dad's morning routine would start with putting the kettle on and making some toast, which he would cover in a thick layer of butter and jam. He would then open the front door so Sheba could run down the stairs at the front of the house and collect the newspaper in her mouth. She would carry it back up the stairs into the house and deliver it to Dad, who was by now back in bed with his toast and coffee, ready to start reading the morning papers.

Dad always came home from his travels bearing gifts, creating great suspense as he slowly opened his bags to reveal the presents. We loved it when he came home. I definitely performed better on the cricket field when he was there to watch me play. However, I am amazed he bothered after his first experience. I was playing for The Scots College at

Dover Heights Reservoir. Dad was quite excited when we won the toss and I was asked to open the batting – he was optimistic I might score a hundred. Unbeknown to Dad we had funny rules similar to those used in indoor cricket: each pair of batsmen batted for four overs and it didn't matter how many times they were dismissed. I faced three balls in my four overs and was two not out. At the end of the game Dad asked me who had won and to his horror I said, 'They haven't worked it out.' I then explained that they divided the number of runs by the number of wickets. Scots won 2.43 runs to Cranbrook's 2.045 runs.

Dad couldn't believe it. He had come from a schoolboy background where you travelled overnight to play games and played all day. And if you were out, you were out, and if the opposition couldn't get you out, that was their bad luck. He reckoned the communists had taken over Australian cricket and said the game's future didn't look good in Australia if that's how it was being played in schools.

I could well have been playing in the Cranbrook side that day. When my family first arrived in Sydney I attended Cranbrook's preschool, St Michael's. I have vivid memories of my mum dropping me off on my first day and tears rolling down my cheeks as I watched her through the window walking away.

Dad told me I was supposed to attend Cranbrook prep school the following year – until his first meeting with the then Cranbrook headmaster, Mark Bishop. Dad had heard good things about the school from Kerry Packer, as his son James was in the senior school. After being given a tour of the school, Dad asked Mr Bishop how many Test cricketers had been educated at Cranbrook. He was surprised when

Mr Bishop wasn't able to name a single old boy who had worn the Baggy Green cap. The headmaster was a cricket fanatic and was probably just as concerned about this as Dad. Maybe Mr Bishop was hoping I would be the first.

The following week, Dad was up the road having a tour of another school, The Scots College. The Scots headmaster at the time was Graeme Renney, a short, unassuming man with big plans for the school who was regarded as a visionary. Mr Renney's answer to Dad's question was that Scots had produced a few fine cricketers over the years, but the school had most certainly delivered plenty of great Rugby players. These included Ken Catchpole, whom Dad idolised from the 1963 Wallabies tour of South Africa. He'd missed two of the Tests through injury, but Dr Danie Craven, the Don Bradman of the Rugby world, had said Catchpole was the best scrum-half ever. On the back of Catchpole attending Scots, Dad decided to send me there. I don't think he even asked about the academic record of either school.

Despite his desire for me to attend a good sporting school, Dad actually never forced cricket on me as a kid. I thoroughly enjoyed playing the game and the camaraderie it gave me with my mates. Having Dad's involvement in my school cricket meant that my friends and I were fortunate enough to have some fantastic cricket tours at a young age. Before I turned eleven I had toured Melbourne and Adelaide, and Dad even organised a tour to England in 1985. Scots Prep 1st XI played five matches against some of England's top public schools. It was an amazing experience afforded to such a young group of boys. Dad never officially coached any of my cricket sides, but I loved watching him make a special effort to give advice and cricketing tips to my close friends. To them he was just Greigy's Dad and I don't think they realised the extent of his fame until later years. Dad instilled in me the love of sport and good sportsmanship, and for that I am truly grateful.

Since Dad had such warm memories of his time at Queen's College, sending us to good schools was important to him. He was big on us having an all-round education and was never particularly fussed about Sam and I having to be straight-'A' students. To him a school should be the kind of place where even if a kid was a hopeless runner, he or she would be willing to run their little legs off to make a contribution. Mum and Dad constantly encouraged us to do as much as possible at school. I played all sports, tried learning four different musical instruments, attempted a few different languages, was in all the school plays, led the Scots' Pipes and Drums as Drum Major, and also somehow managed to earn myself a prefect's tie. I always felt honoured and proud when leading the Scots' Pipes and Drums because of Sandy's Scottish roots. This was particularly the case in the Sydney Anzac Day march.

In 1985, the year before Sam started boarding school at Frensham in the Southern Highlands, Mum and Dad gave her a farewell disco party with all her school friends. We had an enormous timber-floored room at home we used to call the 'ballroom'. Mum took such pride in her home and had beautiful home decorating skills. I can still remember how wonderful the room looked that night. This was no ordinary party either; it was Sam's first mixed party.

The boys were reluctant to get up and dance when the music started, so Dad jumped in and taught them a couple of dances to get everyone going. In the first dance, Dad and

Sam started dancing together, then they split up, he chose a girl and Sam chose a boy. They danced for a couple of minutes before splitting again to find new partners, and so on. They continued doing this until everyone was on the dancefloor. He called this 'snowball', and apparently it was something he and his sisters did as teenagers in South Africa. Sam was extremely embarrassed at first, but when all the parents arrived to pick up their children they had trouble getting them off the dancefloor, as the snowball had turned into an avalanche. Sam still gets some of the guys, now aged 40, coming up to her and telling her how much fun they had at that party.

Dad had an extremely soft side. I remember the day in 1986 when Sam, then aged twelve, first left for Frensham, which was about two hours' drive south-west of Sydney. This was the first day I saw my dad cry. He gave his 'little girl' a big hug goodbye at the steps of her new boarding house, released her, then we quickly jumped back into our car to drive home to Sydney. I saw in the rear-vision mirror that he had tears in his eyes. Sam did have the knack of bringing out his soft side. Even his voice would soften when I heard him telephone his 'little girl' at boarding school, saying, 'How are you, sweetheart?'

Recently, when we were reminiscing about our childhood, Sam told me these stories:

> I can remember every time Dad took me back
> to school for a new term. The first thing he did
> was check my bed had a board under it. He was
> concerned that if my bed was too soft I would have
> back problems later in life. If there was no board

under my bed, he would go around checking the other girls' beds until he found one, which he slid out and then moved under my mattress!

When Mum and Dad came to visit me at boarding school they always took my friends and me out to lunch. On my 16th birthday I had invited too many friends and we couldn't fit them all in the car so Dad opened up the boot and piled three more girls in there. They loved it, needless to say everyone wanted to travel in the boot on the way home.

When I think about Dad's involvement in my schooling, the thing that stands out is how much he enjoyed watching me play rugby. He tried to be at every one of my games, and often talked about how he loved the pace of schoolboy rugby. I wore my Scots' 1st XV jersey with great pride. Running out onto Scots' main oval to the sound of bagpipes and the entire school singing war cries was without a doubt the best memory I have of my time at school.

Apparently Dad was a highly talented young rugby player and an exceptional lineout jumper – back in the days when lifting in the lineout was not permitted. Although Dad had grown up in South Africa, he was a vocal Wallabies supporter, and I used to love going to Rugby Tests with him. I recall watching the Wallabies play France at the SCG in 1986. Dad had been given fantastic tickets, and we were seated in the front row. Before the game started the French fullback, Serge Blanco, walked past us rubbing his boots in his hands. Dad told me he was one of the world's best kickers and that he was probably rubbing some sort of leather cream into his boots to make them softer for kicking.

He did such a great job building up the excitement in me. By the time it was kick-off I had nearly wet my pants with anticipation. I used to sit on the edge of my seat and point out to Dad every time Serge Blanco joined his backline in an attacking position or David Campese did his famous goose-step. To this day when I smell hot chips with vinegar I think of my dad and the bucket we often shared covered in salt and vinegar at the rugby.

It is worth noting that in all that time I spent with Dad I never saw him have an epileptic seizure. I obviously knew he was an epileptic, but only because I watched him take his epilepsy pills every day and because of his involvement with the Epilepsy Association. It was something that just never seemed to impact on his life, from my perspective. What I came to find out in later years is that Dad's epilepsy was influenced by sleep and stress. If he was short on sleep, or high on stress, he was more likely to suffer an aura, or giddiness. Around 1987, he was so obsessed with getting sufficient sleep that he started taking Mogadon sleeping tablets. Initially he would just take one tablet to help him get off to sleep more quickly, particularly if he had been travelling and his sleep pattern was out of kilter. Gradually over time he increased the number of tablets he was taking, until one day he realised he was taking four or five tablets at once. He was addicted and now completely reliant on the tablets to sleep. Fortunately he was able to get help and slowly wean himself off. He also sought advice from various sleep specialists and changed some of his habits, such as not drinking coffee in the afternoon or ice cold water before going to bed.

On reflection, it was about 1990, when I was mid-way through senior school, that Dad started having more giddy spells than usual. I don't think it was just because of his sleep issues. That was the start of a very difficult time for Dad. He was devastated by the loss of his dad, he had separated from Mum and had fallen into financial trouble through trying to help an old school friend who'd migrated to Australia. Dad also found it difficult to share his precious time with so many people and 'keep everyone happy', as he used to say. Apart from the fact that he travelled abroad regularly, he had to make time for fellow cricketers, business colleagues, bosses, friends, family and the general public, who all wanted their own time with him. His epilepsy started playing hovoc.

Mum and Dad had a long history. They fell in love when they were very young, long before Dad found fame through cricket. They had a special bond that had its roots in South Africa, where Mum attended school with Dad's sister Molly Joy. As Mum didn't marry into the fame, she found it difficult to embrace Dad's new lifestyle and 'distractions' in the years after their marriage. Although Mum made some close friendships with mothers of Sam and my school friends, the vast majority of Mum's life in Australia revolved around Dad's friends and his requirements. However, in the rare moments Mum had to herself, she invariably acted as a counsellor to others.

Mum helped so many people through hard times. She gave people the time and attention they needed, and deserved, and she was a wonderful listener. In England she supported fellow cricketing wives who struggled with loneliness when their husbands were away from home for long periods of time. In Australia she provided love and warmth, and our home became a safe haven for many family members and friends. She supported her work colleagues through tough times and even our school friends would seek her out for advice on different matters. Sam remembers a friend of hers ringing one night. As Sam lay on her bed to get comfortable for a friendly chat, her friend asked if she could talk to her mum as she wanted her advice about a problem. Sam never asked what the problem was, but felt so fortunate to have a caring mother whom others sought out for wisdom and advice.

When I was fourteen a close schoolfriend, Courtney Anderson, drowned in a tragic canoeing accident. I was with him when he died and was devastated. Not only did Mum help me through the terrible trauma of this tragedy, but somehow, over many, many months, she also helped Courtney's parents, Susie and Bill, through their darkest hours. More than a decade later, Susie wrote a heartfelt letter to Mum, expressing her gratitude for Mum's friendship and support during that deeply sad time in her life. These are some of the words she wrote in that letter:

I was just thinking how often Bill and I have passed over our thoughts onto others – but never to you. You see Donna darling, I don't think you ever knew just how much you helped us through the darkest, most painful time in our lives. It's strange because we still talk about it – how you would just appear and quietly sit with us – long drives when I hadn't ventured out of the house – our beautiful day at the Botanical Gardens – I don't know how long we sat on that garden bench – mostly we didn't even talk, and when we did, I talked and cried and you held me gently and listened … I've since tried to find that special quality you possess but it doesn't seem to come. I've tried to dig deep to help others the way you did me, in spite of your own problems. But I've since realised darling Donna that yours is a gift so unique that it can't be manufactured.

Mum was great with people. I think she enjoyed starting to work again, particularly the mental stimulation it provided. It must have taken some adjusting for her, though, as she had been a full-time mother for twelve years before starting work in 1985 with Advance Bank. Initially her job was as a sales representative, but it wasn't long before she found her way into the marketing department. In August 1987, Mum moved to National Benefits Consulting Group (NBCG), a company that provided advice to organisations on the design and management of superannuation and insurance plans. She was initially employed in a marketing role, but in July 1988 NBCG was acquired by FAI Insurances Limited and following internal restructuring she was appointed as Manager–Corporate Administration. She stayed at NBCG until 1990. A colleague and dear friend of Mum's from NBCG, Laura Murphy, remembers the difference Mum made to another family's life. Ian Ralph worked in the Perth branch office and needed to bring his wife, Elaine, to Sydney for a lung transplant. Mum knew the family of four was struggling financially so she organised through her contacts at ACP for the company to fly them from Perth to Sydney. When they arrived Mum opened her door and heart in true Donna fashion, assisting them in every way she could.

It was a long wait for the transplant, around 21 months. Unfortunately it was not successful, with Elaine passing away shortly after coming out of surgery. Ian was deeply grateful for the support and care Mum gave him and his family during the 21 months and the difficult time after the loss of his wife. The family wrote at the time of Mum's passing: 'We feel privileged to have known such a beautiful and generous lady. We have such good memories of your mum and these memories will remain forever.'

Mum was fulfilled through her total devotion to Sam and me. Sam left a loving family home for boarding school in 1986 and unfortunately, over the next couple of years, things started falling apart. Even though Mum worked extremely hard over many years to hold her marriage together, the time came when she had to make the most difficult decision she had ever made, to leave the love of her life.

The separation caused Mum severe anguish on two fronts. First, she had to leave a house she had turned into a wonderful, warm, welcoming home. Secondly, her much-loved parents-in-law, Sandy and Joycie, had to leave their home so Mum, Sam and I would have somewhere to live when we moved out of the family home. Sandy and Joycie moved in with Dad.

Because of the arrangement Dad had with Kerry Packer on the financing of our house, it wasn't possible for Dad to leave and us to stay, which would most often be the case in these situations. Whatever the reasons, Mum and Dad both agreed on Dad staying in the family home, leaving him to find a way to pay Mum out her share. In the end it was Kerry who helped sort out Dad's settlement with Mum, something I know Dad was extremely grateful for. Dad's lifestyle didn't change, but ours did. Our family home in Vaucluse had been the perfect house for entertaining, with its enormous garden, swimming pool and even a ballroom.

Although Sam was absolutely devastated by the divorce, she handled it much better than I did. Whether this was because she was not subjected to the day-to-day goings-on while she was away at school or she dealt with it by focusing on her studies, she didn't let her anger and pain get in the way of giving Mum the best support and comfort possible, while not distancing herself from Dad. I was, however, disappointed with Dad for causing Mum so much grief and for not giving her proper recognition for the role she played as his wife and mother of his children. I was also angry when an inappropriate and distressing telephone call at school from a complete stranger made Sam extremely upset. I was also distraught at only being able to see Dad every second weekend.

I know the divorce caused Dad much stress, and for a long time he found it difficult to deal with the fact that he had let his family down. But, like all of us, he had to move on and looking back on it now his guilt at the breakdown of his marriage may have hardened him a little, almost as a defence mechanism.

Now on her own and with an uncertain future, my mother, understandably, was also under a lot of stress. She had some close friends, in whom I am sure she confided, but she considered this her own problem and she was facing it head-on.

Sadly, it didn't take long before our old family home lost that lovely warm feeling when we visited Dad there. It was like the windows had been opened and the happiness had just floated away, letting in cold air. Most meals with Dad were basic, usually meat and three veg. Often this involved Dad getting the coals in the Weber alight to cook steak or lamb chops and Sam and I would lend a hand by preparing a salad, boiling peas or making some mashed potato. To see Dad loading our dirty clothes into the washing machine was a pretty strange sight – having divorced parents certainly took some getting used to. Nowadays, being separated with children is just another kind of family and living in two households is so normal that school application forms have space for two addresses.

We had some fantastic overseas family holidays over the years. It would be unfair to single one out, but our first holiday with Dad after he and Mum separated will always have special meaning because it helped put our relationship back on track. Dad flew Sam and me to London in 1989. I was fourteen and Sam was sixteen. Working in England during the Ashes Test series, Dad was really missing his family and I recall seeing his big smile high above all the other heads when we walked through the arrivals gate at Heathrow Airport.

Dad went to a huge amount of trouble to organise a special visit back to Brighton, where we had lived twelve years earlier. He showed us Brighton General Hospital in which we were both born, and we also visited our family home at Dyke Close in Hove. He knocked on the door and when the owner answered he recognised Dad instantly. 'I was wondering if you would ever come back to visit this house,' he said, then gave us a full tour through our old home. Dad got a real kick out of that visit and told us countless stories as we walked around and his memories came flooding back.

He told us of the time Imran Khan came to visit and how Mum let him lie down on the floor next to the record player and play music all day. In the back garden he pointed out where Mum's vegetable patch was once located. Apparently this was a common hiding spot for Sam's pet tortoise, Charlie. When Sam, aged three, called out for Charlie, he would make his way out of the vegie patch at a tortoise equivalent of a gallop, hoping for his favourite treat: a ripe tomato. Sam and I loved hearing about the fun times Mum and Dad enjoyed with us during those years in Hove.

Dad also drove us up to Scotland and gave us the full tour of Grandpa Sandy's home town, Bathgate. We stayed a night with Sandy's sister, Isobel Carlaw, and visited his nephew Greig Carlaw. We went to the buildings which once housed Greig Bros and Greig's Garage and TV Maintenance where Dad worked all those year ago. At Scotscraig, we took photos of all the different houses … my great-grandmother Granny Greig's house and the cottages in which Sandy and Isobel were born, near Sandy's first school. After a big trip down memory lane for Dad, we then flew to Paris, where he gave us a condensed tour of everything – the Mona Lisa at the Louvre, the Palace of Versailles and the Eiffel Tower. Dad refused to take the lift up the tower and challenged me to a race climbing up the stairs to the top. Everything was a competition for him. He was 42 at the time and, as I reflect on this now, he did an incredible job running all the way to the top that day. I remember him introducing us to the Impressionist paintings of Claude Monet at the Musée d'Orsay and encouraging us to try frogs' legs and snails for the first time. He had an adventurous palate, and for the shock factor liked trying unusual foods.

Going to a museum with Dad as a kid was easy for me – we were always in and out quickly. Sometimes it felt more like we were just ticking it off a list when he made a beeline for the main attractions. While Dad appreciated art and history, he had a short attention span and was easily bored.

It was different travelling with Dad in countries where he wasn't recognised – he certainly wasn't used to being turned away if a restaurant was full. No one had a clue who he was in Paris and none of us could speak a word of French. Dad trying to speak broken French expressions with a South African accent sounded terrible! Staying in hotels in Australia or England everyone recognised him and made him feel special. I remember him on occasion being abrupt with hotel staff if he didn't get crispy bacon at breakfast, having already made a special request for it. Crispy bacon or soft eggs sometimes seemed like a life or death situation. Sam and I would get embarrassed if he made a fuss and would say, 'Dad, don't take it out on the waiters, it's not their fault.' However, he suggested that as he was the one paying for breakfast, not the waiter, he was entitled to make a fuss.

From Paris we drove south to Nice, where we went parasailing and jet-ski riding off the beach ... so much fun for teenage kids. We drove across to Italy and arrived in Florence late one night to find there was a big festival on and no accommodation to be had. Eventually we booked into a tiny little hotel in some back laneway. The room was cramped and only had one bed which squeaked every time one of us moved. The bathroom was so small Dad took a shower while he sat on the toilet and brushed his teeth all at the same time. We all laughed so much on that holiday.

Back at home, life began improving as Mum slowly started to smile again. She was such a superb host and encouraged us to bring our friends home, so on weekends I often had four or five friends over for a roast dinner. She was a great cook and always made sure Sam and I could handle ourselves in the kitchen, like her own mother had done for her.

After the divorce, Mum's focus was on her continuing care of Sam and me. Sam, as always, remained very close to her. Mum needed her daughter's companionship and wanted to maintain a strong sense of family. While Sam always stuck by Mum, she also made sure she retained a good relationship with Dad. She let the sensitivities 'go through to the keeper' as Dad would say. Of course in every broken family some level of conflict is to be expected, and ours was no different. I am blessed, though, with so many fond and happy memories of my childhood.

Mum never remarried. Though she was the one to leave the marriage, I believe she never stopped loving Dad and witnessing her inherent sadness during my teenage years has brought me great anguish over the years. In all that sadness, I never heard Mum talk badly of Dad; she was an incredibly strong and loyal woman. Looking back, I know she bottled up any anger or resentment she had – protecting her children was her number-one priority.

At the turn of the millennium things were really moving on for everyone in the family; we were all having a fresh start. Mum had set up a luxury homewares and bed linen retail business on the New South Wales Central Coast; I was living and working in London; and Sam had moved to Sri Lanka, where she was teaching at an international school in Colombo. Life for Dad was also moving on. He'd remarried and his new wife, Vivian, had given birth to my little sister, Beau, in Sydney on 11 January 2000. Her birth brought great joy and excitement into Dad's life.

Mum's fresh start was to receive a major setback, however, when just over a year later, before her 52nd birthday, she began feeling strange pains in her stomach. The early tests indicated something was not right, and I think she knew she had cancer but she didn't mention those dark thoughts to us. I remember the moment Mum told me she had an appointment with a specialist who was concerned about a large lump in her lower stomach. She tried to play it down, explaining she'd been advised to have surgery to remove the lump, that no one was sure what it was, and that her doctors would have a better idea once a biopsy had been taken. At no stage did she tell me anyone had indicated it was cancer, but somehow I knew. Perhaps I felt it in her voice. I was terrified and tried not to show my deep sense of foreboding.

I was due to marry my fiancée, Angela, ten days later. Mum insisted we did not push back our wedding, and she promised us she would do whatever she could to recover from the surgery in time to be at our wedding, even if it meant being pushed into the church in a wheelchair. The surgeons operated and performed a hysterectomy, and with it removed a tumour described as being the size of a large grapefruit.

The following week Mum was in bed recovering at Prince of Wales Hospital in Sydney. Her focus was to get better and be up walking by Sunday 30 September, my wedding day. When the doctors told her she wouldn't be well enough to attend the wedding, she wouldn't hear of it – nothing was going to stop her from being there on her son's special day. There was even talk about organising a helicopter to fly her up to the Hunter Valley if she didn't feel well enough for the long journey by car with Sam.

How my sister got Mum to my wedding is beyond my comprehension. She was desperately ill and in a lot of pain. Despite it all she managed to walk down the aisle alongside my mother-in-law, Imelda Roche, both carrying a candle with the respective family surname. Mum and Imelda then used their candles to light a single candle labelled 'Angela & Mark'. It was an incredibly moving moment.

Somehow Mum managed to sit through the wedding reception, which involved a three-course meal and speeches that went well into the evening. Her presence was highly symbolic: she had sacrificed her whole adult life for Sam and me and now she was still doing it, literally, on my wedding day.

When I made my speech my mind was like a washing machine. Whirling around were thoughts of a great future with Ange, the wonderful times with Mum and Dad, of lamenting their divorce and wondering whether the stress caused by it had contributed to her illness.

Mum initially kept the details of her diagnosis very vague, saying she was waiting on more test results before we would know what she was dealing with. She sounded so positive that I let my fears dissipate and didn't really have concerns for her life at this stage. She encouraged me to go on my honeymoon to South Africa, the country in which she grew up and fell in love with my father. She promised that by the time I returned she would have more details about her health and a plan to get better.

Ange and I returned from our honeymoon in late October 2001 to the most distressing news. We could tell from Mum's appearance and demeanour in her hospital bed that things were not good. She told me the doctor would be talking to Sam and me in the morning. I didn't sleep that night. I somehow knew what the morning and the doctor would bring.

Mum was diagnosed with a rare and aggressive stage 4 clear cell carcinoma (cancer). The surgeon had removed the tumour, but it was too late, the cancer had spread throughout her body. We were told she had six months to live. We were devastated. I couldn't accept it was true. I recall initially being angry at Mum's oncologist when he broke the terrible news, handing down his verdict in such a matter-of-fact manner, almost like he was giving up on her there and then.

Sam and I just couldn't come to terms with this news, yet Mum seemed at peace with it. It was as if she wasn't hearing the same words we were hearing – 'six months to live'. She declared she was prepared to fight it and her life would now be in the hands of her oncologist, and God.

Mum underwent what turned out to be an unsuccessful, physically and emotionally draining, chemotherapy course.

Initially, she convalesced with Sam's loving attention at her beautiful home in the Matcham Valley on the Central Coast. My parents-in-law, Bill and Imelda Roche, then kindly insisted that Mum move into their home at the Finger Wharf in Woolloomooloo, where she would be closer to her doctors. Sam took leave from her schoolteaching and moved with Mum to Woolloomooloo to become her full-time carer.

On 5 March 2002, our stepmother Vivian, who was heavily pregnant with Dad's and her second child, phoned Sam to say she was being admitted to hospital for an emergency caesarean. Dad was overseas at the time, so Vivian was asking Sam to look after our little sister, Beau, for a couple of days until Dad returned home. Fortunately, neither Vivian nor Sam had time to be concerned about the fact that Sam had no experience looking after children so young. We all rallied around. Ange and I reorganised our work commitments so we could be more available to Mum, and we called on a few of Mum's close friends to help out. Sam moved back into Dad's house, and with the help of our cousin William, who was visiting from the UK, she looked after adorable little Beau, who until that point had hardly ever left her mother's side. Our brother, Tom, was born later that day, coincidentally, and movingly, sharing the same birth date as our grandfather Sandy. Dad was deeply grateful that Sam on one hand could jump in and help out his young family while she was also attending to the needs of her own ill mother. Sam's caring nature and concern for others was something he made an effort to acknowledge with her. He was always very thankful to her.

Although Mum was desperately ill and we all subconsciously knew she was dying, I refused to accept it. It was soon clear she would have to be moved to a hospice but in my naïvety and refusal to admit the inevitable, I didn't even know that a hospice was a one-way street. I had never been inside one before.

It's impossible to describe my shock and anguish when we took Mum to St Vincent's Hospice two weeks before she died. She was 52 years old and we were taken to a ward containing three elderly patients, two men and one lady. The room was full of nurses, testing vital signs, cleaning up after their patients, trying to ease their pain in their last moments.

It hit me like a cement truck that our dear mother was only days away from death. The despair was exacerbated by knowing Mum was spending her last few days surrounded by constant death. Sam and I were inconsolable. I phoned Imelda and said to her, 'We have to bring Mum home.' Imelda knew that was impossible – Mum was in need of professional care. But there was another solution. She immediately phoned her close friend Sister Bernice Elphick at St Vincent's and soon Mum was moved to her own single, private room where she could maintain some sort of dignity in her suffering. Sam, Ange and I were constantly by her side in her last two weeks. Mum's sister Eleanor and her mother Jean joined us in our bedside vigil in her last days.

No one can know how someone else is feeling about their own imminent death, but Mum's unfailing faith suggested she was comfortable with it. Although she knew she wouldn't be with Sam in person for any more special family occasions, she wanted to be at these events in spirit, so she asked me to buy Sam a pair of diamond teardrop earrings. When I showed Mum what I had purchased she cried uncontrollably with joy, and also sadness. We decided I would give them to Sam on her 30th birthday the coming year, as a gift from Mum. Mum's original idea had been that the earrings would be a wedding gift for Sam to open on the morning of her big day but Sam was single at the time and there was a possibility she might not get married for some years. Also, on reflection, Mum decided she wouldn't want Sam in tears on the morning of her wedding day.

So we agreed a birthday gift would be more appropriate. Mum just lay there staring at these precious little diamond earrings, her last gift to her daughter. She looked up at me with her beautiful, sad brown eyes, swimming in tears, and said, 'Perfect. They're lovely. Thank you, darling.'

I told Mum I also wanted her to record a message for Sam, something she could listen to in the years ahead and reflect on how much she meant to her mother in those final days of her life. At this stage, Mum was finding it difficult to talk; she was not just emotional, her voice was husky and you could see the pain caused by every spoken word. She muscled up some courage and we recorded these words for Sam:

> *My darling Sam*
> *Sweetheart, I just wanted to let you know how precious you are to me.*
> *Thank you for all the love, the support and the generosity that you have shown over the years.*
> *I would never have got through this thing without you.*
> *And I just love you so much.*
> *Take care my darling,*
> *Mum*

There is nothing more saddening than seeing a loved one suffering in pain, and waiting for them to slowly die. Paradoxically, the plight of the man in the room next to Mum's put her situation into perspective. His name was Matthew and he was dying of AIDS. He had neither family nor friends and seemed emotionally moved when I said hello and asked him his name. When Mum dozed off I went next door to chat to him. I took every opportunity to reach out to him and I hope I made a small impact in his time of need.

Mum, on the other hand, was surrounded by her loved ones, who visited her every day. Matthew felt he needed to put his feelings in writing and handed me a heartfelt letter in which he commented on the huge amount of love he knew we had for our mother, and how lucky she was for this.

I was so comforted by the fact that Mum had the opportunity to forgive Dad in person in her final weeks and release him from the guilt he had been carrying for so many years. They had a wonderful few hours alone together at St Vincent's Hospice.

I know Mum gained much peace from her meeting with Dad. It was two days before she passed away. My pain over the divorce had evaporated ever so slowly over the years, but Mum's forgiveness of Dad in her final days, and Dad's response in the following letter, brought Sam and me great joy. (My father wrote the year incorrectly on the letter. The year is in fact 2002.)

4th April 2003

Dearest Donna,

Thank you ever so much for sharing some of your precious time with me today. Your forgiveness is genuinely appreciated and rest assured I will do my best to uphold the values you have tried so hard to instil in our two lovely children. I will watch over them and be there for them when needed the way you have always been and we will keep you in our midst. We did share many wonderful years and many good times together and you will always have a special place in my heart.

If I dont see you again go in peace and in the knowledge that there are those of us who will remember you with great fondness

Till we meet again.... lots of love

Tony.

What I didn't realise until Dad told me years later is that Mum had asked Dad for three promises. The first was always to remember to acknowledge her at every special family event in some way, whether by raising a glass of champagne or mentioning her in a speech. She just wanted some sort of gesture in her memory that would mean she was 'present'. The next promise was to give Sam a beautiful wedding day that she and her future husband would remember as the happiest day of their lives. The final promise was to buy me some Tiffany cufflinks for my 30th birthday, as a gift from her.

That last week of March 2002 was without doubt the saddest time Sam and I have ever experienced. Our darling mother was dying and it was time to say goodbye. To see her suffering so badly tore into our hearts. Sam and I would leave the hospice at the end of each day confused, depressed and lost for options. After leaving Mum to rest, we would just cry, holding each other, lost in a world of emotional pain and uncertainty. We didn't know what the next day would bring for the precious woman who had dedicated her life to her children and to our father when we were a family. There wasn't a day when she did not think about her children, who were now entering the next stage of life as adults, soon to have families of our own. It was as if her sole purpose in life was to make her children happy and to prepare us to be good people. She was looking forward to one day being a grandmother, and continuing that love and nurturing for her grandchildren. Her greatest sadness, apart from leaving us, was knowing that she would now not see this day.

When you are about to lose a loved one, so many memories come rushing into your mind. Every thought or reflection comes with a flow of tears. That special holiday, those kind words on a birthday, or the thought of a future event without that person. One of those events that Mum had on her mind, as did Sam, was Sam's wedding day. This is not normal crying like you might experience when you watch a sad movie. It's a deep, stomach-clenching sob which is very hard to stop once you start. Sam and I cried like this many times in that last week, as we watched our mother tirelessly put up a fight against the pain and suffering now consuming every minute she was awake.

On the afternoon of 5 April 2002, we could see Mum was giving up this fight. She could no longer find the energy; she wanted to go and was floating in and out of consciousness. We were all there, the people she loved so much. Her mother, Jean, was lost in despair. No one should ever have to watch their child suffer like this. A woman of strong faith, Granny Reed was praying to God to take her daughter in His arms and release her from this terrible suffering. She could not watch it anymore and was highly emotional. Mum's sister Eleanor was so strong for us all. Having worked as a sister in the oncology ward at Royal North Shore Hospital for a number of years, she had a better understanding of what Mum was going through and knew that her time was coming to an end. Sam and I received great comfort from Eleanor. These were two people Mum had known longest in life. They had followed her out to Australia and always been close by through her life. We all just sat around Mum's bed, feeling helpless and not knowing what to do, just needing to be there with her.

The nurse came in that evening and gave Mum an injection of morphine to reduce her pain and settle her down for the night. With that Mum went off to sleep and the family moved outside into a little visitors' enclave around the corner where we planned to sit through the night. We all had a strong feeling that her time had come. I didn't want Mum to be on her own so I offered to take the midnight shift, and sat at her bedside holding her hand. Ange also came in with me and we sat together, just staring at Mum lying there. Ange nodded off to sleep in her chair while I sat there, staring, watching Mum's chest rise and fall with every breath. Then it happened. Her chest rose and fell one last time. She was gone. I woke Ange. I remember her look like it was yesterday. She didn't have to say anything. I could tell she was so distressed. We both bawled.

I went outside and woke everyone. I looked at them all as they rose from an uncomfortable slumber on the couches. 'She's gone, Mum's gone,' I said, as tears rolled down my face. It was as if no one believed me. They had to see for themselves. We all walked back into Mum's room and reality kicked in. She was so still. Not a breath. No more coughing or pain. She was at peace. One by one we sat with her and said our final goodbyes. As I leant forward and gave her that last kiss I remember my tears rolling down onto her face. Seeing those tears on her face looked like she was crying, too. And with that my final words to my darling mum: 'Thank you for everything you have done for me. You have been such a wonderful mother. I love you and will miss you so much. Goodbye, Mum.'

Our overwhelming sadness was partially softened by the relief that Mum was no longer suffering. Trying to do justice to such a wonderful, loving mother is a forlorn task, but Sam and I gave it a go when we wrote the following poem through a waterfall of tears. We read it together at Mum's funeral.

To our darling mother,
There are times when our hearts are full of sorrow,
But we must let the pain go and invite on tomorrow.
Because our lives have been touched by someone so dear,

It's strange to feel your spirit so near.
To have one more touch, kiss or a hug,
Or to share one last sip from the same coffee mug,
To feel the warmth of the place where you peacefully
     slept,
Or to see your smile when we have been happy or wept.
Just to hear your wisdom when we needed advice,
Or the smell of your cooking was ever so nice.
You had so many stories and many more to tell,
But they stay with you now, yet you told them so well.
Now the time has come for us to let you go,
You've helped us so much, you really don't know.
To see your beautiful face, or have one last touch,
I know we are both asking way too much.
You will always be close and your memories will last,
Look back and be proud of your wonderful past,
For God has picked the most beautiful rose,
To keep in his garden, where lots of love grows.
Farewell our dear mother on your journey from here,
We know you're in heaven, though you still feel so near.
We are not burdened in this hard time of sorrow
For we know you will bring the sunshine of tomorrow.
Farewell our dear mother, go off on your way,
Open your wings now as we sit here and pray,
Lift up your heart and peace to thee
God wanted you now; He has set you free.

Shortly after Mum's passing, Sam moved back into Dad's house – our former family home – for a short while. It was a busy and stressful time, as Sam was helping Vivian with little Beau and baby Tom, while also winding up

Mum's businesses and organising the sale of Mum's house in Matcham Valley. I know Sam was grateful to Dad for his support at this sad and difficult time in her life.

Fortunately Mum had actually met Sam's future husband on a number of occasions several years earlier. Mick Kennedy was a university friend whom Sam ended up dating while studying to be a teacher. I know Mum would have been delighted that Sam and Mick got back together years later when they were both ready to settle down. In fact, it was Joycie who first spotted the keen eye Mick had for Sam before they started dating. In 1995 when Joycie was on holiday in Australia with her brother Toland, Dad took them on a trip out to Bathurst to visit Sam at Charles Sturt University. I know Sam enjoyed showing them around the university campus, which opened the eyes of these two 70-somethings as to what modern-day student life was like. After walking around the campus, they joined some of Sam's friends at one of the university bars and settled in to watch Australia playing in a Rugby World Cup match. During the game, Joycie turned to Dad and pointed out a young man who seemed to be watching more of Sam's movements than those of the Wallabies on television. Little did Joycie know she had set eyes on Sam's future husband.

Mick is an agricultural pilot from Gunnedah in country New South Wales. Most of his flying today is done as a contractor to NSW Rural Fire Services – he and his brother help extinguish many of the big bushfires that flare up across the state during the Australian summer. A traditional sort of guy, Mick felt it important to have Tony's blessing before he proposed to Sam, so in 2004, when Dad was visiting his daughter in Gunnedah, he took him for a flight in one of his small planes. Dad said he was gripping his seat when Mick flew the plane about five metres off the ground, travelling at around 250 kilometres per hour. Dad wasn't usually scared of anything but on this occasion his adrenalin was definitely flowing. Mick turned to Dad, as calm as you could imagine, and said, 'Tony, you may find this a strange time to ask this question, but would you mind if I married your daughter?' As Mick said this, he grabbed the controls and pulled the plane into a vertical climb.

Dad's 'yes' could be heard reverberating for miles across the Liverpool Plains.

I was the master of ceremonies at Sam and Mick's wedding in 2004 and introduced Dad as father of the bride. It was a role he took seriously, and he did a great job. His role of professional wedding coordinator had been an interesting transition for someone who had captained England and faced bouncers from the quickest bowlers that had ever played the game.

I also took the mickey out of Dad by sending up his accent a couple of times during my MC-ing duties. It was something I did on the odd occasion with my friends, but this was the first time I did it in public. Dad seemed to get a kick out of me taking him off and when he started his speech he said, 'In the Greig family we have a wonderful ability to take the mickey out of each other; it has gone on for years. We all give as good as we get.' He then proceeded to raise the microphone stand higher and said, 'It's all right for the short guys,' relishing the fact that he was taller than me.

Sam's wedding was the first time in 30 years Dad was together in one room with his mother and all his siblings. It was such a special occasion for Sam, but even more significant that all of Dad's family had made the effort to fly in to attend her big day. At the same time it was a sad day for us all as we had lost Mum to cancer eighteen months beforehand. Dad also had to carry out the role of mother of the bride. Sam felt Dad went above and beyond the normal role of father of the bride and was extremely grateful for the amount of time and energy he put in to help her plan the day.

Dad commented, during his speech, on his daughter's caring nature. 'Sam's mum, Donna, was a wonderful lady,' he said. 'It was Donna who provided the stability in Sam's life. The love and nurturing she gave to Sam, that great trait called caring, Sam got that from her mum.'

Dad also told a few stories about Sam as a young girl. One story everyone enjoyed involved Bishan Singh Bedi, the former captain of the Indian cricket team, who came to stay with us in England in 1978. Sam was five years old at the time. The doorbell rang and in walked Bishan, who is a Sikh and was wearing a huge silk turban. He was very graceful and polite and leant down to say a warm hello to little Sam.

'Hello little girl, what's your name?'

'Hello, my name is Samantha,' she replied. 'My mummy and daddy always say you should take your hat off when you are in someone's house.'

He smiled at Sam and looked at Dad with a gesture that implied he was impressed with Sam's directness. 'OK, then,' he said. 'But you need to come over here to help me take it off, as it is not a usual kind of hat.' Sam sat there on his knee as he proceeded to unwind ten metres of turban, letting it slowly drop onto the carpet beside them. Eventually, he started to undo all the little bits and pieces holding his beard and hair together. By the time he was done, Sam was looking up at what resembled a little Indian Father Christmas. She was mesmerised.

Bishan looked at Sam and said, 'Is that better?'

Sam looked at him, screwed up her face and said, 'I think you should put it back on.'

Dad went on to tell another story that demonstrated Sam's caring nature. She was about eleven years old, and getting set to run in the 100-metre sprint at her school athletics carnival. The whole family had come to watch her big race. Dad thought he needed to give her some pre-race advice.

'Sam, you have to be competitive,' Dad told her. 'Don't worry about anyone else in the race. Just keep your head down and go for it. If you need to nudge a few out of the way, then so be it. I will be standing at the finish line and I want you to be there first.'

The starter's flag came down and off she went. Putting her head down, she was far out in front of the other girls. Halfway into the race she couldn't help herself. After turning around and seeing that her best mate was coming stone last, she stopped and waited for her friend to catch up, took her by the hand and they crossed the finish line together. Dad said he was tearing his hair out.

My favourite time with Dad was on the golf course. It was the only time we were together on our own, so we could talk honestly and freely without any interruption. During our rounds of golf we updated each other on what was going on in our lives and would always end up reflecting on the terrific family memories we had from my childhood. I loved those moments with just the two of us, and will cherish those memories forever.

Dad was a good golfer and had aspirations of bringing his handicap down to single figures. I recall the first time I beat him in a game. We were in Scotland and playing at the home of golf, the Old Course at St Andrews Links. It was an unforgettable experience, walking around in the Scottish mist, followed closely by our own caddies. I felt like a professional, and the extra confidence helped my swing that day. As I putted into the hole on the eighteenth green, I looked up at Dad and with a cheeky smile said, 'It looks like you're buying the beers, mate.'

'That's fine,' he said, 'but just remember, you haven't really beaten me until you have won off the stick.' Fair enough, I guess, given my handicap gave me an extra six shots on him. But that's golf, and I thought I deserved a little more recognition for my first victory over him. The next day we played at Carnoustie Golf Links; the wind was howling and he gave me an absolute thrashing. Unfortunately I never did beat Dad off the stick. It certainly wasn't for the lack of trying.

Like his own father, Sandy, Dad rarely gave me a compliment without attaching some sort of constructive criticism – but I don't think he was as harsh on me as Sandy was on him. Dad told me that when he scored a century on the cricket field, Sandy would make a comment about the silly shot he played while on 48, rather than pat him on the back and say 'well done'. Perhaps I sometimes confused Dad's lack of compliments with his competitive nature. Golf with Dad as a kid felt as if he were grooming me to be someone he could compete against for the rest of his life. Which is exactly what golf became for us, a friendly bonding opportunity, but always a fierce competition in which all I wanted to do was win.

On one occasion we were playing with Grandpa Sandy. By then in his mid-sixties, Sandy had a fantastic temperament on the golf course. He would pull out his ancient three-wood with its tiny timber head – how he connected with the ball I have no idea. He hit the ball with such grace; it never went very far, but always straight down the middle. Dad and I would then proceed to try to hit the cover off our balls, often slicing or hooking them into the rough. During this game, Sandy suggested the reason I wasn't hitting the ball straight was because my balls were wrong. He said, 'Try this one' as he teed up one of his balls for me. I addressed the ball with my driver and gave it an almighty whack. The ball exploded and I was covered from head to toe in white powder. Sandy and Dad laughed all the way back to the clubhouse.

As wonderful as all our overseas trips were, some of our best holidays were in Australia. One standout for me was when we joined Dad's cousin Roy Taylor and his family on a 4WD trip to the northernmost tip of Australia, Cape York. Dad loved sitting around the campfire in the evening and entertained us all with his storytelling. He and Roy had a close bond and I sensed Roy brought the best out in his personality, particularly in an environment like the Australian outback.

Dad's brother, Ian, had a similar effect on him. Dad and I once joined Ian on his annual fishing trip to Fraser Island, just off the coast of south-east Queensland. Ian gets together with a group of mates each winter for the annual 'Tailor Run'. The group consists of ten blokes, all different ages and from different walks of life, a really good bunch of guys.

On our first morning on Fraser, the alarm went off at 5am. It was still dark outside. We threw some water on our faces to wake up before jumping into our waders. Dad had to have his specially made for his long legs. The plan was to be on the beach with our fishing rods in the water before sunrise. As we walked down to the water's edge with our rods, Ian turned to Dad and said, 'Now mate, I want you to know that I have a reputation for being a very good fisherman on this island. I've told everyone that you can cast. You have said you can. So don't let me down.'

Dad placed a pilchard on his hook. The entire beach stopped and looked at him as he readied himself to cast. They had recognised his hat and came closer in to watch. There was a mighty flurry of arms and legs, similar to his bowling action, and the pilchard was launched. Everyone waited to see how far he could cast it out through the waves. After what seemed like an eternity, his baited hook came thudding into the water next to him in a tangled mess.

I enjoyed the evenings at Fraser Island the most. After everyone had risen from an afternoon siesta, we would put our waders back on and return to the beach to fish until sunset. It was a marvellous time of day – unbelievably serene. The first sips of beer would be followed by sighs of satisfaction from the tired fishermen. Dad was in his element, and it was here he was introduced to the Bundy rum chaser. We were all standing around with our drinks when Dad asked the most senior member of our group, Roy King, why he had two drinks and everyone else had only one. Roy explained about the rum chaser, then added, 'Tony, this is not the Sheraton where you get waited on – if you want a rum chaser get your f…ing own!' From then on after each gulp of beer it became customary to follow it with a little sip of neat Bundy rum. Dad took to this tradition like a fish to water – he absolutely loved it. It wasn't long before he was launching into some of his best stories and would have the group completely captivated while standing in a tight circle on the beach. There probably wasn't a person for some miles down the beach, but I'm sure our laughter would have carried right across the island.

We had seriously fished ourselves to a standstill and when the last day arrived, most of the guys said they'd had enough and were not interested in driving down to the beach for the late afternoon session. We also happened to be out of bait. Dad was mortified, and as had always been the case, he got everyone motivated and keen to go down. He said, 'I'm going to buy some more bait because having a drink on the beach is the best part of the day,' and off he went.

Bait supplies replenished, we headed back out with our Esky packed with all the necessary supplies. After the fishing had ended and we were all enjoying our drinks, Dad got a milk crate out and suggested everyone get up onto it and have their say about the week. He was last to talk and made an emotional speech about what a fantastic time he'd had, and what the trip had meant to him. Dad and I had drifted slightly apart since his and Mum's divorce, and our European holiday with Sam notwithstanding, this was the first real quality time we had spent together for some time.

Dad said: 'What has made this trip so special is the fact that Mark and I have been able to rekindle our father and son relationship, something I have missed so terribly in recent times, and I don't intend to let that happen again. To do this with Ian here as well has been so very, very special.' This was one of the fondest times I had with my dad and Uncle Ian.

Dad respected smart people with strong views – people such as broadcaster Alan Jones. Dad thoroughly enjoyed catching up with Alan for dinner, and Alan often invited along interesting dinner guests. The last dinner they had together was with Jeffrey Archer, the famous English author. Lord Archer recalled the evening in an email to me recently, writing, 'I spent a memorable and very enjoyable evening with Tony as guests of a mutual friend, Australian broadcaster Alan Jones, in his apartment overlooking Sydney Harbour. Tony was a man of passion and firm beliefs, and was one of the great all-rounders.'

Dad loved having stimulating conversations and encouraged me from a young age to read the newspaper and form my own views on current affairs. I remember he was impressed when I told him after my first date with my wife, Angela, that she made a habit of reading the newspaper every morning. I left out that she usually skipped over the sport section.

Dad loved action and pushing thrills to the limit. He could never go too fast, whether it was in a boat, a car, a go-kart or facing the bowling machine in Kerry Packer's backyard. He was the master of fun and enjoyed sharing that fun with people. He approached life in a way that it felt like he was creating a fun story to tell tomorrow. I think he thought he was invincible. In my mind, he was!

Dad always took an interest in how Sam's and my married lives were going. He was very fond of his daughter-in-law and son-in-law, Ange and Mick. He also delighted in visits from his grandchildren, watching with interest how each of them was developing. Jessica, Mia, Georgia, Hugh and Sophie all adored the time they had with their grandpa, too. Dad was big on manners and good behaviour. I wanted him to be proud of me as a father, and loved it when he complimented my kids on their manners.

For Sam and me, the last ten years have seen many changes in our lives. As life goes on, you have to start juggling work with new family and old. We did not see Dad as much as we would have liked during that time, and respected the fact that he, too, had young children, with whom he needed to spend time given he was still away a lot with his work.

I loved talking with Dad about my younger sister and brother, Beau and Tom, and he spoke of them with such pride. At first it amazed me when he decided to become a father again in his fifties. Apparently Dad never changed Sam's and my nappies, and I don't think he was any more helpful in the nappy department the second time around. However, he had so much love for Beau and Tom, and they made him incredibly happy.

I loved sharing a good red wine with Dad during sessions chatting in his lounge room at home. As the wine kicked in, we would both get louder and talk over the top of each other, and others. This seems to be an unfortunate trait of most men in the Greig family. However, Dad always knew his limits and rarely overindulged.

He had a great library of stories, but few of them could match those involving the man who created World Series Cricket, changed the game forever and had a significant impact on the life of Anthony William Greig and his family.

This man was Kerry Packer.

14

Kerry and Dad

KERRY FRANCIS BULLMORE PACKER WAS A GIANT PRESENCE in Dad's life, and consequently in all our lives. Dad had enormous respect for this larger-than-life character who dominated every room he entered. Dad dropped everything for him, which sometimes made me think Kerry Packer was the most important person in his life. The respect seemed mutual – Kerry included Dad in many things he did, whether it was overseas holidays with golfing legends Jack Nicklaus and Ben Crenshaw or deep-sea fishing with New South Wales Attorney-General Paul Landa or hunting trips to Africa.

Kerry would regularly ring early on a Saturday or Sunday morning and ask Dad to drop over. Dad would go, often not arriving home until mid-evening. When Kerry first became a serious part of Dad's life, Mum accepted and respected the time he needed to devote to building their relationship. As time went on, however, she found it more and more difficult. As anyone with little ones would understand, it's not easy caring for young children mostly on your own; I'm sure it was lonely for Mum in those days with Dad away from home so much.

This was a very busy period for Dad. His time was never really his own. When he was not away with cricket he was working hard, making speeches, or socialising in connection with his work and appeared to always be at Kerry's side. Dad was in demand by so many people, restricting the time he was able to give to us. He was ambitious and he loved his work. We craved his attention but tried to understand. When not engaged with other formal business-related commitments of an evening, Dad would generally join other key executives at the Tap Room, a 'watering hole' at Kerry's Consolidated Press Holdings headquarters. Although he learnt priceless lessons about business, he seldom arrived home before 8.30pm. Over time, Mum became more and more distressed by this, as Dad was so rarely there to have dinner with us as a family, something that was extremely important to her.

To Dad, Kerry Packer's opinion of him was very important. One of the only serious hidings I ever received from my father was over some childish behaviour of mine while he was on the phone to Kerry, discussing a particularly important matter. I was seven years old and as a young boy I thought it would be funny to pick up the other receiver in the house and blow a big raspberry down the line. I heard Dad apologise for the interruption and ask if he could call Kerry back in five minutes after he'd dealt with me. The next thing I heard was Dad's big feet thumping up the stairs to where I was sitting in trepidation next to our second phone. He was absolutely furious, grabbing me by the arm and dragging me into his dressing room. Reaching for one of his leather belts, he told me to bend over and touch my toes. I remember feeling the burn within seconds of the leather connecting with my backside. You might call it my Mason and Pearson brush moment.

The hiding had the desired outcome – I never, ever picked up the home phone again when someone was on a call. It also made me realise that Dad's phone discussions with Kerry were exceptionally important to him and were not to be interrupted.

As young kids, we were always put on notice to be on our best behaviour when we were around Kerry, but it wasn't all fear and intimidation. He treated us in a kind and warm manner at all times and I thought of him as a charming and caring person.

I have some very fond memories of the times we spent as a family with the Packers at their home in Bellevue Hill, their beach house at Palm Beach and their property in the Barrington Tops. They are such a warm family and were always so welcoming of us. Unfortunately the Rottweilers at the Packers' Bellevue Hill compound were not so welcoming. I would start to panic as we drove up the driveway and Dad would tell me to pull myself together as the dogs were unlikely to hurt me. As I stepped out of the car I remember the biggest Rottweiler, Pinky, bounding over to me growling and slobbering saliva all over the place. No matter how many times I experienced it, I remained unnerved in the early minutes of every visit. Pinky probably found it very amusing.

I was absolutely terrified of those dogs. I remember being so glad every time my father suggested I pad up and have a turn batting in front of Kerry's bowling machine – the dogs couldn't get to me once I was inside the cricket net. We spent hours in that net. Once while Kerry was having a bat he asked Dad to let a few go through the bowling machine at the same speed as the bowling of Jeff Thomson or Michael 'The Whispering Death' Holding. I was amazed he was able to get bat to ball, let alone produce some beautiful strokes – which he did – as I could hardly see the ball travelling through the air at 150 kilometres per hour.

In my many and various contacts with Kerry in my younger years, I found him most relaxed either on the golf course at the Australian Golf Club, or when he was at his beach house at Palm Beach. For a young boy who loved the water, the Packers' Palm Beach house was like Disneyland. I recall the first time I walked into their garage. It wasn't a garage for cars, as Kerry used to park his Audi Quattro on the front lawn – the first car I ever heard actually talk. I remember thinking it was like 'Kit', the car from the 1980s TV series 'Knight Rider' starring David Hasselhoff. The car was great, but the garage was absolute heaven. It was a boy's paradise, with a 'rubber ducky' inflatable boat, jet skis, water skis, surfboards and wetsuits for all ages and sizes. Over the next couple of years, between the ages of about eight and ten, I would learn to use all those toys and even have a go at driving a tractor down Ocean Road, Palm Beach – the means to transport the water craft to the water's edge. With Kerry it was always a competition against my father, and often also James, who was about seventeen at the time. A challenge would invariably be thrown down to see who could do the best tricks on the jet skis, manoeuvring them on Pittwater, or the highest jumps through the waves at Palm Beach. Looking back on it now, Dad and Kerry were just like big kids.

On most of our visits, Kerry would offer me an ice-cream from what surely had to be the largest ice-cream and soft drink fridge in Australia. It was enormous. Afterwards, we would all pile into the hot tub at the back of the beach house. I was witness to some great conversations in that hot tub and it was there that I developed my insatiable appetite to learn every minute detail about World Series Cricket. Obviously proud of their achievements with WSC, Kerry and Dad were more than happy for me to listen to their stories. I think it also gave them an opportunity to relive some of the adventure of it all.

It was obvious listening to these intimate conversations that the admiration and affection Dad felt for Kerry was returned. Kerry clearly respected Dad's abilities and achievements in the sport of cricket. Close associates of Kerry's have mentioned in recent years that he felt a great indebtedness to Dad for giving up the captaincy of England to join WSC, and for his support in convincing others to join the truly professional ranks. He said once in my company that he admired Dad for the way he was able to reassure the world players who signed that they had nothing to worry about, despite the vicious media campaign waged against them.

Watching others wilt under the pressure placed on them by the cricketing establishment, Kerry clearly admired Dad's ability to handle all the vitriol thrown at him, particularly by large sections of the media. Dad became the frontman for the new order and didn't flinch a muscle under the assault from so many different quarters. A bit like Kerry himself.

Though Dad had to be one of the closest to him, over time I realised that Kerry admired all high-achieving sportspeople and loved all sports. He enjoyed sitting with world-class players listening to their stories, how they achieved greatness, and discussing the skills of their sport. He and Dad also had strong views about changes that would benefit not just cricket but all sports and were not afraid of expressing them in front of these sporting legends in relation to their specific sport, whether golf, rugby league, tennis, cricket or polo.

He also spent hours in front of the three televisions stacked on top of each other in the front room at Bellevue Hill. I guess as a media magnate, with a television station of his own, he had a vested interest in keeping in touch with TV broadcasting. Interesting that it always seemed to be sport on the screens, however!

If I remember correctly, Kerry was originally an Easts Rugby League supporter who swapped sides when Rugby League legend Bob Fulton returned to the Manly Sea Eagles after a stint at Easts. I always assumed it was Dad's attachment to Kerry and Bob Fulton that had him barracking along with Kerry for the Manly team, as I can find no other logical reason. Both seemed to shift their loyalty back to the Roosters in later years, and would often attend games together at the Sydney Sports Ground.

As I mentioned earlier, Dad's relationship with Kerry wasn't just based on acquiescence to a more powerful figure – Dad certainly admired Kerry, but it was obvious the admiration was mutual. Well known for his love of cricket, Kerry respected Dad's professionalism on and off the field and his ever-present desire to win. They thoroughly enjoyed each other's company. Though Dad and Kerry got on very well and rarely had a disagreement, Dad was apparently one of very few people prepared to tell the boss when he was wrong about something. He always stood up to him, even knowing he'd be angry. Though those moments were unpleasant, I'm sure Kerry respected Dad for his willingness to speak out.

I recall one instance when James had broken the rules regarding the use of golf carts at the Australian Golf Club. When Darrell Welch, the club professional, complained to Kerry, the inevitable result was a tongue-lashing for James. Dad spoke out in defence of James when he walked off the 18th green, suggesting to Kerry that he was being too tough on James after the very public dressing down.

'Kerry, that was a bit harsh,' Dad said, 'the best thing you can do is put your arm around Jamie, take him for a walk and explain why etiquette on the golf course is important to you. You can't just leave it like you have. For Christ's sake, the kid is a nervous wreck.'

'How dare you try and tell me how to father my son! F*** off, Tony,' was the colourful and rather to-the-point response.

Having decided the conversation was probably best left there, Dad went for a beer in the members' locker room, pondering whether Kerry would be joining him, or leave immediately for home on the rather sour note between them. He glanced out the window and smiled to himself when he saw Kerry walking down towards the practice fairway with his arm around James's shoulder. He had taken Dad's advice.

Although Kerry had planned his son's career in the family conglomerate, he still felt it very important that James kept his feet firmly on the ground and that he knew how to get his hands dirty. I recall listening to Kerry explaining to James that when he finished school he would be going up north to work at their Newcastle Waters property, a huge cattle station about 700 kilometres south of Darwin. Among many other lessons and skills, this is where James really learnt to ride a horse, which he displayed with great competence years later on the polo field.

Mum had her own horse-riding experience with Kerry at Ellerston. This is one of the most amazing rural properties I have ever seen, situated in a lush valley framed by the rocky peaks surrounding Mount Barrington. Being a polo stud, it has some magnificent horse facilities. I recall Kerry asking Mum during lunch whether she could ride. She told him she used to be an extremely competent rider until she was thrown off a horse a few years earlier, landing on a timber fence and fracturing three vertebrae in her back. She was in traction for weeks and hadn't been on a horse since.

It was always obvious that Kerry liked Mum immensely and wanted her to be a part of whatever was going on. Determined to get her back on a horse, he threw her a challenge. 'Donna,' he said, 'if you can ride as well as you say you can, the time has come for you to get back on a horse. In fact, I will bring my own horse around after lunch and you can show me just how well you can ride.' What could Mum say to that? Sure enough, as soon as we'd finished eating, Kerry had his huge black Quarter Horse brought around. Amazed by the size of the animal, I didn't think Mum would be able to get her legs around the width of its back, let alone have her feet reaching the stirrups. She later told me that the stablehand told her Kerry never let anyone else ride his personal horse. This seemingly small but meaningful gesture indicated how fond he was of Mum. She was greatly touched. I recall the horse's name being Shaka, I assume after the famous African Zulu warrior.

Mum seemed so confident as she mounted the horse with ease, then gave it a gentle kick and took off around the riding arena for a few figure-eights. She certainly was putting on a brave act, as I think she was most likely terrified. I felt so proud of her for her courage and her skill. After she had proved her point, she pulled Shaka up alongside Kerry, jumped off and handed him the reins with a big, proud grin. He was as pleased as she was, and grinned with her.

It was at Ellerston that my sister and I rode our first horse, in fact it was a little pony called Bindi. I think Bindi actually belonged to James or Gretel, but they made us feel she belonged to us whenever we stayed with them.

There was always something exciting happening on the property. Apart from horseriding, James would often have a couple of quad bikes going. During one of our visits to Ellerston, around the time we were mastering Bindi, Mum wouldn't let me join in with James and his mates, saying I was too young to ride a quad bike. James made sure I wasn't left out of the fun, suggesting I jump on the back of one of his mate's bikes.

We chased James up a big hill near the homestead. Our bike was at full throttle flying along as I hung on for my life. I remember feeling a little anxious as we reached the top of the hill and saw James tearing down the other side. Our bike followed after him, but as we started our descent on a slight angle against the downslope of the hill, our left wheels started to lift off the ground. Thinking we were about to tip over, I jumped off the back of the bike and landed flat on my back. To my horror, James's mate didn't have enough time to plan his own escape route as the bike rolled over and sent him flying down the hill, with the bike tumbling dangerously after him. Remarkably, he managed to get away without serious injury and only a few grazes, though he was extremely shaken up, as I was, watching helplessly as it all unfolded in front of me.

Kerry heard the noise of the bike rolling down the hill and came running over to see what had happened. James quietly disappeared, anticipating that 'someone' was about to get in big trouble. Dad told me later that the boy I was riding with was one of Trevor Kennedy's sons. Trevor was managing editor of the *Bulletin* magazine, then managing director of Consolidated Press Holdings and served on the boards of CPH and Qantas.

That was not the last time a Greig family visit to Ellerston put someone's life at risk. On another occasion Dad found himself flying through the Barrington Tops behind Kerry in one of his brand-new ultralights. Dad had never flown a remote control aeroplane, let alone an actual aircraft. I recall his hardly hidden nervousness at the house when Kerry announced that they would be flying after breakfast – if Dad were up to the challenge. Nervous or not, Dad never declined a Kerry Packer challenge.

I think Kerry was the only person in the world who may have been more competitive than Dad. After Dad asked when he'd be getting his couple of days' flying instructions, Kerry's chopper pilot was called in to give him a fifteen-minute briefing, before letting him loose in the sky. I sat on a fence alongside one of the large polo fields watching my father sheepishly climb into his ultralight as the two-stroke engine came to life and let off a few dark puffs of exhaust fumes. Kerry was already out on the grass runway and started off by bunny-hopping up and down the polo field, practising his landings.

Eventually Kerry's machine climbed quickly into the air as Dad's ultralight was moved forward to get set for his own take-off. My heart was racing, and I think it was only at that moment I realised the danger he was putting himself in. His engine got louder and louder as he moved off his mark and prepared for his own take-off. He must have been so nervous as he slowly built up speed. I suspect he simply said to himself, 'Bugger this, I've had a good life and I'm going to heaven,' and pulled his machine into the air, chasing Kerry down the valley. What he wasn't expecting was a thermal updraft that took him into the clouds in a matter of minutes after take-off.

They were so high and so far down the valley that I could hardly see them. Soon they were out of sight, and I had to sit patiently waiting for them to come back into view. About 30 minutes later, I spotted one of the ultralights returning and on descent towards us. It was Kerry. He landed his machine with ease and pulled up alongside the shed where I was now sitting. As he removed his flying helmet, he looked over to me and shrugged his shoulders, as if to say he had no idea where my father was.

The next twenty minutes felt like hours to me. I sat and waited, increasingly anxious about my father. Finally,

I could hear the purring of his little motor down the valley as he appeared in the distance and set himself up to land. Apparently he had struggled to work out how to turn his ultralight around once in the air. He seemed to be gliding about a metre off the ground and hesitating, obviously nervous about putting his machine down. Finally he dropped to the ground with a big thud and bounced a couple of times, looking like he was desperately trying to gain control and get all three wheels flat on the ground. He was coming in at a rapid speed, so Kerry yelled out to him to use his foot on the front wheel as the brake. I can't believe no one had thought to tell him how to stop once he had landed.

Dad pointed his machine at one of the fences on the side of the polo field, which he thought would bring him to a halt. None of us knew what the impact would be like. I was terrified for him. He crashed into the fence and the ultralight came to an immediate and unceremonious stop. I could see movement, so I knew he was alive, but I was still shaken. And so was he. He was clearly desperate for the reassurance of firm ground beneath his feet, literally springing out of his flimsy flying machine and landing gingerly and with an audible groan. His right foot had taken the full force of impact in the unconventional landing. Even from a bit of a distance I could see him wincing as he limped towards me. His big frame looked so fragile as his painful ankle distorted his gait.

It could have been so much worse. We were all just glad he'd lived to tell the story. And tell the 'Ellerston ultralight' story he did in the years to come – hundreds of times. As it was probably one of the scariest experiences of my father's life – even scarier than facing bouncers from Lillee and

Thommo – his desire to share the experience with whomever was happy to listen is pretty understandable. Dad's ability to tell a great story, with or without embellishment, was another reason Kerry loved his company. They would spend hours together trying to top each other with anecdotes.

The fact that Dad was cavalier in everything he did appealed greatly to Kerry, who also had a 'wild' streak in his character. They both believed there was nothing they could not do and so whatever the impetuous idea was at that time, they did it, regardless of the potential consequences. They became soldiers of fortune together in all sorts of dangerous pursuits. As well as the ultralights, they raced cars, went deepsea fishing, hunted in Africa, and shared all kinds of adventure holidays.

From memory, the African hunting trip was to the Okavango Delta in Botswana in the mid-80s, and involved the pursuit of a sick bull elephant. The Botswana government wanted to put the elephant out of its misery, with the benefit of raising money for conservation from the hunting fee that was paid by Kerry. Dad and Kerry spent days with a professional hunter and some trackers trying to track the poor animal and eventually Kerry found the trek tiresome so decided to return to camp. When Dad was reluctant to give up the hunt, Kerry encouraged him to continue with the hunter and the trackers for a couple more days.

Soon enough they found the animal and Dad put it out of its misery, but not without a bruise or two from the recoil of the big elephant gun. Kerry had insisted that the tusks be brought back if the elephant were eventually found but that wasn't going to be easy as they were a long way from camp. The hunter and the trackers left Dad to guard the dead elephant overnight while they drove back to the camp for the equipment to remove the tusks. As the sun went down and the sounds of the night animals kicked in, Dad started to worry that lions or hyenas might try to make a meal of the elephant. It's amazing to me that he didn't consider the lions at least might be quite happy to make a meal of him. But then, perhaps that's just what he told me. He climbed up on top of the elephant's massive body and at the first sound of a hyena he let off a shot with the elephant gun, learning quickly to keep his face and other body parts well away from the recoil. He spent the whole night listening to the noises of the African night wildlife, occasionally succumbing to slumber until the next noise that sounded like a lion or a hyena jolted him awake and he'd let off another shot. He'd never been so glad to see anyone as he was early the next morning with the arrival of the hunter.

On this same trip Kerry had the trackers place a dead crocodile in Dad's tent early one morning. He found a strong stick and propped its mouth open just wide enough to make it look threatening – and alive. To everyone's merriment, Dad got a hell of a shock when he stepped out of bed, letting out an involuntary shriek and breaking all backward long jump records.

Towards the end of the trip, and following Kerry's return home, Dad was attending a sportsmen's dinner in Johannesburg. A leading Afrikaner army official approached him. He expressed disappointment that Dad and Kerry were 'unting African animals. Dad tried to protest that he'd only killed one animal that was sick, when the army officer interrupted him. 'It's only true 'unting when they shoot back,' he said. Dad was not quite sure how to respond to that in any politically correct way, so after a painful pause, chose to take it as a joke and burst out laughing. The officer smiled, but enigmatically. South Africa was involved in wars with Mozambique and Angola at the time and the officer offered to take Dad and Kerry up to the Angola border to fight the People's Movement for the Liberation of Angola (MPLA), who had ruled Angola since its independence in 1975. Dad decided to decline the offer with thanks, but when he relayed the invitation to his fellow hunter on his return to Sydney, Kerry paused pensively and said with some passion, 'That would definitely be an interesting trip.'

When Dad arrived home he had a huge beard. I almost didn't recognise him. He soon got rid of it but left a moustache for a few more days. Mum didn't like the beard and wasn't too keen on the moustache, either – probably the main reason neither bit of fuzz lasted very long.

Those of us left behind didn't have quite the excitement of spending nights alone with a jungle full of wild animals, but I did witness many close shaves in the pursuit of fun by the two Packer men, father and son. On one occasion, James had a near escape at Ellerston while racing against the clock on the go-kart track. I was about fifteen years old at the time, and James was seven years my senior. We had gathered around the go-kart shed with Tony Clark, the manager of Ellerston at the time. Tony gave us an overview of the people who had previously recorded the fastest lap times since the track was opened. There was a list of well-known Australian names written up on the wall. From memory, I think Rugby League legend Bob Fulton held the record for the fastest time.

James was first cab off the rank and was screaming around the first couple of laps. By his third lap he had built up such a speed that his go-kart became airborne on one of the rises, with all four wheels well and truly off the ground. He came down hard on the nose and lost control, flying off to the side of the track in a big puff of dust. He jumped out of his kart faster than Dad had jumped out of his ultralight and cursed loudly as he walked back up to the group of us watching. 'Someone is going to farken kill themselves on these farken things,' he said. After what I'd just witnessed from someone who knew the lay of the land, I certainly wasn't that excited about being next, and in fact was quite unnerved – my excuse for particularly slow lap times.

All the terror in our young lives was not saved for Ellerston, however. Another go-kart race I will never forget was at Kerry's farm in Stedham, England. In addition to polo facilities, the property was equipped with a first-class go-kart track. I was in London in 1997 to join Dad for The Ashes series and we drove out to see Kerry during the break between Tests. When we arrived Kerry was in the middle of watching satellite television. Just as in his front room at Bellevue Hill, he seemed captivated by some sporting event or other and said he would be finished watching shortly, suggesting to Dad that he take me down to the track to get warmed up so he could take me on in a race. When Dad and I reached the garage where all the go-karts were stored it wasn't hard to guess which go-kart I'd be racing against, as the largest one there was painted gold and had KP number plates. The others looked about half its size. Dad pulled one out and reassured me that I was five times lighter than Kerry and therefore had a good chance of winning the race. He told me it was all about my driving lines and how I handled the corners.

I was able to get in about ten warm-up laps before I saw Kerry's big frame walking down to join us. He asked one of his staff to get his go-kart ready so he could 'take on young Greig', no doubt with every intention of giving me a lesson. He then offered me a half-lap head start, which I eagerly accepted. The race would be five laps.

My heart was already racing. I shot off as quickly as I could, nearly losing control on the first corner. As I hit the halfway mark, I could hear Kerry's superior engine roar around the track in pursuit. It was about the fourth lap when I noticed the gardener standing on the final bend giving the track a light spray with a hose. On the second-last corner Kerry gave me a little bump from behind, to let me know he was there. By the time I was on my last lap, I could feel the big man breathing down my neck. I was now travelling at such speed that I had to brake heavily into the last corner, the wet corner. Dad's advice was right, the race would be won or lost on how I handled the corners. I spun violently off the track as Kerry slowly drove over the finish line with a big smile across his face and pumping his fist high in the air. It was obvious to me on this and many other occasions before and since, that he and my dad had a common interest – winning.

Despite his sometimes overwhelming competitive streak, Kerry was always caring to me, as he was to my mum and my sister Sam. I had a lot of fun with the Packers, and just wish the public knew the Kerry Packer my family knew. Apart from achieving a great deal with World Series Cricket, Dad and Kerry had a huge amount of fun together. They were also bound by a strong loyalty towards each other.

How much Dad and Kerry meant to each other, and depended upon each other, was highlighted when Paul Landa, the New South Wales Attorney-General, died suddenly in November 1984. Paul had been a close friend and Kerry was shocked and distraught over his death. Dad was so concerned about Kerry's emotional state that he offered to come home from the Test in Brisbane to be with him. When Kerry refused the offer in no uncertain terms, Dad phoned Bruce Francis and asked him to keep Kerry company the next day.

The loyalty wasn't all one way. When an old school-friend of Dad's migrated to Australia from Germany, Dad went out of his way to help him set up a branch office of his business. In a moment of madness, and an indication of Dad's trusting nature, he signed a personal guarantee on a $10 million business loan for his 'friend'. When the business faltered, the friend took off, leaving Dad with the debt. The bank called in the loan. Though this cowardly act surely meant bankruptcy for Dad, he was as much distressed over the betrayal as the money. Dad handed over everything, which was considerably less than the $10 million. In a remarkable gesture, Kerry stepped in and took care of Dad's outstanding debt.

Kerry's generosity knew no bounds. Although Kerry was a substantial contributor to charity, he did it in a very low-key way and eschewed publicity. One of Dad's favourite stories, of hundreds regarding Kerry's generosity, concerned a trip to the new Sydney Football Stadium. Dad and Kerry were sitting just in front of half a dozen disabled children in wheelchairs and decided to have something to eat. Kerry asked the kids if they would mind their seats for them while they were away. Kerry and Dad got a real kick out of watching the kids fight off attempts by other patrons to 'steal' their seats. At the end of the match, Kerry gave one of the carers his phone number and asked him to ring him at the office the next day. When he rang, Kerry told him he had organised a trip to Disneyland for the six children and their parents.

Kerry loved watching live sport. He once made a trip to Brisbane to watch the Australia v England Test. He asked Dad if he would like to bring a few mates to have dinner with him. Dad brought South African-born England batsman Allan Lamb and two others, whose names escape me. On the completion of dinner at 10pm, Kerry asked Allan whether he had a curfew. When he said 'no', Kerry suggested they head to Jupiters on the Gold Coast for a little gambling under normal Packer rules. Allan queried what that meant and Kerry explained that he bought the chips and they shared in the profits. Allan liked those rules and said he was in, despite the fact that he had to bat the next day.

Kerry bought $100,000 worth of chips and gave each of them $20,000. After a short while they were $200,000 in front and Kerry asked them whether they wanted to cash in or bat on. Dad and Allan wanted to declare a dividend but reluctantly said, 'It's your call, Kerry.' He decided to bat on and by 1.30am they had lost the lot. As if that wasn't bad enough, when they returned to the hotel at 2.30am they bumped into a number of cricket writers who were having a quiet drink.

I think some people found it difficult to deal with Dad, or to relate to him naturally, knowing he had direct access to Kerry, and later to James. In recent years, Dad had a few private run-ins with various people. He told me that people at Channel Nine would sometimes get upset if he went directly to Kerry with an idea or a problem, or anything at all, rather than through what they considered the 'appropriate' channels.

Dad was a great storyteller, right up until his passing, and among the endless array were stories about Kerry. They were fantastic! While he loved telling these ever-colourful tales to the multitudes, and getting the laughs or the gasps of awe, he made a point of never divulging private matters. Dad's stories were more about Kerry's huge personality and the adventures they had together. I felt proud that my dad was so close to such a powerful, globally respected businessman. But much more than that, I also really liked him and his family.

I am so grateful to Kerry for the opportunities he gave my father and the privileged life I have in Australia. During my childhood I was always appreciative of his warmth and hospitality, perhaps over-effusively so, whenever we stayed with him on holidays, but I now regret not having attempted to thank him as an adult. It's so easy to think there will be time and opportunity to express gratitude, admiration, even quiet affection, to people who've had an impact on our lives, but too often those people leave our lives in one way or another before we've made the appropriate effort. Kerry had less of a presence in Sam's and my life once Mum and Dad separated, but there were still occasions when I could have spoken up, and I always could have written, but sooner than we could bear to imagine, he was gone from everyone's lives, too young, like Dad, and even younger … Mum.

15

Behind the Mic

WHEN KERRY ASKED DAD TO COMMENTATE FOR THE NINE Network in 1980 he thought all his Christmases had come at once as it enabled him to keep on with his passion for cricket.

Dad had three heroes – his father; singer Vera Lynn, because of what she did for the troops during World War Two; and the Harlequin-capped Douglas Jardine because of the way he stuck it up the Australians during the Bodyline series in 1932–33. Dad knew that commentary work would provide him with a platform to take the mickey out of Australian viewers through the provocation of the Aussie commentators. Instead of signalling his own boundaries, as he did in the summer of 1974–75 to antagonise Lillee and stir up the crowd at the 'Gabba, he could come into their living rooms and irritate them by pointing out that their cricketers might not be as good as they thought they were. The showmanship he enjoyed in front of big crowds would continue to an even bigger audience through television.

Dad always felt cricket was part of the entertainment business, and he saw himself as an entertainer. That, as much as anything, was the reason for the exaggerated appeals or going down to the boundary to banter with the crowds. Commentators, as well as cricketers, he believed, had to be entertainers.

My father also had an infinite passion for talking about cricket. It didn't matter when, where or with whom, Dad just loved talking cricket. I could give a thousand examples of Dad's passion but this one probably best exemplifies it. The house was full of visitors and Mum was too exhausted to cook, so Dad said he would get take-away fish and chips. When he walked into the shop four cricket lovers recognised him and started firing off questions about cricket. Dad was happy to indulge them as he was enjoying the conversation and their passion for the game. In fact, he was enjoying the discussion so much, that when his order was ready he suggested they come home with him so they could finish their chat. Mum had to hide her displeasure when Dad returned home, fish and chips in hand, followed by four complete strangers.

The best place of all to talk cricket was in the comm box. Dad regarded commentating as an opportunity for him to educate the viewers, something that would enable them to get more out of watching the cricket broadcast. He wanted to be informative.

No one enjoyed travelling and mixing with other cultures more than Dad. He knew that commentating, if he worked hard and became good at it, could provide the chance for him to do something he loved for the rest of his life.

He created his own style, which was no doubt influenced from time to time by suggestions from Kerry. It amused Dad when people attacked him for being too verbose, provocative or excitable, because he knew Kerry had no issues with it. In fact Kerry encouraged it, and Dad's view was that Kerry knew more about television than most.

Dad, Bill Lawry and Keith Stackpole became close friends when they joined the Nine commentary team after World Series Cricket ended. Dad loved taking the mickey out of Bill and Stackie. The first time he met William Morris Lawry he said, 'You're the Australian captain who lost a series 4–0 in South Africa, aren't you?' To which Bill replied, 'Yeah, and you're the guy who gave up the captaincy of England for money.'

All my life people have asked me the question: 'What is it like being the son of Tony Greig?' My standard response is that it is very normal and probably not all that different from their situation with their own father. I have not known any different. I was born to the man, not the famous cricketer or commentator.

I obviously saw and heard my father on TV all the time during summer, but that had always been that way. It has never felt strange to me, just normal. Though I didn't enjoy being Tony Greig's son when I was about 11 years old and Billy Birmingham released his first Wide World of Sports tape. In fact, the first one we had was actually a record. I arrived at school one Monday morning and was greeted as a 'pigeon-toed pea-brain' by one of my friends. Like Dad, I was slightly pigeon-toed and I became very embarrassed about it after being branded with this nickname, courtesy of Billy Birmingham. Slowly my new name made its way around my school. For the next few months I recall sleeping on my stomach with my feet pointing outwards trying to reverse my pigeon-toes. Somehow it must have worked, as I miraculously grew out of my pigeon-toes during my early teenage years.

Dad didn't have any problems with the Billy Birmingham 12th Man tapes. Mum, however, seemed more concerned by all the swearing her children were listening to with our friends. Maybe she was also worried that people would think that was how we spoke at home. Of course, it wasn't.

A couple of Dad's colleagues in the commentary box were very annoyed by the tapes, and I would not be surprised if Billy Birmingham received a letter or two of complaint. Over time, Dad came to recognise that those tapes were having a very positive impact on his public profile. Tony and Bill Lawry's famous duels in the commentary box were now becoming iconic during the Australian summer. Personally, I think Billy Birmingham is extremely talented and should be commended for his commercial success.

During one of my first dates with my wife, Ange, I was to be reminded of just how all-pervasive the Billy Birmingham tapes became. Ange used a line which I recognised from 'The 12th Man'. Her comment involved using my father's name disparagingly. I laughed and asked her if she knew what she had just said? She told me it was an expression that she had heard her brother use many times growing up. I then had to explain to her that the said 'Tony' was my father!

In later years Dad was challenged by the constantly evolving technology, but enjoyed it as it gave him access to a wealth of information and research. He was always looking for help to change the settings on his mobile phone, or to fix an issue he was having with his laptop computer. He kept the Nine IT helpdesk very busy. The internet made Dad a smarter and more informed commentator. I got a kick out of helping him become more comfortable with computers and the internet, and it occupied much of our discussion in recent years. He wanted to be the best he could be at everything, particularly commentating. He thought he was the best, and talked about this with me, though not in an arrogant or boastful way. I think he believed he worked harder than anyone else with his research. He had a unique skill in his ability to build up an atmosphere of excitement with his audience – his commentary during Shane Warne's hat-trick at the MCG in 1994 is a perfect example of this.

Channel Nine's cricket statistician, Max Kruger, told me that in the history of Test cricket there have been 39 hat-tricks, eleven of which pre-date television. They are rare. To call one is a real badge of honour for a commentator. Imagine what it must be like to call more than one.

Back on 29 December 1994, Shane Warne was at the peak of his powers and England was in disarray. Dad was in the lead chair in the commentary box. In came the big England fast bowler Devon Malcolm – a real tail-ender. There was an air of expectancy. The hat-trick was on. Warne bowled, found the edge, then the stout figure of David Boon dived and held the catch and Dad went off. It was brilliant. He was in the moment and yet the commentary lives on: 'It's a hat-trick!' he yelled into the mic. 'It's a hat-trick! Shane Warne's done it! He's got a hat-trick!'

Go forward eight years to 11 March 2001. Australia scored a seemingly comfortable 4–252 against India in the second Test at Kolkata, but then it was 'caaaarnage'. Harbhajan Singh dismissed Ricky Ponting and Adam Gilchrist with successive deliveries. Shane Warne made his way to the middle. Dad was going off, echoing the passion of the baying Bengalis on the terraces. They wanted Warne's wicket to complete this historic event. This was just the setting Dad relished. The big moments brought out his best commentary.

Max Kruger told me that as Shane Warne took his guard, he mentioned to Dad no Indian bowler to that point had taken a Test hat-trick. Dad shared this fact through his mic, building further excitement: Harbhajan bowls and the edge is found. Warney stands there, stunned. It was another hat-trick for Dad – another great moment in his broadcasting career.

Over the past twenty years, Max Kruger has worked alongside the Channel Nine commentators and has got to know them and their families extremely well. I spent hours sitting next to him in the commentary box as a kid, and this is something my little brother, Tom, is now also doing at almost every Test match in Sydney.

Max feeds the commentators all the cricketing facts that they then use on air to inform the viewers. He has a huge amount of cricket knowledge, a walking and breathing *Wisden* if you like. Recently I asked Max about his relationship with my father, as I know Dad was very fond of him. I feel it is best I step back for a moment and let Max speak for himself:

The Tony Greig I grew to know had high standards. He cared. He had a wonderful sense of family and he regarded the commentary box as an extension of his family values. Yes, it was a workplace but it is where strong friendships existed and others evolved.

When I was appointed statistician in 1992, Tony challenged me about my credentials for the job. He impressed upon me the importance of the role. I assured him I was up to the task.

How it works at Channel Nine is the lead commentator sits next to the statistician. It is expected that you interact a lot. If Tony felt I was being a bit quiet, he would say so. He always encouraged me to contribute.

One moment that is a standout for me came after 1993, when Brian Lara had made his breakthrough at international level. His innings of 277 at the SCG will always be spoken of in reverential tones. Tony had a great regard for the entertaining players. One of the best was Brian Lara.

Anyway, a few years later Tony was commentating with Michael Holding and Brian Lara was again at the wicket. Tony was looking for something about Lara to work with, so I mentioned to him that Brian named his daughter Sydney in recognition of that spectacular double century. He dutifully referred to this in his commentary. There was an extended pause. Michael picked up his microphone and in his deep West Indian accent said, 'Tony, it is a good thing he did not make that score in Lahore.' Tony and I looked at each other. What could you say?

When I think of my dad's commentary career, one thing really stands out for me: his on-air duels with Bill Lawry. The 'Tony and Bill Show' didn't happen by chance, but then again, it wasn't planned. It evolved. They found each other. It was just meant to be.

What came first, the rapport or the friendship? Max Kruger is well placed to answer that question, as he witnessed Dad's personal relationship with Bill up close, working with them both on more than 180 Tests, 450 one-day internationals and an assortment of other matches. To the viewers, Tony and Bill were frequently offering different opinions, but to Max there was a common ground. Both were callers and they liked to be entertaining.

Max told me he thought it was all the time the duo spent in each other's company, over three decades of Australian summers, that strengthened the developing friendship. You could say it was an unlikely friendship, considering their respective backgrounds and playing personas. Max had these words to say of their relationship:

There was the rock-solid opening batsman – serious yet excitable. Then there was the brash all-rounder who loved to engage the crowd and who was happy to be portrayed as the villain. Different people but united by a love of the great game.

The rapport developed over time. Cricket at Test level stretches over five days. That is a long time to be around each other in the confines of the commentary box. It was clear that they enjoyed working together. Bill would go with the moment. If Tony disagreed, he would say so. This would invoke an exchange of views. Who would win? Bill thrived on the right of veto – the final word. It really depended on who was the lead commentator, that is, who led the call and, significantly, who would throw to the commercial break.

This would result in vigorous debate in the break. Back on air and the lead man would pick up the call. Depending on what had triggered the discussion in the first place, it may be left there or it could be the catalyst for round two, for it is fair to say that both men liked to have the final word. It was fun to be around when something controversial happened on their watch. Tony loved to stir the pot. Just as he did in his playing days, he liked to keep people on their toes. And Bill had his agenda items. Tony knew he would always get an immediate reaction if he criticised one of Bill's beloved fellow Victorians.

Both relished the opportunity to commentate when the game had hit a flat spot; it seemed they had the power to make something happen out of nowhere. You sensed they both had their checklists – the topics that would always get a reaction. Sitting alongside them, this was how I thought they would assess each other and find the points that would create a conversation.

There was Eastern Suburbs Tony: posh school education; mercenary cricketer and company man; career commentator; former England captain; shared allegiances between South Africa, England and Sri Lanka; and probably the one that irritated Bill the most – proud Sydney-ite.

Alongside that was Blue-Collar Bill: state school education; plumber by trade; pigeon fancier; part-time commentator; former Australian captain; parochial Victorian.

Tony enjoyed highlighting that Bill was the skipper when Australia was thrashed four–nil by South Africa in 1970. If someone started batting slowly, Bill's career résumé would be revisited. A close-up on a pigeon was always well received by Tony.

Bill would love to talk about the real people – the battlers. To him, they were a world away from Greigy's cushy existence. And didn't Bill just love it when Tony commented on the attractiveness of a lovely young lady in the crowd.

It seemed uncanny how often a wicket would fall soon after Bill took over the call. Tony would feed off this and another memorable stint would be underway.

There was an innate competitiveness between them, but what unified them was the shared desire to entertain. Many a time Tony would say, 'Come on, Bill, let's stir it up.' Tony would look at me and ask me to give them something to bring it alive. I don't know why he would say that because, as sure as night followed day, something would always happen as soon as they took up the call.

Boxing Day Tests in Melbourne have been a tradition for most of the Channel Nine era. Who could ever forget Tony Greig's dramatic call of the final ball when Dennis Lillee knocked over Viv Richards to have the mighty West Indies reeling at 4–10 at stumps on Boxing Day 1981? Tony loved the big stage but Bill would always remind him, 'This is the sporting capital of Australia,' when he was feeling subdued. When he was on a roll, Melbourne was elevated to the 'sporting capital of the world'. No false modesty from Bill.

This was Bill's playground. He would be eager to talk about the big occasion; the size and the passion of the crowd; and all things Victorian. However, there was a key 'variable' – Melbourne's fickle weather. Rain interruptions were perfect fodder for Tony. Many of the first days were rain-affected.

Then another New Year would come around and Sydney would play host to its annual New Year's Test. I'm sure Tony would hold his breath and hope for favourable weather. If rain was in the air, Bill was ready to pounce.

Tony would wax lyrical about Sydney. He would have his fun and then seek a concession from Bill that this was indeed God's own country. Bill would be most likely to say: 'Okay, Tony Greig, you've had your fun. Let's get back to the cricket.' As soon as he could Bill would request a pointer, a graphic of upcoming matches, for the next one-day international in Melbourne. He would always talk of an expected crowd way beyond the SCG's capacity. That was their sense of occasion.

Max shared a personal story with me that demonstrated the bond he developed with Dad and Bill over the years. In early 1997, Max was 'considering his future' at Nine. They were in Perth. Dad had heard Max was thinking about 'moving on' and he wasn't pleased. He called Max and told him he would be having dinner with Bill and himself that evening.

They went out for a steak. The discussion was stagnating because Max had dug his heels in. Bill became indignant, and apparently banged his hand on the table and said emphatically to Max: 'Principles don't pay bills!' Dad said, 'We enjoy working with you. We don't want you to leave.' Max says that night left a lasting impression on him. 'The fact they and the other commentators cared proved persuasive,' he said. 'I'm so glad I elected to stay. I got to work closely with these wonderful men for another fifteen years.'

Max always felt like he was part of the family working with Dad and Bill.

I remember the first game one summer was at the 'Gabba. Early on, Tony and Bill were commentating together. Tony spoke of what it was like to see familiar faces at the start of another summer. He suggested several of us were like family and Bill agreed. From our perspective, the feeling was mutual.

At the start of a Test match, Bill would be on edge; Tony would be the voice of calm: 'Settle down, Bill.' When an lbw appeal went up, you'd often hear Bill say, 'That wasn't even close.' That would prompt Tony to dwell for a while on Bill's record of never having been given out lbw in a Test in Australia. So the jousting continued.

For more than 30 years it was the best show in town. To have a ringside seat was a great honour. Tony Greig and Bill Lawry are to cricket commentary what Bud Abbott and Lou Costello are to comedy – a legendary partnership.

Dad loved his dinners with Bill. One day he and Dad were out for dinner with some other friends and a waitress approached him at the table, and said, 'You look very familiar, are you Mark Greig's father?' He looked at her with amusement and realised she had absolutely no clue about cricket or who he was. I got a real buzz when I heard this story because for once Dad was not recognised for being Tony Greig, but because he was my dad. He played it down, but the others talked it up when they told me the story.

I loved joining Dad on his travels and staying in hotels together. When I was twelve, I joined him in Adelaide for an Australian Test series against New Zealand in 1987–88. Dad attended a charity dinner at a popular local restaurant called Ferrett's Place. The owner, Graham Ferrett, a former WSC manager, had invited the entire Nine commentary team. The proceeds from the evening were going to handicapped children. Richie Benaud had been invited to run the kitchen as the guest chef.

I wasn't invited to the restaurant, but instead stayed in our hotel room with Dad's approval to order room service and in-house movies. Dad told me that Richie had taken ages to get the food out to the tables, which meant that he and his commentary mates polished off more alcohol than usual on empty stomachs. Dad was surprised that even Bill Lawry was getting into the champagne, given he was never one to drink. No doubt Bill struggled to keep up with Dad's drinking pace as Richie's fettuccine hit the tables. To top it off, a nice bottle of sauternes was kindly provided by their host to wash down dessert. They were all legless.

When Dad finally made it back to our hotel room, he woke me up as he stumbled into the room and switched the lights on. It was obvious to me that something was wrong. He was leaning up against the wall trying desperately to keep himself upright. I helped him get his clothes off and he fell into bed. After about fifteen minutes lying on his back, I heard him groan as he kicked his long leg out of bed and placed one foot on the floor. I think he must have been trying to stop his bed from spinning around the room. Suddenly he sprang out of bed and made off for the bathroom. He only just got his head in the door when he brought back up everything he had consumed at Ferrett's Place that evening. He completely covered the bathroom in fettuccine.

On his way back to his bed, he said: 'Hey mate, would you mind doing me a big favour and clean up that mess in the bathroom? Richie's fettuccine has made me terribly sick!' So, feeling sorry for him, I spent the next hour cleaning up the bathroom. This included pushing chunks of fettuccine down the drain in the sink. The intense smell of vomit made me want to bring up the three-course room service meal I had consumed earlier.

The next morning Dad was struggling, but he managed to get himself dressed and out the door on time. On the way down to the foyer, the lift opened on Bill Lawry's floor.

'Good morning, Mr Lawry. How are you today?' I said.

'Mmmm … I'm not feeling very well thanks, Mark,' Bill replied.

'That's no good,' I said. 'You must have eaten Mr Benaud's fettuccine as well.'

Typical of Dad, he turned this into another great story to tell whenever he got the chance.

When Dad died, Bill paid the most wonderful tribute to him:

We had different views on cricket. Tony's views were sometimes completely different from mine. But the point was we could have a bit of a challenge on air and as soon as we walked away we were the best of friends. We didn't have a cross word in the 33 years I've known him. He was just a gentleman.

He was fantastic because if you threw something out there he'd come in boots and all. There was no holding back with Tony. We laugh because originally he was well known for putting the key in the big cracks while doing the pitch report, but his knowledge of cricket was outstanding. His record as an all-round cricketer was excellent and if you made a blue about something he was right on to you. He was always challenging but always a great friend.

One 'key in the crack' story is part of the commentary team's legend. Players had used keys to test the amount of moisture in the pitch for years. If the key goes into the pitch easily, it's moist. Dad incorporated the key into his pitch reports. On this particular day at the WACA in 1994, Dad was just about to do the pitch report when he realised he didn't have a key. Mike Procter, the former South African all-rounder, was standing nearby so Dad asked him if he had a key. He did, his key from his hotel room. Dad took it and as he started to do the pitch report, the key dropped into a great crack in the WACA wicket, and is still there to this day.

In addition to the pitch reports, which also showcased his passion for perfect footwear, Dad was associated with other innovations as part of the Nine cricket summer. There was the Weather Wall, something that looked like it had failed an audition for the 'Doctor Who' television series, and the Player Comfort Meter, which Billy Birmingham so mercilessly sent up. I don't think Dad minded what people said about those innovations, so long as they were talking about them.

Dad also was well aware of the responsibility he had to the players when he was talking about them, particularly the pronunciation of their names. He was impeccable with his pronunciation of the names of the Sri Lankans, the Indians and the Pakistanis. Before every tour, he went to the source to make sure he had those pronunciations clear in his mind. Perhaps being able to speak Afrikaans helped him get his tongue around the many syllables in those names from the subcontinent. Whatever, Dad's commitment to getting those details right was another reason he endeared himself to the people of India and Sri Lanka.

My dad was forthright and had strong opinions which often went against the views of his fellow commentators. However, collectively, the Nine commentary team achieved something very special – they became not just household names, but part of the Australian sporting fabric.

After Dad died there was some speculation this would be the end of the team and the legend that had grown up around them. Steve Crawley, the head of Nine Sport, denied this would be the case, if only for one reason – Dad would not want it that way.

'Like Bill Lawry, we will all miss Anthony William Greig, even though he will be with us forever – one of the true sounds of summer,' Steve said.

'And, make no mistake, this is not the beginning of the end. Greigy wouldn't have any of that: "Just get on with it, you lot, toughen up."'

16

Subcontinent and Serenity

DAD WAS A MIXTURE OF MANY INFLUENCES. OBVIOUSLY, growing up as the son of a decorated war hero had an impact on him: it helped him put fear into perspective. Another influence was the wonderful outdoor life he enjoyed growing up in South Africa. While Mum attended a proper finishing school in Switzerland, in many ways England was Dad's finishing school. As captain of England he walked among many fine people and he would have absorbed their better characteristics. In fact, absorb is a good word to think of the way Dad embraced different cultures. When he got to India, he found a people who loved the game of cricket as much as he did. He immediately warmed to them and they to him. On his first tour to India in 1972–73, the crowd roared its approval when Dad picked up Gundappa Viswanath, one of the smallest people ever to play Test cricket, and rocked him like a baby after he scored a century at the Brabourne Stadium in Bombay.

India also taught Dad patience, off the field and on it, as his marathon innings in Calcutta showed in 1977. He made his first trip to Sri Lanka after that series, and again was smitten by the serene people of the 'teardrop' nation. Here was another cricket-mad country he could share his love for the game with. Some might raise an eyebrow at the thought of the highly excitable Tony Greig absorbing the serenity of Sri Lanka, but in a crisis there would always be a certain calmness about Dad.

In 1977, he visited Sri Lanka briefly, during a stopover on the way from India to Australia for the Centenary Test. At that stage Sri Lanka was on the cusp of being admitted into Test cricket, and this visit by the MCC was to be an important part of that. Over the years, Dad not only went back to Sri Lanka many times, he also urged others to go there to see its wonders for themselves.

One of the people who responded to his urgings to go to Sri Lanka was my sister, Sam. The time she spent there is a highlight in her career as a school teacher. I will let her tell her story:

> It had always been a dream of mine to work (teach) in a foreign country. I had planned to go to Turkey and then to Nepal, but just as I was organising my trip in 1999 there was a terrible earthquake in Turkey and for a short while the advice was that it was not a safe place to visit. That's when Dad suggested I look at Sri Lanka. I can remember him saying, 'Have you considered Sri Lanka? It is the most wonderful country, you would love it and I have friends there I can put you in contact with.' I thought it funny that

he would recommend Sri Lanka because there was
a lot of civil unrest there and I was eventually to
experience a lot of police checkpoints, curfews and
lockdowns.

I sent my CVs off and before I knew it I had
secured a teaching position at the Elizabeth Moir
School in Colombo. I had only planned on being in
Sri Lanka for about three months before moving to
Nepal but, like Dad, I fell in love with the country
and stayed a full year. I had no idea Dad was so well
known and so highly respected in Sri Lanka before I
moved there in 2000. He certainly made some very
special friends in Sri Lanka and I feel extremely
fortunate to have shared some wonderful times with
him in this part of the world. All I can say is that
Dad just loved Sri Lanka and the Sri Lankan people
adored him.

Since my dad's passing, I have heard many stories about
him and the way the people of Sri Lanka felt about him. On
the ESPN Cricinfo website, Andrew Fernando summarised
this connection so well when, the day after Dad passed, he
wrote about Tony Greig's special bond with the little island:

For many people, especially in the provinces of Sri
Lanka, it is common practice to have the radio on
alongside the cricket on television, providing the
Sinhala commentary they understand. Often six or
seven neighbours sit cloistered together in a small
room, in front of one of the few television sets in the
village. When Greig's name appears on the bottom of

screen, though, someone calls it out. Nothing more
needs to be said. The radio is turned down and the
TV volume cranked up. Perhaps no one in the room
understands Greig, but they feel like they know him.
He is an old friend. He has been part of their lives for
so long now, and to leave his commentary unheard is
like leaving him on the doorstep to wither in the heat.

Sri Lanka's love affair with Greig began during
the 1996 World Cup, though he himself had admired
its cricketers and their country for some time by then,
even consoling the side after Muttiah Muralitharan
had been called for chucking on Boxing Day 1995.

Sri Lanka were barely better than minnows in
most estimations then. Talented, perhaps, to a point,
but far too young and erratic still to make a genuine
play for a title as coveted as this. Greig nailed his
colours to the mast early in the tournament. 'I just
love the way these little Sri Lankans play,' he declared
during one of Sri Lanka's group matches. 'I really
think they can win this World Cup if they play well.'

'These little Sri Lankans' was to become his
catchphrase during the tournament, alongside his
nickname for Romesh Kaluwitharana – 'little Kalu'.
Perhaps on the lips of any other, those words may
have seemed tinged with condescension, but the
affection in Greig's voice was unmistakable. He is
remembered as a combative man and cricketer, but
he only ever had love for Sri Lanka.

It was fitting that he was on air as Arjuna
Ranatunga and Aravinda de Silva took Sri Lanka
close to triumph in the final. 'These Sri Lankans

are giving the Aussies a real hiding,' Greig boomed, after Ranatunga hit a Shane Warne full toss over the square-leg rope – a cricketing moment almost every Sri Lankan remembers.

After the winning runs had been hit, Greig dubbed the victory 'a little fairy-tale'. 'The thing that I like about these guys is that they not only win, but they win in style. It is only a small place, Sri Lanka, and what a moment this is for Sri Lankan people.'

Over the years Greig's love for the island grew irresistible, and the nation embraced him as one of their own. Sri Lanka perhaps suffers from a condition that might be termed small-nation syndrome. Locals feel they are perennially overlooked and constantly lumped with neighbours from the north they have little in common with. Greig was Sri Lanka's relentless champion, proclaiming the wonder of her beaches, the sweetness of her seafood, and the hospitality of her people, even while the country was in the grip of an ugly civil war.

Both in the cricketing universe and elsewhere, Greig believed in Sri Lanka before she even believed in herself.

When he announced his illness in October, Sri Lankans were sympathetic and sincere. A Buddhist blessing ceremony was organised for Greig in Colombo, with Mahela Jayawardene and Kumar Sangakkara in attendance.

Dad was blown away by that blessing ceremony and the fact that two such high-profile players were there. He sent back a message to the people of Sri Lanka saying how much it had meant to him.

One of Dad's best mates in Sri Lanka was Shiran Manukulasuriya, who first met Dad in 1992 during the Australian tour of Sri Lanka. Shiran has lots of stories about Dad's visits there. In the late 1990s, the now famous ICC elite panel umpire Kumar Dharmasena was playing for Sri Lanka in a Test match on a spinning wicket in Galle. He had taken four wickets with his right-arm offbreaks, and there were only tail-enders to come. He walked up to the captain, Arjuna Ranatunga, and asked to be taken off. Ranatunga asked him what he was talking about – with only the tail to come, Dharmasena was likely to get five wickets, a five-for. Dharmasena said, 'If I get a five-for, I will have to face an interview with Tony Greig.'

In 2010, Dad and Shiran visited Trincomalee, a major resort port city in Sri Lanka's Eastern Province. In the evening, Vice-Admiral Jayanath Colombage, who was at the time the Director Eastern Operations of the Sri Lanka Navy (he later became commander of the Sri Lanka Navy) hosted them for dinner on the beach at Coral Cove. Shiran takes up the story:

> It was a beautiful evening. I told Tony I was taking
> my swimmers along, just in case. Tony said, 'No way
> am I swimming at this time of the night!' Anyway,
> half an hour into the cocktails. I had got into my
> swimmers and was sitting in a partially submerged
> sand bar in the water. Tony was envious so he asked
> the host to make sure all cameras were out of the
> way, to 'keep these Facebook chaps at bay'. The host

agreed and barked out a few orders. Next thing I see is this huge figure of Tony in his equally huge white Y-fronts, glass of red in one hand and a cigar in the other, broad smile, coming to join me.

In about May 2012, we went on a tour of Mullaitivu, where the final and terrible saga of a 30-year war was fought to a bitter end. One must remember that this same area was absolutely devastated by the tsunami some years before. During this tour, which was arranged as a 'Tony, can you help us rebuild this area?' by the Secretary of Defence Mr Gotabaya Rajapaksa we were taken to a school for little kids. The children were aged from three to seven, mainly war orphans and other destitute kids.

They had put together a little musical theatre just for Tony. It was 'wonderful' as Tony put it. He kept nudging me and asking me to look at this little girl who was singing. Tony was fascinated by her beautiful and piercing light brown eyes. After the performance Tony stood among the kids, held their hands and posed for pictures. He almost did not want to leave.

That night, sitting alone outside our rooms in Trincomalee, Tony said, 'Sit down, keep quiet and listen to me. I want to talk about what I experienced in that school today.' He slugged down a huge gulp of wine and in a very unusual, soft and shaky voice said, 'Mate, that was so incredible and so very sad, I have to do something for those kids, they have no one.'

The next few days bordered on annoying for Shiran as Dad repeated this story to everyone he met. Shiran thinks

Dad kept a small part of his heart there in that little school, and those piercing brown eyes.

Shiran also said Dad enjoyed his golf in Sri Lanka:

Tony's passion for golf was paramount. The Royal Colombo Golf Club always gave him courtesy of the course. Through golf, dinner at my house and his own affection for the Air Force, he became friends with Harsha Abeywickrama, who was appointed Commander of the Sri Lanka Air Force in 2011. In fact, on invitation of the Commander, Tony was one of the first to play the Eagles golf course in Trincomalee. Sadly, the last game of golf Tony played was when he teamed up with his little sister Sally Ann and took on Harsha and me in Colombo.

When we stayed outside Colombo, I would always request the hosts to have a bed long enough for Tony to fit into. One time in Jaffna, he was given a really large room with three beds in it. The next morning while having coffee, I asked him if the bed was comfortable. He said, 'Yes, I made it comfortable, come take a look.' So I went into the room to see that he had piled the mattresses from all three beds onto one. He had spent an elevated and comfortable night.

Tony loved to drive himself around Sri Lanka. It is now very quick to get from Colombo to Galle on a new expressway, only it's a bit complicated to get to the start of the expressway. In September 2012, after detailed instructions from me on how to get to the expressway, Tony sped off. Twenty minutes later, he calls me.

Tony: 'Mate, no worries, I am on the expressway, thanks.'

Me: 'Oh that's great, watch out for the cops.'

Tony: 'Oh! OK, why?'

Me: 'There's a speed limit.'

Tony: 'Oh, OK. What's the speed limit?'

Me: 'One hundred kilometres per hour, but 110 is OK.'

Tony: 'Ok thanks!'

Me: 'What speed are you at now?'

Tony: 'Eh, let me see. 145-ish, I think!'

Me: 'Oh god, I give up.'

Tony bellows with laughter.

Once when Tony arrived in Sri Lanka, he gave me a cardboard box full of old videotapes of different sizes and shapes and asked me if I could find someone to restore and digitise as much of them as possible. It took about six months but we did restore some of them.

When Tony returned to Sri Lanka the next time, I gave him the DVDs with the resurrected video on it. He was really excited. That evening when he came for his customary roast pork dinner at home with my family, he pulled out one of the DVDs and said, 'Mate, you gotta see this.' We sat in front of the TV for a good part of the next hour and watched the footage, which was of his dad's funeral. This was the first time I met the Tony Greig who was sentimental, emotional and so proud of his family.

I had the good fortune of meeting Joyce, but this DVD was the first time I had seen Molly Joy,

Sally Ann and Ian. Tony paused and rewound, painstakingly telling me about almost everyone of the maybe 100 or so people on that video. He explained how the hearse was driven away, and how as per his Dad's wishes they just stood and watched. His voice trembled at times but he was so immersed in this whole nostalgia trip that, since it was just my wife and me as an audience, he probably did not care to hide his feelings. He covered everything, who was who, who married whom, their kids, the church, the aunts and uncles, the old school and mates. It was enthralling, I felt that was the point where he took me into his family, like an honorary membership of sorts.

The day after the Twenty20 World Cup final in early October 2012 was sadly the last time Shiran saw Dad. They had lunch in Colombo at the Cheers pub at the Cinnamon Grand Hotel. Most of the teams taking part in the World Cup had stayed there, including the victorious West Indians, and the team they beat in the final, the Sri Lankans.

Shiran says Dad was at his mischievous best that day:

While we were sipping a beer, the sales manager of the hotel strides up to us and says, 'Guess what!' Apparently the hotel had given the West Indies boys a private function room to party and celebrate in. However, when the hotel staff dared enter the function room to clean up the next morning they found the team had (in their pooped state) left the World Cup trophy behind. So the hotel management had tracked down the manager of the team and returned it.

Tony was appalled. He said, 'Why did you do that? If it were me I would have snuck into Mahela Jayawardene's room and put it next to him on his bedside table, and then when Mahela woke up, he would have seen it and thought losing the final was only a bad dream.' I gave myself a stitch laughing.

During 2000 when Sam was living in Sri Lanka, Dad was in Colombo on a cricket tour. Shiran was hosting yet another party but by now apparently Dad was tiring of these late-ending Sri Lankan parties. So he said to Shiran, 'Mate, why can't we be civilised and start at 6pm instead of 8.30pm, so we can finish at a decent hour?'

It was a decent crowd and following Tony's subtle instructions, most came early. The crowd included Dad and Sam; Shiran and his wife, Amalini; South African cricketer Pat Symcox and his family; former Sri Lankan captain Arjuna Ranatunga and his wife; and also former Pakistani player Rameez Raja and his family. The party was superb, some 30–35 guests in total. The food was great – a huge leg of wild boar on a spit, many types of bread and salads, and rice of course. Sam apparently also cooked up some beautiful prawns on the barbie. But alas, Shiran tells me, the party ended only after they had downed four litres of scotch, two litres of Bacardi, a bottle of vodka, a good portion of a bottle of cognac, a slab of beer and thirteen bottles of red wine. And, as per Dad's well laid out plans, they wound up early, too, as in early in the morning – 2.30am.

W

After Dad's death our family received a wonderful letter from Air Marshal Harsha Abeywickrama, Commander of the Sri Lanka Air Force.

He wrote:

> I cannot recollect any celebrity who carved out for himself so deep and sacred a place in the hearts and minds of 'all people' of our highly diverse society in the recent past, so much so [Tony] ranks with the greatest and fondest cricketing idols this country has ever produced. What was most impressive was his humbleness. He loved the history, culture, traditions, hospitality, natural beauty, food and people of this country and we loved him back; and it will be so for centuries to come.

As Shiran said, Harsha was a good friend of Dad's, and they had enjoyed that game of golf together at Colombo Golf Club with Sally Ann only a couple of months before his death. After golf they ended up at Harsha's home for lunch. Their mutual love for golf and cricket, and Dad's own background as the son of a decorated RAF officer, made the bond even stronger.

There was also a letter dated 14 January 2013 from Air Chief Marshal WDRMJ Goonetileke, the Sri Lankan Chief of Defence Staff. Below is an excerpt from the letter he wrote to our family:

Only a few people in this world are gifted with the ability to reach out, touch hearts and influence people to strive harder to achieve greatness. The people who possess this ability and also persevere to help mankind are a further minority in this world. To us Sri Lankans, Tony was an exceptional personality who belonged to this small minority. To us Sri Lankans, cricket is a part of our life's routine, and Tony was a powerful influence that strengthened our cricketing resolve to take on the world.

Sri Lankans took to the internet to express their feelings of love and loss after Dad's death on 29 December 2012. These are just a few of the tributes I read online:

Cricket would not be the same without Tony Greig. You are the one who defended Sri Lanka when everyone [mocked] our little nation and our ability. You are the one who [described] Sanath as Master Blaster, Kaluwitharana as Little Kalu, Arjuna as Captain Cool. You are the one who [said] that Sri Lankan pineapple and King coconut is best in the world. Some games we watched just because we love your commentary. When we go to watch a match at Premadasa (Stadium) we always want to see this tall white fellow who is wearing a top hat with a microphone in his hand. We always want to see you in press box. For us you are a Sri Lankan! A true gentlemen! You will surely be missed for decades to come, as we will remember you as the best commentator ever!

– Tharanga Nuwan Chandrasekara.

ABOVE LEFT Tony in his Sussex jumper in 1968, aged 21.

ABOVE RIGHT Tony with Kerry Packer after a press conference at the Dorchester Hotel in London in August 1977. Kerry had just announced that he was going to take the cricketing bodies to court over the dispute regarding his World Series Cricket competition.

BELOW Tony narrowly avoids being hit in the face by a Jeff Thomson bouncer during the second Test match at Old Trafford in Manchester, 8 July 1977. Tony went on to score 76 runs. England won by 9 wickets.

ABOVE West Indies captain Clive Lloyd and Tony share a drink after the fourth Test at Heading ̣y in Leeds, 27 July 1976. West Indies won by 55 runs to win the series and retain the Wisden Tro ̣y.

BELOW Tony batting during his innings of 91 runs, watched by Australians Rick McCosker *(cent ̣* and wicketkeeper Rod Marsh during the Jubilee Test at Lord's cricket ground, 21 June 1977. The match ended in a draw.

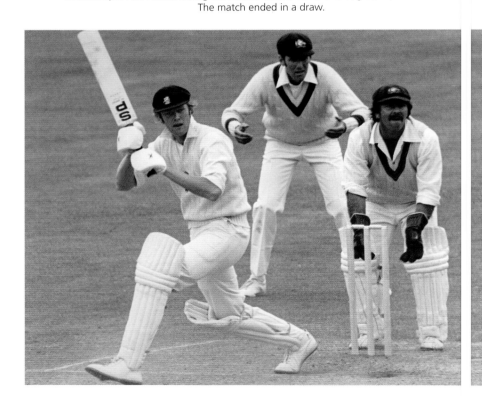

ABOVE Sussex county cricket team, May 1969. *Back row* (L-R): Terry Racionzer, John Snow, Tony Buss, Tony Greig, Mike Buss, Graham Cooper, Peter Graves. *Front row* (L-R): Les Lenham, Jim Parks, Mike Griffith, Ken Suttle and Don Bates.

BELOW Tony coaching his younger brother Ian, aged eleven, in the nets at Hove in May 1967.

RIGHT An article by Ian Todd published in *The Sun* on 17 August 1976, following the fifth Test at The Oval. West Indies won by 231 runs leaving Tony to eat his words and do some of his own grovelling!

BELOW Tony and Ian Chappell inspect the vandalised pitch on the morning of the fifth day of the third Test at Headingley in August 1975. England had the upper hand, but the captains mutually agreed to abandon the match due to the damaged wicket.

Sport OKAY, SO I'M GROVELLING NOW!

Joker Greig cheered as he goes on his knees

Tuesday, August 17, 1976
Telephone: 01-353 3030

By IAN TODD

TONY GREIG finally got down on his knees and grovelled before the West Indies fans at The Oval yesterday just before Clive Lloyd's declaration.

And so once the knee and jeers turned to cheers for the England captain. Later Greig confessed that his "grovel" remark that caused resentment before the start of the series was an "unfortunate mistake."

DOWN goes Greig . . . on hands and knees, in front of the West Indian supporters, who enjoyed the laugh with the England skipper. Picture: PETER JAY

HOLDING READY TO PUT

By CLIVE TAYLOR

MICHAEL HOLDING, tall, cool, casual and deadly, will today close the series against England with a final onslaught at The Oval.

Thinker Giles is all out to direct

By HUGH JAMIESON

WEST BROM player-manager Johnny Giles last night revealed the reason behind his shock decision to rank a long-term future outside League management—he wants to be a director.

Pledge 5p for Chelsea!

ABOVE Tony examines a waxwork of himself by Madame Tussaud's on display at Hove before a County Championship match, Sussex v Lancashire in September 1975.

OPPOSITE Kerry Packer and Tony outside the High Court in London at the end of the first day's hearing on 26 September 1977.

ABOVE WSC World XI team photo taken at Waverly Park in Melbourne, 1977. *Standing* (L-R) Mike Denness (Manager), Mike Procter, Imran Khan, Bob Woolmer, Derek Underwood, Barry Richards, Zaheer Abbas, Dennis Amiss. *Seated* (L-R) Majid Khan, Alan Knott, Asif Iqbal, Tony Greig, Eddie Barlow, John Snow, Mustaq Mohammed.

RIGHT Tony pours Viv Richards and Clive Lloyd some champagne to celebrate WSC World XI's win against WSC Australia XI in the second Super Test at Gloucester Park, Perth, in January 1978.

BELOW When men were men. No helmet. No arm guard. No chest pad. Tony hooking Dennis Lillee during the first Super Test of World Series Cricket in Melbourne in November 1978.

ABOVE Tony doing his first-ever pitch report for Kerry Packer and his son Jamie, on a drop-in wicket at the Sydney Showground in December 1977.

RIGHT As Captain of Surrey, Ian Greig met Queen Elizabeth II on 31 July 1991 at The Oval, in the NatWest Trophy Quarter Final v Essex.

BELOW Queen Elizabeth II being introduced to the England cricket team by captain Tony Greig, before the start of the Centenary Test against Australia in March 1977 at the MCG.

OPPOSITE Tony sits on the bonnet of his sponsored white Jaguar at the Sussex CCC ground at Hove in April 1976.

BELOW England team photo 5 August 1975, on day five of the second Test v Australia at Lord's. This was Tony's first Test as captain of England. He brought David Steele into the side, when Steele was close to retirement from county cricket for Northamptonshire. *Back* (L-R): Bob Woolmer, Graham Gooch, Chris Old, Peter Lever, Dennis Amiss, David Steele, Barry Wood. *Front* (L-R): John Snow, Allan Knott, Tony Greig, John Edrich, Derek Underwood.

RIGHT Tony 94 not out at Eden Gardens at the close of play on day three of the second Test India v England, in Calcutta, 3 January 1977.

BELOW Tony having some fun on the field during his century, pretending his bat is a rifle during the second test, India v England in Calcutta in January 1977.

KEN KELLY

ABOVE Ian Greig was selected in the England team that beat Pakistan at Edgbaston in August 1982. *Standing* (L-R): Allan Lamb, Mike Gatting, Chris Tavare, Derek Pringle, Geoff Miller, Ian Greig, Eddie Hemmings. *Seated* (L-R): Bob Taylor, David Gower, Bob Willis (captain), Ian Botham and Derek Randall.

LEFT Robert Langer looks on as Tony, wearing an early motorcycle-style crash helmet, cuts the ball at VFL Park in Melbourne during a WSC Super Test in early 1978. Helmets became popular after Dennis Amiss had some made in Birmingham, UK, for players to trial during WSC against the deadly bowling of Lillee, Thomson, Holding and Roberts.

BELOW Tony Greig salutes a cheering crowd after the MCC's victory over India in the second Test in January 1973 at Eden Gardens, Calcutta.

CHANNEL NINE / PBL MARKETING

PA/AAP

OPPOSITE Tony plays up to the 100,000 plus crowd at Eden Gardens after a firecracker was thrown onto the field during the second test, India v England in Calcutta in January 1977. Tony scored 103, the other batsman is Roger Tolchard (67).

ABOVE Channel Nine commentators (L-R) Ian Healy, Mark Taylor, Mark Nicholas, James Brayshaw, Michael Slater and Tony Greig pose before game one of the Commonwealth Bank One Day International Series between Australia and England at the MCG on 16 January 2011. The '70s theme was in celebration of the first one-day international played 40 years before.

LEFT In May 2012, Tony visited an orphanage in Mullaitivu, on the north-eastern coast of Sri Lanka with close friend Shiran Manukulasyria. The children were mainly war orphans and other destitute kids. Tony was moved that they had put together a little musical theatre just for him.

RIGHT Richie Benaud and Tony at the release of the DVD 'Benaud's greatest XI' at the SCG in December 2004.

TOP Tony doing his pitch report in his trademark Panama hat at the WACA in the early 1990s. It is regarded as one of the quickest and bounciest pitches in the world.

ABOVE Ian and Tony in May 1990 at The Oval following Ian's 291 runs off 251 balls in a four-day match against Lancashire. Ian's innings was the highest by any Surrey batsman in 64 years. Surrey's 9-707 declared was the highest score ever made against Lancashire.

RIGHT Tony with Michael Holding at his 50th birthday party which was held at Tony's home in Sydney's eastern suburbs in 1996.

ABOVE (L-R) Tony Greig, Mark Taylor, Richie Benaud, Ian Chappell and Bill Lawry pose during the Channel Nine 2010/11 Ashes Series launch at the SCG on 16 November 2010 in Sydney.

RIGHT Australian captain Michael Clarke is presented with Tony's neckerchief by Tony's youngest son, Tom, prior to the start of play on day one of the third Test between Australia and Sri Lanka at the SCG on 3 January 2013.

ABOVE The Channel Nine commentary team, Tony's family and fans observe
a minute's silence in Tony's honour at the SCG, 3 January 2013.

BELOW Beau, Tom, Sam and Mark speak on stage in remembrance of their father
during the Tony Greig memorial service at the SCG on 20 January 2013.

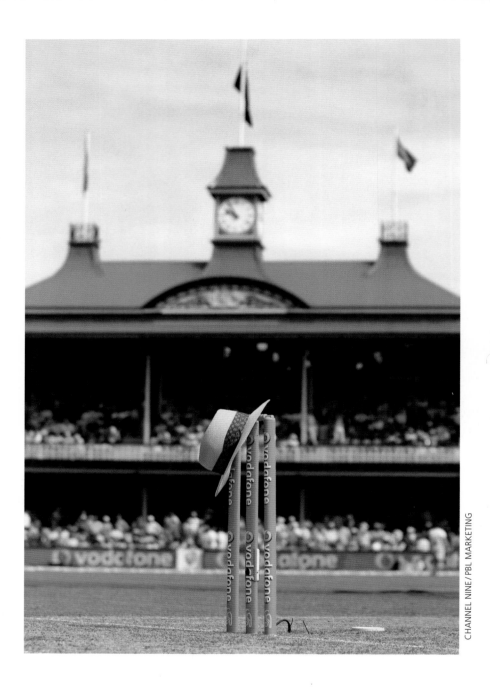

Tony's Panama hat sits on the stumps
prior to play commencing on day one of
the Sydney Test in January 2013.

was a genuine friend of Sri Lanka. His passion
and support for Sri Lanka was most evident during
the final of the 1996 World Cup. When Tony realised
that Sri Lanka would win the final, he was excited
and commented, 'These little Sri Lankans are giving
the Aussies a hiding.' Every Sri Lankan loved him for
that kind of morale-boosting support for Sri Lanka
who was the overwhelming underdog at the time.
No doubt Sri Lanka has lost an ally in international
cricket. May he RI.P.
– Kanchana Perera

My mother, who has very little knowledge of cricket
in general, was in tears after hearing the news! That's
how infectious he was in our tiny little country of
Sri Lanka! His comment of Little Kalu and the
pineapple and mangoes were words that every Sri
Lankan cherished! As they say Tony, 'Thanks for the
memories Tony, you will never be forgotten!'
– Changa

There are literally thousands of messages on the internet
like these, which were great words of comfort at the time
of Dad's death, and we will always be grateful to the Sri
Lankan people for them.

On one of his last trips to Sri Lanka during the
Australian tour there in 2012, Dad again showed his
willingness to go above and beyond to help out an old
friend. A colleague of Bruce Francis's had approached
asking for a favour. Two young girls he knew, Sophie and
Emily Parratt, were finishing off their backpacking trip

through India and Sri Lanka and were now in Colombo, venue for one of the Tests. Could Tony get them tickets to the Test? Could he! Not only did Sophie and Emily get tickets, they got tickets in the premium air-conditioned box. Dad invited them to have drinks and dinner with the teams before the match; drove them to and from the cricket ground each day they attended; took them to the commentary box to see how it all worked; organised drinks for them with Tom Moody and other identities, including the umpires; and on their last day in Sri Lanka organised a team car to take them to the airport. Dad also mentioned them in the commentary, which caused their parents back home no end of joy.

Dad's attitude has always been that many, many people have done things for him over the years which he hasn't been able to reciprocate directly but when he helps others he feels he is indirectly thanking those who have helped him. By giving Sophie and Emily such a good experience in Sri Lanka, as well as reciprocating indirectly, he might have also hoped they would go home and tell more people about the country.

It was the same with India. As far back as the 1970s, he urged people to go and see for themselves what a wonderful place it was. Dad was frustrated that people dismissed India as a third-world country with poor quality hotels. He acknowledged that people needed to be careful with food and water, but he thought Indian hotels generally had a very high standard of service.

In 2011 I helped Dad set up his Twitter account. He quickly discovered he could increase his followers by as many as 2000 overnight simply by mentioning the Board of Control for Cricket in India, the BCCI, or the Decision Referral System (DRS) which the Indians refused to implement, a real sore point with Dad.

This tweet got one of those huge responses: 'Most Indian, and many overseas commentators, are scared to criticise BCCI because if they do they will be dropped as commentators.' It was re-tweeted more than 100 times, including by @ESPNcricinfo (which at the time had 128,328 followers) and @LalitKModi (who had 366,658 followers). Lalit K Modi is a powerful former Indian cricket administrator.

Something else that really pushed the numbers up was the mere mention of India's most famous cricketer, Sachin Tendulkar, in a tweet.

It wasn't long before Dad went past 70,000 Twitter followers. Generally, he was not frightened to be critical of India and some of the directions in which Indian officials were taking the game. That was to be one of the central themes of his 2012 MCC Spirit of Cricket Cowdrey Lecture at Lord's. Since he was full of praise for India and Indians in the lecture, he was disappointed that so many people chose to ignore those words and attack him for what he thought were important constructive criticisms of Indian cricket.

Dad's MCC Spirit of Cricket Cowdrey Lecture remains a must-read for anyone who loves the game of cricket, and particularly for anyone who wants to be involved in its administration. It has been included in the appendices of this book.

17

Siblings

It's hard to know which was the greater, Dad's pride in his young brother, or Ian's hero-worship of his big brother. Although there was quite an age difference between them – Dad was born in 1946, Ian in 1955 – they had an incredibly close relationship.

Dad played a huge part in Ian's development as a cricketer right from the moment he made him face up to his bowling in the backyard to make the point that Dad's school friend Paul Ensor was soft. Dad was a coach and a role model and once Ian's career began to take off, an important adviser. When Dad left for Sussex in 1966, eleven-year-old Ian set himself the goal of following his brother.

As a schoolboy, Ian was exceptionally talented at cricket and rugby, the first boy from Queen's College to represent South African Schools at both sports.

Thanks to Sally Ann's husband, Phillip Hodson, Ian was able to secure a place at Cambridge University, where he had an outstanding sporting career. Phillip, a proud Yorkshireman who went on to become president of the MCC, had his own fine cricket career. In fact it was cricket that first brought him into contact with the Greig family, or 'this secret Afro-Scottish society' as he once called it.

Given the heavy Scottish accents involved in both famous meetings in Africa, it was almost another Dr Livingstone/ Morton Stanley moment. I will let Phillip take up the story:

[Former English cricketer] Richard Hutton was to blame. He wanted to visit his fiancée, Charmaine, in Johannesburg and asked if I would replace him on the imminent Staggerers tour to the Eastern Cape [Staggerers were a well-known social nomadic cricket side based in Johannesburg. They played at the Country Club and have been represented by many South African Test players]. Peter van der Merwe, the former South African captain, was to lead the tour, so I accepted with alacrity.

Rather foolishly, I flew into Jan Smuts Airport in September 1974, met the organiser, Blythe Thomson, and was then ferried with several teammates some 700 miles to Queenstown, an old '1820 Settlers' colonial town. With no proper sleep during the past 36 hours of air and car travel, I was asked to open the bowling and promptly hit the square-leg umpire first ball. It got better – marginally!

We beat the local side comfortably and returned to the bar, which on looking back seemed to be the favourite safety net of my 20s. I was ensconced on the bar-stool, talking too loudly as usual, when a tall, imposing gentleman clutching a pint of Coca-Cola approached me.

'I'm Sandy Greig,' he said in a very obvious Scottish accent. 'I believe that you are staying with us. Tony rang me and asked me to look after you. By the way, this is my youngest daughter, Sally Ann.' So, with those few simple words began a 40-year relationship, with not only my wife, Sally Ann, but the whole Greig family – a clan that extends to hundreds of cousins, nieces, nephews and the like; and a more competitive family you could never meet.

Sally Ann was wearing a fashionable, short mini-skirt. We studied each other. I bought her a drink. Apparently, I called her 'a typical English public-school product'. She told me that I lacked breeding; as usual she was right! From those inauspicious beginnings a spark was ignited. She cancelled her date and I took her to dinner that very evening before returning to the Greig apartment in the early hours of the following day.

Sally Ann and I met only twelve times before we married in Queenstown 28 months later. I coached cricket in Klerksdorp, an Afrikaaner town some 1000 kilometres north, and then worked for Anglo American in Johannesburg, while Sally Ann worked in the Standard Bank in Queenstown. Accordingly, it was a slightly surreal courtship, and I only met the rest of the family fleetingly. Nonetheless, some things were very obvious. Joyce was the centrifugal force around which they all gathered. She was the constant 'rock'. She had had to be, as Sandy battled with alcoholism. Money was always tight, but all four children had been brought up to be self-sufficient.

Sandy, of course, was a war hero. His record with 101 Squadron is very well known – DSO, DFC, shot down twice and finally after 54 missions sent to South Africa in 1943 to train pilots and navigators. The only surprise to me would have been if he hadn't drunk; though, I should say that in my time of knowing Sandy, from 1974 to his death in 1990, he never touched a drop of alcohol. He drank Coca-Cola and replaced this addiction with a regular consumption of cigarettes.

While others thought him a forbidding man, I always considered him to be gentle, thoughtful and erudite; albeit he never suffered fools. I think he was pleased that his youngest daughter decided to marry an Englishman, because he was fearful for South African society at that time.

I think that he was also delighted when I managed to help Ian obtain a place at my old Cambridge college, Downing. Ian was then in the South African Army, completing his National Service. While an excellent cricket and rugby player, Ian would be the first to admit that he was most certainly not an academic. Even I was surprised when I rang my old tutor, John Hopkins, the great law guru at Cambridge, and asked if he had a place for Tony Greig's younger brother. He would win three Cricket Blues and three Rugby Blues, I promised. John immediately replied, 'Send him.' 'What?' I queried. 'For an interview?' 'No, just send him,' he replied!

Fortunately, Ian did win those Rugby and Cricket Blues – a very rare achievement indeed; and what is more, he obtained a degree. How? None of us is quite sure. I should really ask John Hopkins; but I never have done.

If Ian wasn't the greatest scholar, his contribution to Cambridge's sporting achievements was substantial. In 1979, his final year at Cambridge, he captained the First XI. He inherited a talented side, which included another future England all-rounder, Derek Pringle. Ian drilled the side hard, assisted by his manager, the infamous Brian 'Tonker' Taylor, former captain of Essex. The hard work paid off, and at Lord's in July they beat Oxford by an innings and 22 runs. That allowed Ian to emulate Phillip Hodson – who had played in 1972, the last time Cambridge had beaten Oxford by an innings.

While at Cambridge, Ian also got the chance to play in the same game as his big brother – albeit on different sides. Ian was picked for the Combined Oxford and Cambridge Universities team that played Sussex in a Benson and Hedges Cup match at The Parks in 1977. Ian bowled a few balls at Dad and remembers an inside edge just missing leg stump. He says, 'Boy, I would have given him a send-off if it had bowled him.'

By 1980, when Ian was ready to play his first county game for Sussex, we were already living in Australia, post World Series Cricket. So the two brothers never played together in England. They did, however, play with Waverley in Sydney grade cricket in 1983.

Ian's rugby career at Cambridge was also quite remarkable as he was asked to play out of position on the wing instead of at fullback. Despite that, he scored a try in each of the first two Varsity matches at Twickenham – a rare achievement.

One of his coaches at Cambridge was the former Scottish international and BBC commentator Ian Robertson who, like my grandfather and Uncle Ian, had been to George Watson's Boys' College in Scotland. This is how, with his tongue in his cheek a fair bit, Ian Robertson summed up Ian's rugby career:

> First of all, his tackling was not as good as the great JPR Williams. Admittedly, he never missed a tackle or dropped a pass or failed to catch an enemy 'up and under' in three years at Cambridge, but I would still have picked JPR before Greig, given the choice.
>
> Similarly he scored loads of spectacular tries on the wing and occasionally in the centre, leaving a trail of high-class opponents floundering in his wake, but I swear Gerald Davies was a more dangerous runner. I know Greig's supporters are going to say that he scored two tremendous tries in his two Varsity games in 1977 and 1978 and Gerald Davies scored none in his three Varsity games but we all know not to trust statistics.
>
> It is worth pointing out his try in 1977 was nothing special. Any player with natural ability, a keen insight and shrewd tactical appreciation of the game blessed with excellent positional sense and blistering acceleration would have scored that try.

All he had to do was work out that the fly-half, Nigel Breakey, would probably fire a kick wide to the corner when he got into trouble and all the wing had to do was anticipate precisely when and where the kick would be made, position himself correctly, outflank and outwit his opponent and then outsprint him and the rest of the cover to score. Believe me, it was really that easy. It was the same sort of story the following year when he joined the exclusive band of players to score tries in successive years.

I would very much like to conclude by writing that apart from being a brilliant sportsman with outrageous talent and a mini-intellectual egg-head, he is also arrogant, conceited, aloof, pretentious and universally unpopular. Sadly, I can't. Regrettably, he is modest, humble, friendly, courteous and hugely popular with everyone who has ever met him.

My father, who had helped meet some of the expenses of sending Ian to Cambridge, was very proud of his little brother's achievements, and also a little envious. He once told me he would have given up all the accolades that came his way to have gone to Cambridge.

After leaving Cambridge in 1979 Ian joined Sussex, where his performances were good enough to earn him selection for England. In 1982, he played the only two Tests of his career against Pakistan. At Edgbaston in the first Test he scored fourteen and seven and took four wickets, opening the bowling in Pakistan's first innings. In fact his first innings figures, 4–53, were exactly the same as Dad's in his first Test. He was less successful in the second Test, and his Test career ended there, although there was a time seven years later when it might have resumed.

Ian played for Sussex until 1985 when, surprisingly, he and the county parted company. The official reason was because the club was going through tough times financially and couldn't afford to keep him on the books. The more likely version was a falling-out with the coach, Stewart Storey. Ian was devastated by the decision, which also upset many of his teammates.

He moved to Brisbane in 1980, where he had a career that had its roots in a Combined Oxford and Cambridge Cricket Tour to Australia in 1979. While in Brisbane for a short stay during that tour, the University of Queensland Cricket Club asked him if he would consider being their coach in the summer of 1980–81. His decision to accept the offer was another life-changing moment. In need of a haircut, he visited a salon recommended to him by a friend. There, he met hairdresser Cheryl Day. Two years later, she became Mrs Ian Greig.

They have two children, Michelle and Andrew. At around the same time Andrew was born, in January 1987, came another turning point in Ian's life. He received a phone call from Geoff Arnold, the former England fast bowler who was now coach of Surrey. Arnold was looking for an experienced all-rounder to boost his squad of players. Ian asked for time to think it over, which Arnold duly granted. Before Ian phoned him back, though, he received another call from Arnold: 'Would you like to captain Surrey?' he asked. Ian sought out his big brother for advice. The advice Dad gave was pretty impressive stuff. He said: 'First, if you're only taking the job because the financial offer is a good one, then don't take it. Second, if you're only taking the job so that you can stick it up Sussex, then don't take it. But if, however, you want to captain Surrey because you want to get back to the game you love and you think you can do a good job, then say yes straight away and start packing.'

Ian led Surrey with great skill, such that in 1989 whispers began that he might be the next captain of England. David Gower's England team had been unceremoniously thumped by Allan Border's Australians that year, a breakthrough moment in Australian cricket which was the beginning of an era of global dominance.

What was needed in England was a thorough reshaping of the team. It was obvious Gower would not be the captain for the upcoming tour of the West Indies and when Ian was sounded out by senior cricket officials he quietly made it known he was available if required. However, the decision to live in Australia after being sacked by Sussex counted against him.

The lawyers were brought in and they determined he needed to do another four-year qualification period. But just to prove the committee that dealt with the issues of these qualifications still hadn't managed to sort out the Greigs, he was to remain recognised as a qualified county player! To this day, Ian still doesn't know what would have happened if the lawyers had decided in his favour. Would he have captained England 'A' on that team's tour of Zimbabwe? Would he have followed in his brother's always oversized boot marks and captained England? That is something to ponder sometime around a campfire on Fraser Island.

These days Ian is heavily involved with the cricket and rugby programs at the Anglican Church Grammar School, or 'Churchie', in Brisbane. He happily says he was never as good a player as his big brother, but he was a highly regarded sportsman and leader of men. And his highest first-class score was 291, against Lancashire for Surrey. Dad's was 'only' 226.

Dad was also proud of the achievements of his two sisters. Because they were the eldest children, he and Molly Joy were very close. When Sandy was transferred to East London in 1962, Dad and Molly Joy, who were then sixteen and thirteen, stayed in Queenstown as boarders at their respective schools. Molly Joy missed her parents and other siblings dreadfully, but as she recounted recently, Dad did his utmost to fill the breach:

> If you had a brother, he was allowed to visit you after church. My brother was such a dish and loved by all the girls. He never missed a Sunday visiting time to see me. At times I cried until one day he said, 'You make me so sad when you cry for Mummy and Daddy and if you carry on, I won't be able to visit you anymore.' The tears were contained after that. It was during these Sunday visits that Tony first saw and met Donna. I can remember Tony commenting on her beauty and regal presence.
>
> Tony was so kind – he worried about my homesickness. He would give Jess, the man who sold doughnuts and cakes from his bicycle, money and ask him to take me a doughnut to my hostel. Jess would arrive, ring his bell, and ask to see me. The handing over of Tony's cake made me cry even more and Jess would comfort me and return to tell Tony that his little sister loved the cake but was still crying!

Molly Joy's education was interrupted by the move to Scotland in 1967, which caused her to miss her final year of school. Despite not matriculating, she has had a stellar career in marketing and promotions, beginning when she returned to South Africa with her family at the end of 1968.

After a few minor jobs she joined the retailer OK Bazaars in Johannesburg and says this was her 'lucky break'. She was the first woman to hold the job of promotions manager at the company, a major retailer with 120 stores in South Africa. While at OK she was 'headhunted' by one of the leading advertising agencies in Johannesburg and subsequently joined AdMark Advertising as managing director of its retail arm. She spent eighteen months in New York representing the company and its clients who were keen to break into the American market. She then returned to South Africa and joined a leading motor dealership in East London. There, her promotional skills again came quickly to the fore. She arranged for world-champion motorcyclist, Kork Ballington, to come to the dealership, which then sold more Kawasaki motorbikes in one weekend than it had for months.

Molly Joy brought another accomplished cricketer into the family when she married Norman Oswald Curry, or 'NO' (pronounced En-O) as he is known, in 1994. He had represented Namibia at cricket. They went on to have two children, Greig and Alexander. Like his uncle Tony, Alexander played cricket for Queen's College First XI for three years, captaining the side in his final school year. He also played rugby in the Queen's First XV and represented Border NR schools. Since leaving school, Alex has been playing Premier League Rugby in South Africa, having represented Natal Midlands XV and also more recently

Natal Wildebeest XV. He looks like he will be a real contender for selection in The Sharks Currie Cup squad next season. Greig, too, is a talented sportsman in cricket, squash, hockey and golf. He followed in his grandfather, Sandy's, footsteps by becoming a pilot and is passionate about aviation.

Molly Joy had her own advertising agency that was part of the Saatchi & Saatchi (Africa) Network and was awarded the Reserve Bank of Namibia's account to launch Namibia's very own currency, the Namibia dollar. She was also a finalist in the Namibia Business Woman of the Year.

Family was always important to Dad and he loved the moments when everyone could come together – his 50th birthday party, his mother's 80th and then her 90th birthday party. These were all amazing experiences for me, just seeing the bond between Dad, Molly Joy, Sally Ann and Ian that had been forged in both the good times and the tough times in Queenstown.

Sally Ann and Dad had become much closer in recent years, mainly because they were meeting up more often. Initially, Mum and Dad were leaving England to make their home in Australia just when Sally Ann and Phillip were returning to Yorkshire from South Africa to carve out their lives. So contact was spasmodic. Phillip was busy building up a substantial business, and Sally Ann was preoccupied with their two boys, Richard and William.

When they went off to school, Sally Ann busied herself with different business interests. She established a flower shop, followed by an estate agency which is still flourishing today. She plays a lot of golf and bridge, and spends a lot of time making beautiful quilts. She is like Joycie, the rock around which Phillip, Richard and William gravitate. She is very proud of her family:

> Richard has married the lovely Zoe Kimberley, the best thing to happen to him and me, a simply wonderful daughter-in-law. Richard is so like my dad, Sandy, in looks, has many of Phillip's mannerisms and has a soft heart, like his mum. Richard has followed Phillip into the insurance business. Thankfully after qualifying as a game warden and a professional hunter, he went to Durham University and saw sense!
>
> William is a Greig in looks. He has finally decided to become a lawyer after many years of study at Durham and a brief sojourn working for a London charity. William amazes us with the good he does on a daily basis. He is a wonderful young man who lives his life to the full. He is a very good cricketer and has captained MCC teams on many occasions.

Sally Ann was also delighted when Phillip was honoured with the MCC presidency in 2012. This not only allowed her to see Tony much more in his last year through visits to Sri Lanka, but it also allowed Dad to come back to Lord's before he died.

One of Dad's proudest moments was being asked to give the MCC Spirit of Cricket Cowdrey Lecture at Lord's in June 2012. Obviously a lot of that pride came from the prestige attached to the event, but also because it carries the name of one of his heroes, Colin Cowdrey. The fact it was a family affair also gave Dad a lot of pleasure. The formal invitation came from his brother-in-law Phillip Hodson, as president of the MCC. It was Phillip who introduced Dad's speech, and that introduction is included in the Appendices. Dad was also able to take his wife Viv and my brother and sister, Tom and Beau, to London for the occasion. Unfortunately, Sam and I couldn't make it to Lord's, but back in Australia our families all listened online.

After Dad's recent death, I believe the family bonds have become even tighter. Emails have flown around the world from my aunts and uncle and my cousins as we have worked on this book.

And there in the centre remains the centrifugal force, as Phillip Hodson calls her – my grandmother Joycie, who will now tell the rest of the story of the Greig clan.

18

End of the Innings

ALTHOUGH SANDY AND I ULTIMATELY CAME TO SUPPORT Tony's decision to join World Series Cricket in 1977, we were over the moon when the settlement between World Series Cricket and the various cricket authorities was finally reached. First, because it was heart-wrenching to read and hear our son being maligned in the media, pubs and homes, day after day, week after week, for nearly three years. How he coped with the vitriol, particularly from former friends and close associates, was beyond us. Secondly, as cricket lovers, it hurt Sandy and me to see the cricketing establishment and WSC denigrating each other. To us, it was like a civil war, and although Tony had no doubt whatsoever that there wouldn't be any lasting damage to cricket, we weren't as confident.

The despair we carried around with us for three years soon turned to exhilaration when we started receiving letters from our eldest boy expressing his joy at his seamless transition from professional cricketer to businessman and commentator. Most parents worry about what their children are going to do with their lives after school. I am sure parents of professional sportsmen and women, who have no qualifications, worry even more. That is why Sandy and Tony had that deal – four years to make it in cricket or back to university and a teaching job at Queen's. To know that Kerry had promised Tony a job for life, and to get reassurances from Tony that he was happy in his new world, lifted a weight off our shoulders.

When Tony signed his contract with Kerry in March 1977, he had no great expectations about what his role in the Packer empire might be – he could have been sharpening the pencils! Fortunately, Tony had impressed Kerry sufficiently during the intervening three years of WSC. Accordingly, Kerry decided to throw him into the deep end as managing director of The Brokers, his new insurance broking company. In addition to that job, much to Tony's great joy, Kerry also asked him to join the Channel Nine cricket commentary team. Towards the end of the 1980s, Tony also compered the Wide World of Sports Weekend program alongside Ken Sutcliffe, one of Channel Nine's most accomplished presenters.

If Tony thought running The Brokers was going to be a doddle, he was badly mistaken. He suddenly found himself back in the all-rounder's role again, having to negotiate contracts with the insurance companies; run the sales force; speak at conferences; and to not only act in the company's television advertisements but negotiate their placement with Channel Nine boss Sam Chisholm. He sent us tapes of the advertisements and reports of how he was going. Sandy, who had worked in insurance for many years, shook his head with disbelief, advising Tony not to take credit for naming the company. He said The Brokers was a generic name and every insurance broker would benefit from the ads, but it was highly unlikely his company would. When Sandy suggested Tony change the name as soon as possible, he chose Lion Insurance Brokers because the lion dominated the African jungle.

Sandy also advised Tony not to take credit for the ads. In fact, he told Tony he didn't think anyone would want to take ownership of the ads. According to Sandy the first ad missed the mark by the proverbial mile. In the belief that high-income earners already had their own insurance brokers, the company decided to pitch the business to the masses on lower incomes who had never used an insurance broker. Despite this, the first ad featured high-profile actor Nick Tate sitting on an upmarket veranda in the posh Sydney suburb of St Ives with an Afghan dog at his feet. Sandy argued it was hardly the image that the working-class families of Sydney would identify with.

Tony was speechless at getting it so wrong. Admitting to himself that when it came to insurance his father knew best, he asked Kerry if he had any problem with bringing Sandy to Australia to help run the marketing campaigns. Kerry thought it was a good idea and Sandy and I moved to Australia in 1984. We had come out the year before for Ian and Cheryl's wedding. As well as attending the wedding, we wanted to see if we thought we could ever live in Australia. The wedding was in Brisbane and the day before, we went to the Breakfast Creek Hotel for a meal with both sets of families. Ian and Cheryl lived in a wonderful Queenslander home in Brisbane, built on stilts to let the cool air flow under the house during the hot Queensland summers. I recall a friendly little kookaburra landing on the balcony and letting out a big 'koo koo kah kah' as if to let everyone inside the house know he was there.

'What on earth is that?' I asked.

'That's Kookie our pet kookaburra,' said Ian and he went outside and began feeding it by hand.

The wedding was wonderful, very formal, the men in top hats and tails. I had a hat that matched my outfit but Sandy told me not to wear it, as nobody would wear hats in Australia. At the wedding, everyone had a hat, and I had to go and find one to keep the sun off me. It was a very hot Brisbane day.

On that trip, Sandy and I felt there was a lot about Australia we liked and living in the same country as both our sons was too appealing to resist, although we knew leaving South Africa would not be easy. It was very sad saying goodbye to everyone, especially to Molly Joy who was seven months pregnant with Alexander, her second child.

I adored her eldest boy Greig and I cuddled him and cuddled him before the time came to leave South Africa. As the train left the station in Queenstown, Molly's husband, Norman Curry, held Greig up for us to see as we waved them goodbye. While still holding up my grandson, he chased the train along the platform, blowing kisses until we were out of sight. Again a very sad departure on a train had become part of my life. Sandy and I ordered our supper to be brought to the compartment, but we didn't touch it. We just clung to each other and cried at leaving Molly Joy and all my family. We wept and wept and wept.

When we arrived in Australia we stayed in the flat out the back of Tony and Donna's house in Towns Road, Vaucluse. The Lion office was in Miller Street, North Sydney, and Sandy left home at 6am to beat traffic on the Sydney Harbour Bridge. I was left on my own, and at times I felt very lonely. I had no car, so I learnt about my new home by walking and taking the bus. I did enjoy very much being close to my grandchildren, Sam and Mark, and after a while I began to make friends. I joined the Rose Bay Bowling Club and had many wonderful times there. With the help of Tony's networks, I organised a ball to raise money for charity.

Then one day Tony rang from the Lion Insurance office. They were in trouble – their receptionist was ill. I quickly took the train to North Sydney from Edgecliff Station and stood in for the receptionist, a job that included operating the switchboard. It was very busy – Lion Insurance was growing fast. The new advertisements were working: everyone was trying to 'get the Lion on the line', as Tony used to say in the ads. The ill receptionist never returned to work, so for a while I took over full-time. But Sandy wasn't happy with me working full-time given I was now in my sixties, so we advertised for a new receptionist. The first one lasted just one day. Then along came Annette Taggart, who fitted in perfectly. I spent a week training her, and then went back to working part-time for the company.

By now both of us had fitted in very well in Australia. Sandy loved going to the Lord Dudley Hotel every Saturday where he would sit and talk to his friends, people such as Alan McGilvray, the cricket commentator. Sandy had heard him talking on the radio many times in South Africa and knew all about him. They were always joined by two or three other friends and would just talk cricket and rugby. Each one bought their own drinks; Sandy, who had not touched alcohol in over ten years, drank Coke. In later years when Sandy was becoming apprehensive about driving himself to the Lord Dudley, Tony or I drove him. He just loved the company of those men, and the things they talked about.

Once when Tony dropped Sandy off at the pub he had two tickets in his pocket to the upcoming Bledisloe Cup Rugby Test which he wasn't able to attend. One of Sandy's drinking buddies, Hamish Grieve, who had also been in the RAF, was an avid Wallabies fan so Tony offered him the tickets. Many years later when Mark ran into Hamish at the Lord Dudley and bought him a beer, he told Mark how chuffed he was that Tony had given him those tickets.

Tony would include me in everything he did. If he were taking the children to Bondi Beach, he would ask me to join them and there would not have been a time when he didn't stop at the shops and buy us all an ice-cream on the way home. When Sandy and I were living in our own unit away from Towns Road, Tony set up a special code for me. He would ring me from his home to say he was going to the beach. He would then drive to the front of our flat and call me from his car phone. There would be just two rings and that was my signal that he was out the front. Sandy didn't go with us to the beach all that often because of his fair skin.

Sadly there were dark times, too. As Mark described in an earlier chapter, Tony went guarantor for an old South African schoolfriend. He had helped him get established, which was typical of my eldest son: he would do anything to help people. However, this time it was to go way beyond helping out a friend, as Tony trustingly agreed to give a personal guarantee on a very large loan. Sandy told him not to but, in a moment of madness, Tony did. While he was commentating in England the bank rang Sandy continually saying the loan repayments were not being paid. Sandy phoned Tony's friend who assured him the money was in the post, but it never was.

Also at this time, things were not going well with Tony and Donna. Tony was working extremely hard and rarely arrived home in time to have dinner with his family. On many occasions Donna had to eat alone. One night she came to me in the flat and said, 'Tony is still not home, I'm going to bed.' I said I would wait up for him, so I went down to the house and sat in the kitchen. Tony's dog Sheba was at my feet. She always got up when Tony came home and made a fuss of him, so I knew the first sign of his arrival would be Sheba's excitement as she heard Tony's key in the front door. I waited and waited until Tony eventually came home. When I asked him where had he been, he pulled up a chair, sat down next to me and said, 'Mum, I have many friends.' Over time this became too much for Donna and in 1988 she moved out with the children, Sam and Mark.

Sandy and I moved back into the house at Towns Road after Tony and Donna had decided to separate. Donna, Samantha and Mark needed somewhere to live and we suggested they move into our unit in Woollahra. We lived with Tony until Sandy died in 1990. Sandy's death at the age of 68, on St Andrew's Day, left me absolutely devastated. He had diced with death many times in his life, even before I met him. He had crashed his plane in Southern Rhodesia when he first joined the RAF. He could have died on any one of those missions over Germany. He might have been a good navigator, but he also needed a lot of luck. More than 55,000 of his fellow Bomber Command comrades didn't share in that luck. He had almost died, too, in 1961, when he tried to take his own life. Only the great work of the medical team in Queenstown saved him on that traumatic night when Tony and I followed the ambulance to the hospital.

In 1989, he had a heart attack when we were holidaying in England and his condition was so critical Tony was told he wasn't expected to make it through the night. Tony immediately flew from Australia hoping to make it to his bedside before he died. Sandy somehow held on until Tony arrived. In a thin voice, he told Tony he loved Australia so much he wanted to die there. It was only slowly, but he did recover from the heart attack well enough for us to travel back to Australia. A friend of Tony's, Mel Gottlieb, flew with us and his kindness will always be remembered and deeply appreciated.

When Sandy went to hospital for the last time in 1990 it was for what even then was a routine operation, to have a cataract removed from his eye. After the operation, the surgeons at St Vincent's said all had gone well and I went home. That evening the phone rang. It was the hospital: Sandy was in a bad way, he had contracted pneumonia. Again Tony and I found ourselves at Sandy's bedside; it was an awful experience. He was on life support in intensive care with three specialists in attendance. They called Tony outside and spoke to him. Then Tony came back inside and told me the specialists wanted to see me, so he stayed with Sandy and I went out to see them. They told me that the life-support system was all that was keeping Sandy alive, that his kidneys had failed him.

At that time the minister from our church, St Andrew's Presbyterian Church in Rose Bay, walked in. His name was Bruce Christian, a wonderful man. I looked at the bag containing Sandy's urine. The amount of urine only measured four and I knew it was supposed to measure eleven. Bruce squeezed the tube attached to the bag to see if it could reach eleven. It didn't, Sandy's kidneys were gone.

Tony then indicated with the tip of his little finger and said to me, 'Can you tell me: has Dad got even this much to live for in this condition?' I turned to the specialists and they said: 'Not in our opinion, he hasn't, but it can only be your decision Mrs Greig.' I looked at Tony in desperation. He said, 'Mum, he's being kept alive, we're not being fair.' I had to agree. When I did, the specialists told us to go and have some last precious moments together. Sandy could only mouth words to me; I could just hear his voice. He said: 'I'm glad you are wearing my favourite dress.' Sandy's last words were to Tony. 'Look after Mum, Tony, take care of Mum.' Then they switched off the machine and he was gone, straight away.

They took us into a little parlour in the hospital where they brought us tea and some food. The sandwiches and tea could still be standing there to this day for all I know because we didn't touch them. Instead, we had the difficult job of phoning Molly Joy, Sally Ann and Ian. Sally Ann was recovering from a major operation so was unable to come to the funeral, which was held at St Andrew's, Rose Bay. Before the funeral, we went to the funeral parlour to see Sandy one last time. By now, Ian had also arrived from London, after trying desperately to be there in time for Sandy's final hours. When we got there, Sandy's coffin was draped in an RAF flag.

He had left special instructions about his funeral. He was not to be buried, and no one was to come to the crematorium. So it was a very emotional moment when the hearse pulled out of the church. For the funeral, Sandy's medals had been placed on a pillow. Mark picked up that pillow and ran to his father. Tony gave him the biggest hug and they just cried.

Afterwards we had a wake at Tony's home. I had never heard of such a thing as a wake. After a funeral in South Africa we would just have a cup of tea, but I was told in Australia it was the tradition to drink something stronger. So we had a wake and that was right, not much tea was drunk as people talked about Sandy and celebrated his life. There were a lot of people there, a lot more than either Sandy or I could have imagined when we first moved to Australia. Sandy had made many, many friends, among them the former Australian Rugby Union coach and radio broadcaster Alan Jones. On Tuesday 5 December, five days after Sandy's passing, Alan read a tribute to Sandy on his radio station. He gave Tony a recording of it and it was played to all the people at the wake. It was a magnificent eulogy played to the background music of Vera Lynn's 'We'll Meet Again' and it brought most of the guests to tears. Alan said:

A Scotsman died last Friday, on St Andrew's Day. He was only 68. He'll be buried today. He was no ordinary Scotsman. This man was, perhaps, the most Scottish you could ever get. He had a distinguished war record. He won the DFC and the DSO. He flew 54 bombing missions into Germany during the war.

341

He had a wife named Joyce, two sons and two daughters. One of the girls lives in Namibia, the other is in the United Kingdom. They won't be here today for their dad's funeral.

This Scotsman was a man of letters. He worked in South Africa for a while. He was fastidious about the use of the English language.

He was heavily involved in sport. He loved rugby and cricket. He coached both sports. He was an administrator of both in South Africa, and he was loved by blacks and whites alike because he was honest and straight. He was never intimidated by anybody. He used to live to the full the maxim of Polonius in his advice to Laertes, when Polonius said:

To thine own self be true
And it must follow as the night the day
Thou canst not then be false to any man.

As I said, he was a Scotsman. He lived in South Africa for many years, but was passionate about Australia because of his relationship with Australians during the war, but he was deep down and always, a Scot. He loved his rugby, and ever since Scotland won the grand slam of rugby in the Five Nations Championship a couple of years ago, this fellow used to wear his tartan trousers and his Scottish jumper almost every Saturday in memory of that great moment. He never went to a rugby international at Concord Oval here in Sydney because he felt that it was demeaning that such a fixture be played at such a ground.

He was ill recently when he went to England about this time last year. He didn't want to die in England. He wanted to come back to Australia.

Two more things about this bloke. He was an alcoholic once, and he told everyone about it because he kicked the habit. And he used to go to AA meetings and he supported AA because he said you needed strength and discipline to beat alcoholism – and he had both.

But I suppose his proudest moments were the fact that his two sons played Test cricket. Both for England. And one of his sons played twice for Cambridge at rugby and should have played international rugby for Scotland.

His sporting moments would have been proudest in his life because these moments involved his two sons.

The grass is a little less green today. An innings is ended. Sandy Greig will be buried today. The father of the former England captain, Tony, and the former England player, Ian. There could be no prouder Australian, nor could there be a prouder Scotsman, and certainly no prouder father.

He deserves to rest in peace.

Sandy's death was marked by a whole range of people in Australia in public tributes and private grief. A local shopkeeper not far from Towns Road, a South African man of colour to whom Sandy had offered advice when he'd first moved to Australia, broke down and cried when Ian told him of his father's death.

Ian stayed with me for a few weeks after the funeral before returning to his young family. Sally Ann replaced Ian, having made a full recovery from her operation, and helped me answer all the lovely letters and cards we received when Sandy died. I needed that help because every time I read a letter the tears would fall. I was lost, it was the most terrible time; I couldn't eat, I couldn't believe that my wonderful, darling Sandy had died. For a time I lived with Tony but eventually, a year or so later, I decided to return to South Africa to see my family and friends, many of whom I had not seen for a long time.

Tony and Donna had divorced by this stage but I felt comfortable leaving Australia because I knew Tony was now happy again and in good hands with Vivian, whom he married just before Christmas 1991. Viv had been very successful in the advertising industry and she and Tony were able to combine their skills and set up a home business together, which included the direct selling of sporting memorabilia. Viv ran the home businesses while Tony took on commentary commitments throughout the world.

Tony also worked for Epilepsy Action Australia's board. He wanted to improve the service available to people who had epilepsy, and also to remove the social stigma that is often attached to it.

Tony and Viv had two wonderful children together, Beau and Tom. Beau is very bright like her mum, and also has a beautiful singing voice. Tom, just like Tony, absolutely loves sport and has natural talent with a bat and ball. Tony took Tom to the rugby and cricket as often as possible and they watched every rugby Test on television together when they couldn't get to the game. Viv and Tony were obsessive about good manners and etiquette – former Wallabies captain Andrew Slack bumped into Beau and Tom with Channel Nine commentator Mark Nicholas on Bondi Beach once and said they were the most well-mannered children he had ever met. Tony also took Viv and the children on many of his overseas commentary trips, so they are very worldly for ones so young.

Tony would only agree to me returning to South Africa if I could be near my sister Adelaide, now Adelaide Hardwick. When the flat next to Adelaide became vacant in 1991, I flew back to South Africa, to Queenstown, my home town. But then Adelaide moved to Jeffreys Bay, on the coast, so Molly Joy arranged for me to move to a flat in Parklands, in East London.

Not long after moving back to South Africa, I went with Molly Joy and Ray and Adelaide Hardwick to the funeral of a family friend, Jimmy Arnott. There I met up with Lionel McKenzie, who was a friend of Charles Barry, my first husband all those years ago. When Lionel saw Charles soon after the funeral, he said, 'I bet you can't guess who I just saw!' Charles couldn't guess, so Lionel had to tell him: 'Joycie, Joycie Taylor.'

Well, that was it. Charles was on the phone to Adelaide's house and he spoke to my nephew, Ray. He didn't say who he was, just an old friend who had heard that Joycie was back in South Africa and he was looking to get in contact. Ray told Charles I was in Namibia with Molly Joy – I spent three months there with her and her family while mourning Sandy's passing. Charles then phoned Molly Joy in Namibia. I remember her coming to me and saying, 'Mum, there's a man on the phone for you.'

It was Charles. He said it was lovely to hear my voice, and then he told me that ever since he'd heard I was back in South Africa he'd wanted to get in contact with me so we could arrange to meet. I told him that unfortunately I couldn't see him any time soon as I was about to travel to England to see Sally Ann, and then on to Australia to sort out my possessions. He was still the old persistent Charles, the man who had convinced my parents we should be married even though he was about to go off to war; the man who had tried to talk me out of divorcing him for Sandy Greig, right up until the last moment.

He rang again the next day. That was the day we talked about a special medal he had given me all those years ago. At the time he told me I was to keep the medal and to give it back to him only when I stopped having feelings for him. It was I who brought up the subject of the medal, not because I had stopped having feelings for him, but because I thought it was something his children might want as a keepsake.

Charles said, 'Does that mean you no longer have feelings for me, Joycie?' I said no and told him again that I thought his children should have it. He then insisted I should only return the medal if I no longer had feelings for him.

Charles also told me he was moving from Johannesburg to live in Durban, on the coast, as his chest couldn't handle Johannesburg's cold climate. He asked me to come and see him in Durban, but I said no. Then not long afterwards Tony was in South Africa to commentate for a series of five Tests. I suggested to my brother Toland that we follow Tony around the country in my car.

By now, Charles was ringing me on a regular basis and asking me to come and visit him. So when Toland and I arrived in Durban for the Test match there, I contacted Charles and made arrangements to meet him at his flat.

Rather than drive myself, Tony offered to drop me off at the Holiday Inn, which was across the road from Charles's flat. I must admit I was a little nervous when I put on my make-up and used the hotel mirrors to make sure I was looking my best. I then walked over to his block of flats and asked the receptionist for Mr Charles Barry. The receptionist told me he was expecting a visitor today and that I should take the lift to his floor. The lift door opened and there he was. He put out his arms and when I walked to him he gave me a big hug and said, 'I have loved you for 50-solid years.'

We went inside his flat and talked for hours. We discussed our lives, our children and reminisced about old South Africa and all our old friends, many of whom were no longer alive. Tony had given me his mobile number so I could ring him if things didn't work out with Charles and he would pick me up. When I hadn't called hours later, he rang me to make sure everything was all right. Things were going so well I had completely lost track of time and couldn't believe we had been chatting away for so long.

Charles told me he had been married twice after our divorce in 1945. He had three children from his second marriage to Jackie. They were Janice, Glenda and Brownlee. It was obvious Charles still had strong feelings for me – I felt his love and it felt right. I knew he was such a lovely man and that love from so many years ago was also still in my heart. It felt like we were supposed to be back together; there was a bond that just pulled us close. Without too much thought we discussed moving in together, in my flat at Parklands Retirement Complex in Berea, East London. He jumped at the opportunity and so it was to be. Joycie and Charles back together again. To me it felt perfectly right as I could feel Charles' love for me. It felt nice to have that companionship after thinking I would never experience a relationship again.

I got to know Charles's family, and his children came to call me 'Magic Mum'. Charles commented to me that he felt I brought him closer to his family, which I think made him very happy in his later years. He was by now an old and frail man – not only had he spent all those years as a prisoner of war, deprived of even the basic necessities of life, he had a terrible road accident in the early 1980s which he had only just survived. To say he had his fair share of physical challenges in life would be an understatement.

Charles quickly fitted in to the community at Parklands, helping out with little jobs. To this day they still use the numbers he made for the bingo evening. So we just picked up from where we had left off all those years ago, when his unit, the Kaffrarian Rifles, had departed Pietermaritzburg and I was left to find my own way back to Queenstown. We had barely had much of a spring, and there was no summer for Charles and me, but in our autumn years, well he had loved me all of those 50-solid years and I still had that medal … I still had feelings for him.

We stayed together right up until his death from a heart attack on 31 May 2001. It was another extremely sad moment in my life. We had finished our dinner and were sitting down to talk and to have a drink. He just looked up at me and cried out, 'Oh Joycie', then slumped forward in his chair. Suddenly, he too was gone.

It is comforting for me that we had had ten final years together. I often still wonder about this wonderfully patient man, Charles Barry, who carried a flame for me for all those years. Even though I had broken his heart, there was no bitterness.

What a strange life. Married to Sandy for 45 years, but spending the last ten years with the man I previously divorced after three years spent apart during the war. It all seemed like a Wilbur Smith story, but it really happened. Life had come full circle, and I had been very fortunate to be loved by two handsome, strong men – one British and one South African.

There had been sad news of another sudden death after I returned to South Africa, that of our gardener and dear friend of the family, Tackies. In 1992 he was horrifically murdered by his girlfriend and her acquaintance. It was a dreadful death, which involved Tackies being tied up with chicken wire and having battery acid poured down his throat. Like so many murders that occur in South Africa, Tackies was killed for his possessions. They had stolen his watch that our family had given him, and also a bike that was a present from Molly Joy.

We all have so many wonderful memories of Tackies, the endless hours in the garden where he bowled to Tony and of course the visit to London in 1977 to be a part of *This Is Your Life*. It was his first time outside South Africa. Because his friends didn't believe his story, Sandy arranged for a huge television screen to be set up in the Greydene Country Club back in South Africa so they could watch Tackies' moment of fame.

In the Green Room, waiting to go into the studio for that program, he'd made a beeline for Sir Garfield

Sobers, a man of similar colour who he thought must have also flown out from Africa for Tony's program. He was desperately needing someone to talk to in his own language and immediately greeted Sir Garry in the Xhosa language. The cricketer replied, 'Sorry, sir, I do not understand a word.'

Every day during that trip to England produced some new surprise for Tackies. He had stories to tell of flying in the big silver bird, watching 'Roots' on television and telling us that Kunta Kinte deserved a beating for being cheeky to the bwana (master). He was fascinated by another television program, 'Jesus of Nazareth'. He had never seen a television before in his life. At that time television had still not come to the regions in South Africa.

After dinner on his first night in London he wanted to go to bed. We said we would follow him and he left. About twenty minutes later we found him sitting on the floor of the lift. He didn't know which button to push.

When Sally Ann took Sam, Mark and Tackies to the aquarium in Brighton people stared at them. Tackies was perplexed until Sally Ann explained to him they were only puzzled as why 'their children' were so fair-haired. The shock and horror of knowing that such a thing could be legal was too much for him!

The pigeons in Trafalgar Square fascinated him. He said that if he had them in South Africa he would never be hungry, he would just grab one, wring its neck and into the pot it would go. That was his favourite story of all the things he encountered in London. There was so much love and friendship between Tackies and the Greigs. It was sad that his life was to end so tragically and suddenly.

Then there was to be another death for which I was not prepared, something a mother can never be ready for, the death of a child, my eldest boy Tony.

The attitude to Tony in England had been mellowing over the years. Although he didn't let the establishment's ostracism worry him, he was overwhelmed when the MCC offered an olive branch by making him an honorary life member in 1998. He was just as excited in 2009 after being so well received when he spoke at a dinner in London for nineteen former England captains. Then, last year, he was asked to deliver that marvellous speech to the MCC in honour of his childhood hero, the Spirit of Cricket Cowdrey Lecture. As he was preparing for that event he had a bad cough. He was told it was bronchitis. It wasn't. Further tests when he was in Sri Lanka covering the cricket revealed he had a small malignant lesion in his right lung. In October, he was diagnosed with lung cancer, or more specifically adenocarcinoma in the pleural cavity (lining) of his lung. He had a couple of serious operations and was planning to undergo a treatment program of chemotherapy. We all knew from the outset his chances were not good, but I prayed and prayed.

It was an extraordinary three months from the diagnosis of the cancer to Tony's death. How Viv coped is beyond me. She had to look after Tony day and night; get Tom and Beau off to school and feed them; look after any overseas and local visitors who wanted to see their old friend; and also handle all the correspondence from those who couldn't make it to his bedside but sent their best wishes.

Sam and Mark were fortunate to spend a lot of time with their dad in those final months and were of great help to Viv in caring for him. She was also assisted by Ian, who would come down from Brisbane to help her with the children and also spend some quality time with his brother. They were all able to have discussions they would not otherwise have had if Tony had died tragically in a sudden accident, so they counted that as a blessing. In those final weeks they talked, laughed, cried or sometimes just sat comfortably in silence. Mark and Ian both told me how their conversations with Tony were filled with stories of family, friends and neighbours and the things they had done together. That was my son's wealth: a lifetime of memories of people and events shared with them. In those, he was truly a rich man. Mark also told me that Sam and her dad had a wonderful connection, describing how he saw much love in the way Tony held her hand during those final days. Tony really let all his children deep into his heart and expressed his love and gratitude to them openly.

Tony also spoke openly with me. I would have done anything to be there with him in person, but he insisted that international travel at my age was just too risky for my own health. He rang me every night at 10pm Sydney time and the call would usually last for about an hour. We talked about anything and everything, growing up in Queenstown, his father, playing Test cricket, what his children were up to. By now as well as Sam and Mark, of course, he had Beau and Tom. Just like Sandy, he had two sons and two daughters and you could tell he loved them all so much and was deeply proud of them.

When Tony ended these nightly conversations with me he would always call Bruce Francis. It was Bruce's job to keep Tony awake until it was time for him to take his last pills for the day, which was just before midnight. They relived every second they'd spent together over the previous 40 years. Bruce enjoyed his banter with Tony, and no doubt tried again to convince Tony that those lbw decisions back in the 1970s, when they had played against each other, were not out. Tony would not have a word of it.

It was in Tony's nature to fight against the cancer and he gave it everything he had. Channel Nine interviewed him via a live cross from the first Test against South Africa in Brisbane in November. When Mark Nicholas asked him how he was going he responded with his usual honesty – he had a fight on his hands.

Every operation was a dangerous one, but he was prepared to have them all, so strong was his desire to go on living. He had so much more he wanted to do. He still loved travelling the world and commentating. Because of his illness, he knew he would have to miss the first series in Australia. That really hurt because it was the South Africans who were touring. He loved upsetting his fellow commentators by barracking for England or South Africa whenever they were in Australia. During his call with Bruce two days before he died he said that David Gyngell, the CEO of Channel Nine, had asked him if he were up to doing one session of commentary during the Sydney Test that was to start on 3 January. Tony thought he was and was desperately keen to do it, not just for himself, but because he wanted to keep the continuity of his employment in the Channel Nine commentary team. It was also a major attraction to Tony that the other team touring Australia that summer was from his beloved Sri Lanka. The Sydney Test would be a chance to catch up with many of his Sri Lankan friends again.

The morning of 29 December 2012 was not all that different from previous mornings of that month. Tony had spent a very emotional Christmas with his family. The reality of his situation was starting to take hold of him. Mark shared with us all overseas a wonderful photo of the family together at Mark and Angela's house in Sydney on Christmas Day. I was thrilled that Tony was up and about after his most recent operation and could join the family for Christmas lunch. Mark set up a video camera in the corner of his lounge room and pointed it at his dad all day, recording Tony's every move. Apparently he was full of joy opening his Christmas presents and interacting with his five young grandchildren. Sam was there as well, having flown down from Gunnedah with her son and daughter, Hugh and Sophie. Tony had all his four children together on Christmas Day. It was really lovely.

However, Tony's breathing was not right, and I now know that some fluid had returned to his lungs. Mark had driven him out to watch Tom play cricket the previous weekend. Just the simple act of walking from the car across the field to where Tom was playing left Tony breathless and exhausted. He so enjoyed being there to support Tom, but he really wasn't well. Apparently it didn't stop him sharing a beer with the other dads, though.

The two operations Tony had on his lungs were supposed to stop the fluid getting in and allow him to get himself well enough to undergo chemotherapy treatment. He had Stage 4 cancer, so there was not a huge amount of confidence among his doctors. However, he was prepared to fight it, and after his first dose of chemo he told me that he was feeling surprisingly well, although he was having some difficulty with his breathing. Mark told me about the terrible morning of 29 December and although I wanted to share Tony's last hours with you, I just couldn't get past the first two sentences before the tears made it impossible for me to write, or even speak. I therefore asked Mark if he could pick up the story before handing back to me to complete our tale.

Dad was still in bed at home on that last day when Sam and I arrived for our morning visit. He was at his best in the morning and often had a rest in the afternoon. He loved his morning coffee, which we usually picked up from his favourite coffee shop in Rose Bay. This time he wanted Sam to make him a home brew, plenty of sugar as always. We spent the next couple of hours talking to him by his bedside. Viv made him a bowl of porridge and Tom brought him up a bowl of diced watermelon. I had found an online video with lots of footage of Bomber Command in World War Two. We lay in Dad's bed and watched this video together on my iPad, pausing it on occasion so he could look closely at the RAF crews to try to identify Sandy in the many photos. Dad shed a tear, and commented to me about how brave his father was, and how terrible it must have been for such young men, some only seventeen years old, to experience the terrors of war.

Dad then received a call from an old friend, Allan Sawyer. Allan was concerned about him and was hoping to pay him a visit. Never one to knock back company, Dad agreed and suggested Allan come immediately so he could have a rest later. When Allan arrived Dad just wasn't feeling well enough to get himself downstairs. However, with a little encouragement from us, he was determined to give it a try so we helped him into his robe. Viv, Sam and I managed to walk him slowly to the top of the stairs, but he couldn't go any further. He was absolutely exhausted and I was worried he might pass out and collapse down the stairs. We quickly brought in the oxygen machine and tried to calm him down, as he was starting to panic about his breathing. After sitting down for five minutes at the top of the stairs, it was decided that he should make his way back to his bed, where he could lie down comfortably and slowly get his breath back.

By the time he was back in his bedroom he was completely spent. We took his dressing gown off and sat him on the side of his bed. He couldn't even pull himself up onto his bed, he just lay on his back diagonally across it. He started to panic about his breathing and then all of a sudden lost consciousness. He was having a seizure. After a few minutes he came round and was feeling a little hazed, though a lot less stressed about his breath than before he went into the seizure. He got comfortable on his bed and I played a few Dean Martin songs on my phone, to try to relax him a little. Dad looked up at me with a big smile and gave me the thumbs-up. He approved of my choice of music and in a soft croaky voice said, 'Lovely, mate.' These were his last words to me.

Dad wasn't back in bed for long, resting without talking, when he started panicking again about his breathing. He couldn't get enough oxygen into his lungs, even with the machine on its highest flow setting. All of a sudden he fell into a big seizure. This one was more serious and he didn't look like he was coming out of it at any stage. We all started to panic. He was now in a serious way. Using my mobile phone I called for an ambulance and took verbal instructions (on loudspeaker) as we tried desperately to revive him. There was no heartbeat. I was told I had to get Dad down onto the floor so that I could do CPR on a hard surface. Somehow I managed to lift my 300-pound father off his bed and place him on the floor. I then started CPR and continued chest compressions for the next five minutes or so. Viv and Sam quickly ran downstairs to open the front and back doors for the paramedics. It felt like eternity before the ambulance arrived and they pulled me off my father, just lying there so helpless. They hooked him up to their equipment and after a few attempts with the defibrillator he had a pulse, though they said it was only faint. He was fighting; that huge heart wasn't going to give up easily. The paramedics tried desperately to keep that pulse going while they carried him down the stairs and out the back gate to where the ambulance was waiting. Before they loaded him in, with tears streaming down my face, I leant over and said, 'I love you, mate, thank you for everything. I love you.' I kissed him on his forehead and squeezed his hand. The ambulance tore off with sirens blaring. They were still working on Dad when he arrived at St Vincent's Hospital, but there was nothing anyone could do for him. He was gone. That big heart that had kept his big body going had stopped. We were all shattered, and the world of cricket was in mourning.

In the weeks that followed many tributes flowed, many fine words were written about my son, what he had done on and off the cricket field. To read them was of some comfort. To know that he was honoured and revered at more than one memorial service was another comfort. I could not have been prouder of him, and I know that if Sandy had been alive he would have felt exactly the same. But I will always miss Tony, I will always miss the way he loved his mum, all those delightful conversations we had when he was a little boy, and all the conversations we had when he was ill, and he would phone me.

And I will always remember the last words I ever spoke to him. They came on 28 December: 'God bless you my darling son, now turn over, say your prayers and go to sleep and remember always that I love you.'

Appendices

2012 MCC Spirit of Cricket Cowdrey Lecture

Delivered by Tony Greig at Lord's on 26 June 2012, introduced by Phillip Hodson, MCC president

I thought it appropriate to remind the assembled audience of Tony's figures because they sometimes get forgotten amidst the hoi polloi of today and the number of games that are played today.

Tony played 58 Test matches for England. He scored 3600 runs at an average of above 40. He then took 141 wickets at 32 and took 87 catches in those 58 matches.

That's quite an astounding all-round record.

More particularly, Tony is not the first guest speaker at this lecture who was born in South Africa. Of course we have had Bishop Tutu and Barry Richards.

He is not the first speaker to have captained England. We had Geoffrey Boycott who from memory we allowed to captain England on two occasions.

He's not the first speaker to reside in Australia. We've had Adam Gilchrist.

He's not the first speaker to have played for World Series Cricket. We've had Clive Lloyd and others.

And he's not the first speaker to have spent the last 30 years absolutely on the front line broadcasting and commentating about the game he loves because we've had Richie Benaud. But I tell you what, he is the first speaker we have had who combines all those attributes.

It is a great pleasure tonight, I can think of nobody better to deliver the Cowdrey Spirit of Cricket Lecture than Tony Greig.

Mr President, My Lords, Ladies and Gentlemen.

Thank you for inviting me to give the MCC Spirit of Cricket Cowdrey Lecture. I consider it an honour to acknowledge Colin and to have the opportunity to share with you some of my experiences as well as some thoughts on the game we all love.

I noticed that both Martin Crowe and Adam Gilchrist paid tribute to their families at the start of their speeches so I trust you will indulge me if I do the same. I should like to thank my wife Vivian for her patience and help in putting this lecture together. I should also like to thank my children Beau and Tom, who are here with me tonight, and Samantha and Mark, who are embracing the spirit of cricket by listening to this lecture the way we used to listen to the Tests 60 years ago in the early hours of the morning. Without their love, support and understanding of the demands cricket makes on family time, I would not have been able to enjoy all that cricket has given me.

When I received my invitation I immediately wrote

down ten topics I wanted to address. However, after a month's reflection, I thought I shouldn't indulge myself and that it was more appropriate to confine my speech to the spirit of cricket. However, since arriving in England, I have been told repeatedly by a wide range of people that before speaking about the spirit of cricket, I must explain my reasons for sacrificing the most coveted role in world cricket, the England captaincy, to become involved with an Australian television tycoon. A quote from the transcript of my meeting with Kerry Packer, five days after the Centenary Test on 22 March 1977, gives the best insight into how I felt at the time:

'Kerry, money is not my major concern. I'm nearly 31 years old. I'm probably two or three Test failures from being dropped from the England team. Ian Botham is going to be a great player and there won't be room in the England Test side for both of us. England captains such as Tony Lewis, Brian Close, Colin Cowdrey, Ray Illingworth and Mike Denness all lost the captaincy long before they expected. I won't be any different. I don't want to finish up in a mundane job when they drop me. I'm not trained to do anything. I went straight from school to playing for Sussex. I am at the stage in my life where my family's future is more important than anything else. If you guarantee me a job for life working for your organisation, I will sign.'

The previous season's cricket with Waverley in the Sydney grade competition created a great thirst to work in Australia. I was not only paid around £50,000 for five months' work but more excitingly, I mixed work-wise and socially with a number of Australia's leading businessmen. This opened my eyes to a world that I didn't know existed.

Obviously, there were also key issues with the England administrators that disturbed me, which I felt would never be resolved. I couldn't understand why we were only paid £210 a Test when we were playing in front of packed houses. The psyche of the administrators, the vast majority of whom I regarded as good friends, was that the honour of playing for England was enough – money shouldn't be a consideration. Consequently, I couldn't see an end to the game underselling itself and there appeared to be no hope of expanding the revenue base for Test and county players alike, unless there was a revolution, or at least a big upheaval. Having to make changes to innocuous sentences in my books and newspaper articles at the behest of the TCCB was a source of irritation. And having to get permission to take wives on tour and paying more for friends' tickets to the Centenary Test than I was paid for playing in it, also didn't help.

I have never had any doubt that I did the right thing by my family and by cricket. I have worked for Kerry Packer's organisation for 35 years and my family's future has been secured. After the initial nastiness and internal feuding, cricket and cricketers also did quite well out of World Series Cricket (WSC):

- WSC ensured cricket reinvented itself to survive the changing world;
- WSC was the jolt the administrators needed, and it flagged the message that they were substantially underselling the sport to the television stations;
- Players immediately received substantially more money at both Test and first-class level, which increased the longevity of their careers;

- Companies saw value in using cricket as a marketing tool;
- TV coverage improved significantly, which increased interest in the sport;
- Night cricket created a new audience, both television-wise and at the ground, and generated significantly more income;
- WSC revolutionised cricket pitch preparation through the drop-in pitches;
- Cricket's success inspired other sports to imitate cricket with things such as TV coverage and sponsorships.

I only have two regrets about World Series Cricket. EW Swanton was very good to me throughout my career and I am saddened that despite numerous attempts by me, I never had a chance to make peace with him after World Series Cricket. Second, I had a wonderful relationship with the chairman of selectors, Alec Bedser, which continued through and beyond World Series Cricket. I know Alec understood why, but I dearly would like to have told him of my plans before they became public. However, I promised Kerry I wouldn't.

I have some great WSC anecdotes and I'm happy to share them with you, as well as address any other WSC issues in question time, if you so wish.

I played with and against Colin. In so many ways he embodied all that is good about cricket. There could be no better person after whom to name this lecture. As a batsman he was calmness and gracefulness themselves. On and off the field, I don't think you could find a more courteous person than Colin. Who else would have called Jeff Thomson 'Mr Thomson'?

In the 1990s, Colin and another hero of mine, former Sussex and England captain Ted Dexter, were so concerned about the decline in sportsmanship in cricket, they campaigned successfully to have a description of the spirit of cricket included in the preamble to the laws of the game. We are indebted to both of them for their work.

When you talk about the spirit of cricket you are talking about not just the game, but a way to live your life; you are talking about embracing the traditions of the game and sharing your experiences with friends and cricket lovers alike; you are talking about caring for people less fortunate than us. This has been done for years through organisations such as the MCC, the Lord's Taverners and the Primary Club, and more recently through foundations and organisations set up by many players.

The spirit of cricket is not just about adhering to the laws of the game. It's about something far more enduring: adhering to a set of values that can elevate you above the humdrum, above the cynicism that can drag you down if you let it. It not only covers uniting the various peoples in countries such as India, Sri Lanka and the countries of the West Indies, but it also brings light into the lives of hundreds of millions of people in those countries as well as in Pakistan and Bangladesh. In particular, the spirit of cricket is also about putting the game's interests before your or your country's interests.

Many people have romanticised our game because it does lend itself to that. Which other sport can generate substantial newspaper column inches over the equivalent of the suspense created by five successive maidens?

Cricket is also a partnership, and like all partnerships there is give and take. Sometimes cricket can feel like it has given you everything, the moment when you score a Test 100 or score the winning run on the village green when you were batting at number eleven. At other times, it gives you nothing. A string of ducks or a dropped catch. But as with all great loves, you never walk away. You accept the bad times, the sacrifices that you make to participate in this wonderful game, the one the poets call the summer game. Give your hand to cricket and it will take you on the most fantastic journey, a lifetime journey both on and off the field. That is what it has done for me and I suspect for most of you.

People around the world love sport, but none, in my experience, in the same profound way that people love cricket and what it stands for. I love cricket because apart from the skill required to succeed, it is a great leveller. It is also a wonderful test of temperament and a test of courage. I love it for the people it has introduced me to − lifelong friendships with people from across the globe. I particularly love it for the opportunities it provides for old folk like us to get together as we have done today. I love it for the wonderful spectacle it continues to be in a world that is changing so fast. In the world of Facebook, the web, Twitter, text messages and tattoos, you still can't see anything to match the rhythms of a Test match. Cricket moves to charm, and even in the 21st century, it still has the grace of timelessness.

Yehudi Menuhin once said of one of Beethoven's greatest works, the 'Pastoral', that Beethoven wrote it, but God approved it. Whether it's a game of cricket on an English green, an Indian maidan, a Caribbean beach, an Australian park, or right here at Lord's with the ancient pavilions looking on, I believe that is so true of cricket. We humans created cricket, but God approved it.

It has its scandals, it has its challenges fitting into a 21st-century world where a lot of me-first values of different generations clash with the distinctive beauty of cricket. But people still play and follow cricket in remarkable numbers because their relationship to it is different from any other game.

We have in our audience people of greatness in their chosen fields, music, the arts, business, science and politics. Offer them the chance to play a village green match tomorrow and they will invent any excuse to get out of the office. You can play and love cricket with the same deep-rooted attachment at any level.

And here's another thing that makes our game unique. One of the first things scientific researchers do when they start a project is to 'read the literature', to find out what is already known. When it comes to 'the literature', no other sport, not even the Americans with Red Smith and Roger Kahn, has ever produced anything as magnificent as cricket's great writers. Heading them up, the incomparable Cardus and the poet Arlott.

I preface the following comments by saying I have only considered our game from the narrow perspective of the ten Full Members of the ICC. Lord Woolf in his recent report to the ICC looked at the global picture and took into account the views of the 95 associate and affiliated members of the ICC and consequently has a more negative view than I.

I believe our game is in reasonably good shape. More people play it than ever before. Run rates are often substantially higher than in the 'golden years' of cricket.

More women are involved as both players and spectators. Television audiences are up substantially. We have expanded our product range – Tests, ODIs and Twenty20s – to cater for the different needs of players and spectators alike. Global revenue has gone through the roof. Substantially more players make a decent living – crikey, the England players even have food tasters and someone to tuck them into bed at night. In the old days people used to say the sun never set on the British Empire. Today, cricket has grown so much that it is probably watched on television somewhere in the world 24 hours a day. Sure there are issues that need attention, some even urgent attention, but this has always been the case. This is part of the evolution of any game.

At the risk of oversimplifying things, the major problems facing cricket at the moment are: the decline in the image of cricket; ICC's control; the international calendar and the mix of different types of cricket; gambling; the Decision Review System; governance; unequal resources; and the possibility of India cherry-picking the Woolf Report to increase its power.

Fortunately, I think most of the problems can generally be addressed if India invokes and adheres to the spirit of cricket. Mahatma Gandhi said, 'A nation's culture resides in the hearts and in the soul of its people.'

As cricket certainly resides in the hearts and souls of Indian people I am optimistic India will lead cricket by acting in the best interests of all countries rather than just for India. If there is proof of the leadership India can provide it is the recent announcement of a one-time benefit payment of $13 million to former national and domestic players for their services to Indian cricket. This certainly exemplifies acting in the spirit of cricket and rewards those players who played before 2003 for little financial reward. That people like Chandrasekhar, Prasanna, Borde and Nadkarni will have this sort of financial support as they cope with the onset of the years is a powerful sign that India can not only generate great wealth for the game, but use it wisely for the benefit of cricket and cricketers.

Almost since its inception cricket has been synonymous with fair play. 'It's not cricket' – another way of saying 'it's not right' – was an expression used throughout the English-speaking world – not just in cricket-playing countries. It was a gentleman's game. More than any other sport, the people who played and the people who followed cricket knew they were special. Along the way my generation decided that the game would be more exciting and more testing if we turned the heat up on the funny quips and used them to intimidate the opposition.

History suggests most players of mine and subsequent generations also embraced the new gladiatorial environment. On reflection, I wouldn't have had it any other way. But I have to acknowledge that we not only breached the spirit of cricket but it was probably a selfish attitude.

As a result of sledging, I don't think following generations inherited a game that was as special in the community's eyes that my generation inherited. Sadly, these days, captains don't earn or receive the same adulation that Richie Benaud and Sir Frank Worrell rightly received in their day. Players also no longer have the same relationships with each other that, say, Keith Miller and Denis Compton had. Crikey, at times when I watched Ricky Ponting and Duncan Fletcher, who was sitting in the stand, and Andrew Symonds and

Harbhajan Singh on the field, I thought I was back in the 1960s and 1970s watching Billy Bremner and Nobby Stiles chopping down opponents.

I suspect who runs cricket and how well it has been run have been contentious issues since the beginning of time. Irrespective of the existence of the ICC or its forerunners, for about the first hundred years cricket was run by England and Australia. Both countries, proud advocates of democracy, ironically even had a veto on the ICC or its equivalent. Unfortunately, on many occasions self-interest was more important than the spirit of cricket and countries such as India and New Zealand were undoubtedly discriminated against.

Before examining the specific issues, we must acknowledge and praise India for embracing the spirit of cricket through the financial opportunities it provides, which has enabled a number of Test-playing countries to survive, and some to thrive. World cricket would be in a sorry state if it weren't for the money shared with other countries from India's television deals. You can imagine the indebtedness to India of those cricket boards, which are able to negotiate a tour with the Board of Control for Cricket in India (BCCI) to their country. It generates a spike in the host country's revenue that they will not see until India chooses to come again.

World cricket would also struggle if India didn't have such sophisticated administrators as it does. More recently, India has found a way to involve its wealthiest entrepreneurs and Bollywood stars through the ownership of its IPL teams.

Today, many people level the problems of the game with the ICC. Technically, they are correct but in practice most members of the ICC have little control over many of the important issues of the game. Currently, there are ten full members of the ICC and the constitution requires the approval of 70 per cent, or seven members, to advance any motion, which means 40 per cent, or four members, can block any motion.

Much of the game is controlled by the BCCI because it controls enough votes to block any proposal put forward at the ICC board meetings. The reason for this is some countries would not survive without the financial opportunities India provides. What is just as disturbing is through the Champions League, South Africa and Australia have a partnership with India and are unlikely to risk offending India. The current Champions League ten-year contract generates just under a billion dollars and is 50 per cent owned by India, with Australia and South Africa sharing the rest.

As a result of the dependence on India the process adopted by the ICC is simply not working. The ICC cricket committee, for example, is made up of a group of top-class current and former players and umpires. They go to great lengths to make recommendations that they consider in the best interests of the game.

These recommendations are then submitted to the CEO's committee for approval, which normally happens as a formality. The recommendations are then raised at the ICC board meeting and if India doesn't like them, they are, at best, modified or thrown out. It's a sorry state of affairs and very frustrating for those who give so much time to getting things right.

India's apparent indifference towards Test cricket and its response towards some of the key issues – the international calendar and the mix of the different types of cricket;

its attitude to the earlier ICC corruption inquiries; its indifference to the urgency to introduce anti-doping rules; the rumoured corruption hanging over the IPL; its attitude to the Decision Review System; and its role in the lack of due process in stopping former Australian prime minister John Howard being appointed vice president of the ICC – are all examples of disappointing decisions. But many of the problems with the ICC could be resolved if India invoked the spirit of cricket and didn't try [to] influence its allies in how to vote.

In my view, every international team should be required to play at least three Tests, three ODIs and three Twenty20 matches against all the other teams in a given home-and-away cycle. The Future Tours Program is managed by the ICC and it provides guidelines to its members. The ICC tries to impose 'minimums'.

However, the various 'big guns' didn't like the idea of being tied to these 'minimums' so they agreed to the minimums but introduced an 'unless otherwise agreed clause', which in effect allows all full members to do as they please.

In a perfect world no consideration should be given to any domestic tournaments – that is IPL, Big Bash, Champions League, etc. – before the international calendar is set in stone. No domestic competitions should take precedence over international matches. Unfortunately, India is preoccupied with money and Twenty20 cricket, and sees its IPL and Champions League as more important than a proper international calendar. To compound the problems, India has not only sold part of the game to private interests but some of her administrators are seen to have a conflict of interest, which makes it more difficult for it to act in the spirit of the game.

Twenty20 has played a crucial role in creating interest in cricket to a new audience. The funds it generates at both international and domestic levels also helps underwrite all other cricket. The IPL has produced a wonderful opportunity for players from all cricketing countries to mix in a way that Martin Luther King would never have dreamed. But the IPL is too long in its current form; many players are paid ridiculous sums of money; young players are brought from other countries when they should be learning their craft in their domestic competitions; and the Indian board is more beholden to the private franchise owners than it is to fellow ICC members.

The net result of this is Test cricket is suffering; some players appear not to have the same feeling for Test matches as their predecessors; there are more and more meaningless ODI matches; governing bodies have lost some control of their players; and some players are abandoning their responsibilities to their home countries.

We can huff and puff as much as we like and have all sorts of external reports but this situation can only be resolved by India accepting that the spirit of cricket is more important than generating billions of dollars; it's more important than turning out multi-millionaire players; and it's more important than getting square with Australia and England for their bully-boy tactics towards India over the years. It's ironic that the world, including India, rightly worships at the Nelson Mandela altar because of his conciliatory attitude but then India eschews his approach by indulging in a little payback.

Although the current Test ranking system is working well, I think a play-off for the Test crown is essential.

Test cricket is still paramount in England, South Africa and Australia but disappointingly it is no longer as important in India as it once was. Sadly, Pakistan can't play Tests at home and the West Indies has big problems, which have diminished the standing of their Tests. The euphoria in India after it won the ODI World Cup was amazing. That euphoria was not duplicated when India became number one in the Test rankings. Cricket will only have its priorities right when Pakistan and the West Indies are given a helping hand and their Tests become more meaningful, and when Indian players and people celebrate success at Test level as much as it did when it won the ODI World Cup. That can probably only happen by having a play-off for Test supremacy, say once every four years. The ICC's internal executive was bitterly disappointed that India was responsible for canning the scheduled 2013 Test championship. Unless India embraces the spirit of cricket I wouldn't hold my breath about the scheduled 2017 Test championship being played.

I was involved in the embryonic stages when Channel Nine developed tools to aid the viewer in judging umpiring decisions, and have been a passionate supporter of the Decision Review System (DRS). I do, however, accept that it is hard to argue against people such as Rodney Cavalier, current chairman of the Sydney Cricket Ground Trust, who, in opposing the DRS, said: 'Cricket is fantasy. It is the intersection of Heaven and Earth, it cannot ever be the slave of certainty. The essence of cricket is honour and accepting the umpire's decision.'

Having acknowledged that, I would still argue that it is just as important to get the decisions correct. It can't be good for the game when the media devotes so many words and so much ink to bad decisions, which ultimately undermines the integrity of some results. The DRS is not perfect, but it does err in favour of the umpires' decisions and according to the ICC, fewer mistakes are made with its use. And furthermore, there is less conflict on the ground.

India has two reasons for opposing it: One, because its superstars had such an embarrassing experience with it in the early days. Two, the BCCI argues that the DRS is too inexact. Ironically, the spirit of cricket is batting on both sides in this one. The Cavalier approach says DRS is not in the spirit of cricket, but on the other hand, the Indian superstars should act in the spirit of cricket and accept the majority viewpoint.

These days you can't talk about cricket without dwelling on the ongoing damage match fixing or game manipulation has caused the sport. I share the world's view that it is repugnant and the cricket administrators should adopt a zero-tolerance policy.

Currently, all ICC Member player contracts contain clauses prohibiting match fixing, etc., and all contracted players are required to sign off on the education program provided by the ICC, prior to taking part in any international match. The boards have also spelt out exactly what a player's obligations are if any approach is made by anyone in relation to corruption. For example, there is an ICC Anti-Corruption and Security representative at every international match. Players are encouraged to go to either their management, or alternatively, go directly to the ICC Anti-Corruption and

Security representative. Sadly, this hasn't been sufficient to eliminate corruption.

Short of all players agreeing to take lie detector tests, I don't know how corruption can be eliminated completely. I think all players should agree to take lie detector tests and all should agree that if they failed the tests, they would give the officials access to their bank account records and phone records. My expectation is that only a handful of players might fail the test and therefore it would not be an onerous commitment by 99.9 per cent of the players.

Some players embrace the bookies or their representatives for financial gain or because of threats to their family or because a young, naïve player feels beholden to a captain he idolises. Ironically, I think taking lie detector tests would be in the interests of the vulnerable players because it would lessen the chances of approaches from bookies and captains. Knowing that they would be caught through the lie detector tests would lessen the chances of the players trying to either make a quick dollar or capitulating to the bookmakers' threats. Obviously, agreeing to take lie detector tests would be a huge invasion of privacy – but no more so than accepting strangers knocking on your door at 5am asking you to provide a urine sample.

It's a huge sacrifice but I think it would be in the spirit of cricket for the players to agree to it.

I should like to express my dismay at not only the proliferation of external reports telling us what changes need to be made, but also governments throughout the cricket world telling us how to run the game. I don't know whether current administrators lack the knowledge and courage to make decisions for the sport. Perhaps it's both or more likely they are being sneaky in pushing responsibility for unpopular decisions to an external source.

In recent times Cricket Australia, the ECB and the ICC all commissioned external reports. The ICC investigation was undertaken by Lord Woolf, and his key recommendations were never going to be accepted.

Basically, Lord Woolf was recommending the equivalent of the United States, Russia, China, United Kingdom and France giving up their vetoes in the Security Council, or the House of Lords voting itself out of existence.

Believe it or not, the reason for outside independent 'expert' reports is that anything put forward by, say, the ICC executive is perceived to be an agenda driven by someone. What a sorry state of affairs. What a copout. I want cricket people running cricket in the best interests of cricket, not outsiders reading from a textbook.

Over the years cricket has been severely damaged by government interference in South Africa, Pakistan, Sri Lanka, Zimbabwe and India. England has been subjected to government interference and recently the Australian government urged Cricket Australia to improve its governance. Obviously, all cricketing boards need to comply with the laws of the land, re corruption, etc., and all need to improve their governance, but the governance should be done at their own initiative and members' behest, and not with governments holding a gun at their heads.

There is obviously a substantial difference in available resources between the haves – India, England, Australia and South Africa – and the have-nots – West Indies, Pakistan, New Zealand, Sri Lanka, Bangladesh and Zimbabwe. This creates many problems. The have-nots' youngsters are less likely to be attracted to cricket; it is far more difficult for those countries to develop the players; and perhaps more importantly, players from the have-not countries are more likely to be attracted to the big money in Twenty20 competitions than in playing Tests for their own countries. Once again, this problem could be addressed if all countries invoked the spirit of cricket and made some sacrifices. The following comments provide a solution to my earlier observations about the International calendar and the IPL, and, paradoxically, the IPL might just provide a solution.

One, India should agree to reduce the length of the IPL in its current form as a trade-off for the other countries not scheduling Internationals in opposition to it. That is, unless it adopts my Asian League proposal, which I shall discuss in a minute.

Two, Sri Lanka, Bangladesh, New Zealand and the West Indies agree not to schedule any Internationals in opposition to the IPL. These countries will never be able to generate enough income to make Internationals in the long term more attractive to their players than the IPL money.

Three, India should agree to expand the IPL to, say, an Asian League and include extra teams from Sri Lanka, Bangladesh and Pakistan. The cricket boards of these countries should be given a financial interest in the competition, which would enable them to underwrite most of their cricket. Those funds would compensate the boards for not running domestic Twenty20 competitions of their own as they are planning to do now.

This expanded league would enable players from the have-not countries to earn good money and still be available for Internationals.

Four, England should set up its equivalent of the IPL and include teams from the West Indies and one team from Ireland, which would have a financial interest in the competition. Similar arrangements should be made by South Africa for Zimbabwe and Kenya. And Australia's Big Bash should include New Zealand teams.

Five, world cricket should do everything possible to not only help the West Indies become a dominant Test force again, but to ensure Pakistan cricket survives the extraordinary situation it finds itself in.

As I have expressed a number of times throughout this speech, I believe most of the existing problems can be solved by India if it embraces the spirit of cricket and leads for world cricket, not just for India. However, there is a potential problem, which would diminish my optimism. Lord Woolf recommended that the President of the ICC become a ceremonial role and that a new position of an independent Chairman be created. He recommended that the Chairman serve for three years and that the position be remunerated.

This person would be the most powerful person in world cricket. Although India has rejected the Woolf Report, I am concerned that it will cherry-pick and support this recommendation, or a watered-down version, in a motion to change the existing constitution. India has enough clout to control the position.

I should like to conclude by saying that cricket, a 19th-century game, has survived and thrived into the 21st century because the spirit of cricket has been just as special to cricket-playing countries as democracy and Shakespeare have been to the world. Cricket as we know and love it has plenty of problems. Most of those problems can best be solved if the ICC members put the game's interests before their own interests; if India accepts the survival of Test cricket is non-negotiable; if India accepts its responsibility as leader of the cricket world; if it embraces Nelson Mandela's philosophy of not seeking retribution; and if it embraces the spirit of cricket and governs in the best interests of world cricket, not just for India and its business partners.

All those things need to be addressed so that cricket's own great journey can continue – the one that began on the Wealds of Kent and the Downs of Hampshire, and of course found its way north, so that that canny Yorkshireman Captain James Cook could set it off towards Australia and New Zealand. And it has found its way to the East and West Indies and my native South Africa and they're beginning to play it in all sorts of other exotic locations.

What we have is a game with its roots deep in the 19th century, but like a magnificent English oak, continues to spread its luxuriant branches in the 21st century. If we want our children's children's children to be able to climb on that tree, share in what we are lucky enough to share in, in this room today, we must do everything in our power to ensure that the tree can live. To do that, no matter where we come from in the world, no matter what our religion or our hue, we must be guided by the paramount and enlightening thing that Colin Cowdrey knew and cherished so well. The Spirit of Cricket.

Tributes to Tony Greig

'I was blessed to know Greigy, we all were', by Bill Lawry, *The Australian*, 31 December 2012

I've lost one of my best mates, the game has lost one of its greats. This is going to be a hard Test.

Sydney was Tony's town and we were all going out to visit him when we got there. Every Sydney Test, he put on a party at his house and it was the highlight of our time up there.

He was a generous man, a gracious host and he loved to bring cricket people together. I find myself talking about him these past few days as a cricketing ambassador.

I'm going to miss the routines we had. For 33 years at every venue other than Sydney or Melbourne he would drive me to the ground, Richie joined us a bit later on in the car, but Tony always drove. He liked to be at the wheel.

He could find his way to any ground in the world.

He was a great friend, we were a lot closer than you might think.

Tony was an entertainer on air, but I hope he is not just remembered for the pitch report or the car keys because his knowledge of the game was fantastic and it started from the fact that he was a very good cricketer.

Greigy played well in India, he scored centuries against almost all countries, he was a wonderful all-rounder, a brilliant slip fieldsman and an agile bat pad.

He was always talking to people at airports, it didn't matter who they were, they got a big smile and a handshake.

I think he would have loved to play cricket all his life, but when he couldn't he threw himself into commentating for us, writing for Cricinfo, working for broadcasters everywhere, he just wanted to be part of the game.

Don't get me wrong, though, he was a tough competitor – as tough as they came on the field.

I remember him in 1974 playing against Thommo and Lillee when he took them on in Brisbane in the first Test of the Ashes.

I think he was as frightened as the rest of us would have been against those two on that wicket, but he put on a brave front and gave as good as he got. He thrashed that magnificent 100 in the first innings. He got them both worked up and they dropped short and he hit fours all over the place.

Chappelli told them in the second that they might be better off pitching it up to the big gangly bloke and Thommo knocked him over with the sandshoe crusher for two.

I remember laughing when he wore that helmet to face Lillee at Gloucester Park in the World Series game, but they're all wearing them now. Tony didn't mind being laughed at.

Australians loved to hate him because they knew he was in their face, but they saw something of themselves in him. I remember him telling me how he turned to a teammate when the England team flew over the harbour into Sydney once and announced that this was the place he was going to live – that was before World Series.

He loved the water, he loved Bondi, he loved those bloody dangerous things, those Jet Skis, he was into snorkelling and all that stuff.

He was larger than life and I can see why Kerry Packer took to him, it wasn't just the cricket connection.

I am really going to miss him and I think we all are. He had taken to bringing his son Tom to the box in Sydney and he was a lovely kid with great manners and his young daughter Beau would come to our place during the Melbourne Test and play with our grandkids. They were a credit to Tony and Viv, those kids.

It's a very sad time, but we had 33 years of great times in Australia and England and I was blessed to know him. I think we all were.

'Outsider Tony Greig made English cricket great through inspirational leadership', by Mike Atherton, *The Times*, 1 January 2013

Mike Selvey, the former England bowler who is now cricket correspondent of *The Guardian*, called Tony Greig the most inspirational captain he had played under – quite a compliment when you consider that Selvey played most of his county career at Middlesex under Mike Brearley, widely considered to be the best England captain of modern times.

It takes all types, of course, but if the character of England captains could be measured on a scale, then Brearley and Greig would be at opposite ends of it. Brearley:

bookish, thoughtful, measured – albeit with a volcanic temper – and apt to winkle the best out of people by psychological assessment. Greig: brash and colourful with a preference for dragging players with him by the force of his personality.

In the 33 years that Greig fashioned himself into something of the voice of cricket for the Nine Network in Australia and the subcontinent, where they preferred his over-the-top style and gimmickry to Richie Benaud's cool dispassion it is sometimes forgotten just what an outstanding cricketer he was. Captain, swashbuckler, medium pacer, fast off spinners, brilliant close catcher, there was little on the field that Greig could not turn his hand to with skill and style and success.

'Fearless' is a word that has been used in many of the tributes paid over the weekend, particularly by Dennis Lillee, to whom Greig squared up in that iconic Ashes battle of 1974–75. If there was one series that ushered in the modern game, then it would have been this one, the savagery of which compelled a move to protective headgear thereafter. Clive Lloyd's West Indies were put through the mill the next summer, prompting a rethink and subsequent decision to challenge teams through fear.

This was a macho world – big hair, big moustaches, cigarettes, booze and no sun-block – in which Greig was entirely at home.

It is hard for the modern cricketer, swaddled in protective gear since childhood, to appreciate that, in Greig's era, raw courage was a crucial ingredient of success. No modern batsman knows what it is like to stand at the crease in the knowledge that one small mistake could kill you.

'Ashes to Ashes, dust to dust, if Lillee don't get you, Thommo must' was rammed down the throat of every England batsman during that 1974–75 Australian summer. More bones were broken in that series than in the Bodyline Tests four decades earlier, and the barracking from the edge was uglier, too. Amid the wreckage of the first Test in Brisbane, Greig stood tall with a mighty hundred.

He refused to be intimidated and even went out of his way to wind up Lillee, signalling boundaries himself, a red rag to Lillee's bull. There was cricketing intelligence behind the matador's apparent suicide, though, as Lillee bowled shorter and faster, and Greig, against convention, stayed inside the line of the ball (rather than getting behind the line, as the coaching manual dictated) and carved away through the off side.

This fearlessness, and refusal to be intimidated, was never more needed three years later when he decided to throw in his lot with Kerry Packer's World Series revolution. It was a move that alienated many observers in England – including *The Times*'s cricket correspondent John Woodcock, who wrote that giving up the national captaincy was easier for someone who was clearly not an Englishman 'through and through'.

Of all the gibes, this was the one that Greig found hardest to ignore – and to forgive. What he never regretted though was his decision. For sure, it was a move that made him financially secure for good, tying himself to Packer's raft so that there was never any danger of submerging in later life. But every cricketer who has made even a half-decent living from the game since then owes Greig and his contemporaries a debt of gratitude for the battle won against the rapacious administrators of three decades ago.

Give the recent hosannas thrown in the path of Alastair Cook's conquering tourists, it is worth recalling Greig's India tour of 1976–77, which remains among his most brilliant achievements. England won the first three Tests by margins of an innings and 25 runs, 10 wickets and 200 runs – this at a time when touring India was a hardship posting rather than an exercise in brand-building.

Greig's flair and feel for the media was highlighted on that tour when he seduced the crowds as expertly as could any local snake charmer. Indian umpires were just one of many roadblocks between a touring team and success, and Greig shrewdly used the pulpit to neutralise the threat by praising them publicly whenever he could, and the crowds loved it when he feigned injury by falling prostrate in the middle when a firecracker went off in Kolkata.

Although occasionally he was apt to misread the mood – most famously in 1976 when he said he would make Lloyd's West Indians 'grovel' – it came as no surprise that his post-playing career came at the microphone and in television. He was made for it.

But if this last role is how he will be remembered by a generation that never saw him play, then it has been deliberately underplayed here. The controversy that ended his international career meant that his playing achievements have been wrongfully understated ever since. After 58 Tests, the differential between his batting and bowling average, for example, remains greater than either Ian Botham's or Andrew Flintoff's.

But he was not easily forgiven for his dalliance with Packer, although there was a homecoming of sorts in the summer when he delivered the MCC's Cowdrey lecture. The recent OBE awarded to Mike Denness, Greig's predecessor as England captain, means that of all the men who have captained England with any longevity since then, only Greig had not received any official recognition, reflecting his outsider status.

For a long time that is how he liked it, but more recently, with his second, young family came a mellowing. It cannot be rectified now.

'Magnificent all-rounder, inspirational captain and true pioneer', by John Etheridge, *The Sun*, 30 December 2012

The game of cricket, as we know it, can be split into two distinct phases – before Tony Greig and after Tony Greig. He was that important.

Greig, who died yesterday aged 66, was a pioneer, visionary and agitator as well as being a magnificent all-rounder, inspirational captain and outspoken commentator.

He courted controversy. While England captain, Greig subversively recruited his own teammates, who turned their backs on traditional cricket and signed to play in a circus funded by an Australian TV magnate called Kerry Packer.

In 1976, he infamously said he would make the West Indies 'grovel' – which, coming from a white man raised in apartheid South Africa, was about the most insulting comment imaginable.

Greig was instrumental in bringing in much of what we take for granted now – helmets for batsmen, coloured clothing, white balls, big money for players, made-for-TV events (think Indian Premier League) and even the idea of a South African captaining England.

Such things might have happened eventually, of course, but Greig blazed the trail.

At 6 feet 7 inches, he was a towering figure in every sense.

Charismatic, brave and, in his playing days at least, a blond Adonis, Greig took on opponents and the establishment with equal relish.

Even 35 years later, current players owe him an enormous debt of gratitude.

He helped improve their lot with his demands and forward-thinking. He was the godfather of the modern game.

Greig overcame personal obstacles, too. He suffered his first epileptic fit at the age of 14 while playing tennis.

Anthony William Greig was a true global figure.

He was the son of a Scottish father, born in South Africa, England captain and a resident of Australia for most of his life.

Greig arrived at Sussex for a trial in 1965. By 1972, he was making his debut for England, scoring a brace of half-centuries against Australia in his first Test.

Because of his height, he stood upright with his bat raised in his stance (another first) and wore distinctive, boxing-style batting gloves manufactured by the St Peter company.

Greig also helped design batting helmets.

As a bowler, he switched from medium pace to off spin and promptly took 13 wickets in a Test in Trinidad in 1974.

He succeeded Mike Denness as England captain in 1975 and scored 96 in his first match in charge against Australia at Lord's. He was a fearless competitor.

The winter after his 'grovel' gaffe, Greig led England to a Test series win in India, something achieved only once in the next 36 years. His players would do anything for him.

Greig scored centuries on turning pitches and fast, bouncy surfaces. He was versatile and always entertaining.

During his hundred in Brisbane in 1974, Greig signalled a four, as though he was an umpire, whenever he hit feared fast bowlers Dennis Lillee or Jeff Thomson to the boundary.

There were other controversies. In that match in Trinidad, Greig caused a near-riot when he ran out West Indies batsman Alvin Kallicharran after the final ball of the day.

He was technically correct because the umpire had not called 'time' but he eventually withdrew his appeal and Kallicharran continued his innings the next day. Greig was undoubtedly one of England's finest all-rounders.

His record is superior to that of Andrew Flintoff, for example, and perhaps only Ian Botham stands ahead of him over the past 50 years.

Greig was removed from the England captaincy as soon as his involvement with World Series Cricket became public, although he did play all five Tests in the summer of 1977 under Mike Brearley. He spent much of the following months in court fighting the TCCB (the old name for the ECB), who wanted to ban the Packer players from first-class cricket. Greig won that battle, too.

Packer liked Greig's ebullient character and he hired him as a TV commentator for his Channel Nine cricket coverage.

He became famous for his wide-brimmed hat, his 'Weather Wall', enthusiastic style and for using his car keys to test the hardness of the pitch.

When Greig suffered financial difficulties after a failed business venture, Packer was there to help.

Greig was hugely popular in Sri Lanka, where he endorsed products ranging from mobile phone networks to pineapple chunks, and the rest of Asia.

He became a director of the rebel and now-defunct Indian Cricket League.

Greig suffered severe coughing earlier this year and was diagnosed with lung cancer in October after commentating on the World Twenty20 in Sri Lanka.

He died from a suspected heart attack.

Greig leaves a wife, Vivian. They had two children and he had two children from his first marriage. His brother, Ian, also played Test cricket for England.

'Cricket loses Tony Greig, one of its giants', by Peter Lalor, *The Australian*, 29 December 2012

Tony Greig will not come back to the cricket, his chair in the commentary box will remain empty, Bill Lawry's excesses will go unchallenged and all of us who love the game will be saddened by this development.

Cricket has lost one of its giants.

The former England captain and an essential part of every Australian summer for almost four decades died today.

The tall, South African-born cricketer and commentator, was diagnosed with lung cancer in October.

He suffered a heart attack at his home in Sydney this morning and died at 1.45pm AEDT with his family at his side. He was 66.

The illness kept him from the Channel Nine commentary box this year, but has been part of Australian cricket from the mid-1970s and one of the great characters of the game.

It could be argued that Tony Greig was the godfather of modern cricket, the man who believed the game should be entertaining and a little irreverent but always ruthlessly competitive. The man who introduced us to the crash helmet at the crease and the wide-brimmed boater.

Most of us grew up with Greigy. Always cast as a pantomime villain, he broke the mould of England cricketers and most particularly England captains. He gave as good as he got and sometimes more.

To Australians his haughty accent and intimidating stature made him sound the height of pomposity, but nothing was further from the truth.

Controversial, abrasive and intelligent, he brought his competitive instincts to the commentary box, always baiting and probing, looking for a weak spot in his colleagues who he needled and niggled relentlessly.

Younger cricket fans will remember his perennial battles with Bill Lawry, Greig always taking the opposite line, delighting in any chance to undermine the exuberant jingoism of the Australian commentator.

For years it seemed his insertion of a car key into the pitch was as important to the starting of a match as the coin toss on day one.

Born in South Africa to Scottish parents, Greig's cricketing prowess is often forgotten. At six foot six he was an imposing character, a dashing batsman, a bowling all-rounder (he took 8–86 against the West Indies in Port of Spain, 1974), a sure slips catch and an inspirational leader whose captaincy of England in India in 1976–77 is remembered fondly by his team and opponents.

He took Australians on at their own game, rejecting the stiff upper lip approach and embracing the one where the lip was your first line of attack.

Greig baited David Hookes on the eve of the Centenary Test, sledging the player on the eve of his debut at an official drinks function, suggesting he was just 'another left-hander who couldn't bat'. On the field he suggested the South Australian's testicles hadn't dropped.

Nobody had heard an England captain speak like this.

The fair-haired Australian had his revenge later in the game on his fair-haired tormenter, striking him for five successive fours and only just being denied a sixth off the last ball. Greig told me some years ago that he had been reminded of that over every week for the rest of his life after taking up residence in Australia.

He was fearless in his taunting of Dennis Lillee and Jeff Thomson and injudicious when he suggested the West Indies pacemen would grovel before him, but that was Greigy – always willing to put on a show, never willing to show weakness.

He shifted here, as people who saw 'Howzat' on television recently would know, when he became Kerry Packer's lieutenant in World Series Cricket. Greig became instantly the most reviled man in English cricket. Banned and bullied by the establishment, he only fled the country when his daughter became victim of the excessive reaction.

Greig loved Australia because it accepted him without snobbery or question, allowed him his abrasive humour and indulged his love of cricket. He fashioned a character for himself in those World Series matches, writing at the time 'the more they hoot me, the more the bowlers throw at me, the better I'll like it'.

In his 1976 book *Cricket* Greig opined that the game needed to change for a new era of fans.

'No matter what one thinks about cricket and cricketers, it has to be realised that the players are basically entertainers,' he wrote. 'The principals in this dramatic comedy are undoubtedly the crowds that flock to Test matches.'

He wrote about baiting crowds around the world and how when the mob on the hill started to get too ugly from the effects of Sydney sun and beer he would take them on. They'd call him a 'pommy bastard' and he would insist they got their facts straight. 'I was born in South Africa' and then he would suggest that they were 'nothing but convicts' and mimic a man carrying ball and chain. They loved it.

Greig played 58 Tests and boasted a handy all-round record of 3599 runs at 40.43 and 141 wickets at 32.20. They are the numbers of a great all-rounder.

His record as a cricketer is often overlooked and his knowledge of the game and love for it was too. Get him away from the commentary box and he was a generous and erudite man who spoke with passion and intelligence.

He was invited back to England a few months before the cancer was detected to deliver the MCC Spirit of Cricket Cowdrey Lecture and used the opportunity to berate the Indian board, suggesting its power and attitude were undermining Test cricket.

Again he was controversial, again he was baiting the bully, aware of the consequences but that was the only way he knew to go about things.

Greig was a character in the game all around the world. During the last Australian tour of Sri Lanka he was ubiquitous. His big head under that big hat stared down at you from billboards and hoardings, insisting you buy this or that, visit here or there

For some reason the Sri Lankans loved Greigy like Australians did. He sold them mobile phones, he sold us breakfast cereal that apparently looked like a cricket bat with little holes in it.

There's a big hole left in the game today, because the big man has gone.

Greig is survived by his wife, Vivian, and two young children, Beau and Tom, and a son, Mark, and daughter, Sam, from his first marriage. Greig's brother, Ian, 57, played two Tests for England and also lives in Australia.

'The anti-hero who cannot be replaced', by Malcolm Conn, *Daily Telegraph*, 30 December 2012

The loss of Tony Greig has taken a dimension away from cricket that cannot be replaced.

Greig was the anti-hero, the contrarian, well beyond the commentary box. He became a caricature of himself as the devil's advocate, Australia's enemy and the touring team's friend.

Born in South Africa and a captain of England, Greig was a ready-made villain at any cricket match involving Australia, even though he spent half his life living here.

Commentary box banter will never be the same again.

Flags flew at half mast on opposite sides of the world

yesterday – at Lord's and the SCG – such was his impact across the cricketing globe.

And NSW fans who may have once booed him in the mid '70s as England's greatest provocateur now have the chance to show their affection.

The SCG Trust will encourage everyone attending the third Test against Sri Lanka, beginning on Thursday, to wear a broad-brimmed hat in honour of Greig, zinc cream following the sudden retirement of Mike Hussey, and a pink shirt in support of the McGrath Foundation.

Cricket Australia, Channel Nine, the SCG Trust and Cricket NSW are working on a joint tribute for Greig around the Test.

An enormous man with an even bigger presence, Greig was full of bluff and thunder behind a microphone, but a fascinating man over a beer or around the dinner table.

He had endless stories about the game and how little had changed in some respects.

Greig was particularly amused by ball tampering. During a long and successful county career, Greig claimed to be aware of all sorts of attempts to gain an advantage by working on the ball.

This included players chewing mints and then applying the sticky saliva – as recent England opening batsman Marcus Trescothick admitted to in his autobiography – bowlers using Vaseline or trying to lift the seam with their thumb or fingernails.

Greig was unconvinced that any of it made much difference.

'You still had to be able to bowl,' he said.

A man of strong opinions, you were left in no doubt when he disagreed with you. But a stoush could come and go in the midst of dinner without anything left lingering.

Greig got on with life. Indeed, he enjoyed the sharper side of a conversation.

He was adored on the subcontinent. And if there was a better connected cricket aficionado in Sri Lanka, I never met them.

Greig was omnipresent in Sri Lanka, looking down from huge signs all around the country advertising a mobile phone network.

'Where's the best place for a traditional Sri Lankan meal?' I asked him in the foyer of the Cinnamon Grand during Australia's most recent Test tour there in September last year.

'Hang on,' he said. 'I've got just the place.'

A quick phone call and he pointed to a nondescript hotel a couple of kilometres up the Galle Road.

Its basement opened up to a dining room that served great food and cold beer at even better prices.

I'll be going back there again the next time I'm in Colombo to remember one of cricket's most imposing characters.

'Greig's a unique cricketing story', by Robert Craddock, *The Courier-Mail*, 29 December 2012

There has never been another cricketing story like Tony Greig's and there never will.

The son of a Scottish migrant was a South African-born, England-finessed, Australian-residing citizen of the world, a Test captain who loved stirring the pot, a revolutionary who fought the establishment, losing some battles but spectacularly winning others.

At times throughout his colourful life all of the nations mentioned above claimed and cursed him but that was the essential flavour of his story as a man who followed in no other man's steps.

In an attempt to intimidate rivals Greig would stand within breathing distance of the batsman and make subtle jibes, making the term silly point as suitable for what he was saying as where he was standing.

He would bait crowds when few of his generation would ever have been so bold and found verbal combat stimulating.

In some ways his trademarks – such as the windmill swings of the bat when he came to the crease – were unforgettable, in other ways the footprints he left on cricket have been underplayed.

He was among the first to wear motorcycle helmets for protection, to stand upright in his batting stance and to slice fast men deliberately over slips … a trailblazer in every sense.

Later in life, with Channel Nine, the playful side of his personality shone through as a commentator who enjoyed playing the contrarian, the man in black.

The cricket world, though hearing Greig as a commentator for more than three decades with the Nine Network, never really heard the best of him.

His finest work was done as perhaps the best dinner company in cricket, a man whose colourful stories ranged from tales of Bradman to Tendulkar, from Shane Warne's brilliance to Muttiah Muralitharan's family biscuit factory in Sri Lanka, to Kerry Packer's private world.

Some of his greatest battles were ones kept mostly away from public view such as his battle with epilepsy which once saw him collapse at Heathrow Airport after the return of the 1975 Australian tour.

As an all-rounder Greig was no Sir Garfield Sobers but certainly he was in one of next drawers down.

He was dynamic and, like Sobers, a master of versatility. His Test record of 3599 runs at 40.4 and 141 wickets at 32.2 in 58 Tests may not make the jaw drop but he was a robust competitive force in everything he did.

As a player he carried himself like a man who had the key to every lock; his body language radiated the vibe 'just watch this' and he often got wickets through the force of his personality.

Greig arrived in England from South Africa having played just one first-class match but such was his exceptional talent he reached 1000 Test runs in just his 14th Test and won Test matches bowling medium pace on some occasions and off spin on others.

No lesser judge than keeping icon Alan Knott rated Greig – at his peak – the best off-spinner in the world.

Sometimes Greig's combative nature got the better of him and he lived to regret a throwaway line made against the West Indies in England in 1977 when he said he intended to 'make them grovel'.

With their sensitivities over the region's slave ancestry raging, the West Indies never forgave or forgot.

After one dismissal of Greig in that series Viv Richards said: 'Who wouldn't want to maybe have one-up on your colonial masters at some point? … I just wanted to send that message we are all equal. It's pretty simple.'

Greig will almost be remembered for his role in quitting English cricket to help Kerry Packer organise the World Series Cricket circus in the late 1970s.

No other cricketer in World Series was closer to Packer than Greig; their mutual admiration knew no bounds.

One theory has it that Packer and Greig gained their rebellious streak from having domineering fathers who they could never please.

Greig once said his father was 'exceptionally critical of every move I made' while Packer could never recall his father praising him to his face.

Greig was given a brutal working over from the English public and media but his final decision to join Packer was made when he felt shattered by a snub to his daughter.

'I went to pick up my daughter, Samantha, from school,' he recalls. 'Her best friend had a party the next day. The mother was handing out invitations and my daughter didn't get one. The mother looked at me and said she's not getting one.

'I was gobsmacked. That caused me to phone up and tell Kerry "I'm out of here." Within three days, we were out of England.'

Greig had a cricketing life like no other. It's hard to know where he fits best in history but one thing is sure — history will never forget him.

'Tony Greig: charismatic, gifted cricketer and the ideal foil for Packer', by Vic Marks, *The Observer*, Saturday 29 December 2012

Think Tony Greig, think Kerry Packer. The two names are

indelibly linked. Yet there is another link in this chain that can easily be forgotten. Why was Greig, who died on Saturday at the age of 66, sought out by Packer to be at the forefront of World Series Cricket in 1977? Because he was one of the most charismatic and gifted cricketers on the planet.

Packer's intervention, which was regarded by many as a cataclysm at the time, has tended to dwarf just how good a cricketer Greig was. In the end the figures don't lie. In 58 Tests for England – and there obviously could have been many more – Greig scored 3599 runs at 40 and took 141 wickets at 32, which does not compare too badly with Ian Botham (5200 runs at 33 and 383 wickets at 28) or Andrew Flintoff (3845 at 31, 226 at 32).

Somehow it is a surprise that we should find him in this same bracket as Botham and Flintoff. He was surely too gangly to be a great batsman and his bowling too bland to trouble Test players. But behind the bluster here was an intelligent, streetwise cricketer at his most formidable when the challenge was at its most extreme.

When he scored a brilliant hundred at the 'Gabba on the 1974–75 tour of Australia he signalled his own boundaries off Dennis Lillee. This was a provocative act, not always appreciated by his colleagues ('Please don't make him mad,' pleaded Derek Underwood at the other end). My guess is that Greig's histrionics did indeed rile Lillee somewhat (actually there is not much guesswork involved here); they made Lillee bowl shorter; they made him lose control. This was brilliant theatre from Greig; it was also shrewd tactics.

In Calcutta, in 1976, Greig was capable of scoring a seven-hour hundred at a strike rate way below the norm for Jonathan Trott while keeping 80,000 spectators entertained in the process. Greig wooed the Indians; they loved it when he fell to the ground poleaxed after a firecracker had been let off. Such adulation eased the path of his team around the subcontinent. Under his leadership that series was won 3–1.

Greig could bat all right. And he was a successful bowler, but more through force of personality than any intrinsic venom. He could swing the ball and, even though he did not make full use of his height, the odd delivery would bounce more than expected. But it was when he improvised with his off-breaks that he had the most remarkable success. In Port of Spain in March 1974 he took thirteen wickets and therefore contrived to square a series against West Indies that England seemed bound to lose. Geoffrey Boycott scored 211 runs in that match and wryly observed that he and Greig had kept Mike Denness in his job as England captain.

But by 1975 Greig had taken over from Denness and he would captain England 14 times. Ask any of his teammates and they speak of an inspirational captain. None of them has a bad word to say about him and the testament of a dressing room is as reliable as it gets. Of course Greig could raise hackles. There was the run-out of Alvin Kallicharran in Trinidad, which might have terminated that tour of 1973–74 rather abruptly if the diplomats had not got to work overnight.

There was the 'grovel' remark, a rare occasion when Greig's PR had disastrous consequences. In half a sentence he managed to galvanise West Indies' tourists of 1976 to even greater resolve. Usually Greig manipulated the press brilliantly. He never shied away from a microphone and he could dictate the news agenda with easy charm. He understood how the media operated and how they could be used to his advantage far better than the current England setup.

And, of course, there was Packer. It took balls to forsake the England captaincy and to take on the establishment, but it was already apparent from his exploits on a cricket field that he had big ones. Greig often protested that he enlisted with World Series Cricket for the greater good. He was also candid enough to admit that he was able to secure his family's future by taking the plunge and aligning with Packer. He procured a job for life with Channel Nine in Australia and younger cricket fans will be more familiar with Greig's ever-enthusiastic commentary than his swaggering strokeplay.

In England he was branded a traitor. The venom seeped from the MCC establishment. In their eyes Greig's decision to join Packer was far worse than any subsequent defection by England cricketers on a South African rebel tour. Even though it transpired that the 'Packer Circus' did not precipitate the end of the cricketing world after all, Greig was ostracised for decades.

There was a homecoming of sorts in the summer of 2012 when he was invited by the MCC to give the Spirit of Cricket Cowdrey Lecture at Lord's. This was the last time I saw him.

He looked a little shackled by the format but he was clearly thrilled to be asked. He delivered a carefully chiselled speech, reading every word. But afterwards there was a forum conducted by Mark Nicholas. Once the question-and-answer session was under way Greig was at his best: instinctive, mischievous, funny, outspoken, enlightening and always engaging.

Greig was different to the run-of-the-mill professional. He was not just a better player than most; he was braver; he operated on a different level, fascinated by successful men beyond cricket; obviously he was prepared to challenge the status quo in a manner that most would never dare. Yet he was never aloof.

I made my debut in first-class cricket against his Sussex side in The Parks in April 1975 (I dropped him and he made a century, as it happens). More importantly I recall this Adonis of the cricketing world, who had just returned from Australia, a battered hero but one who would soon accede to the England captaincy. And I remember how he made time to chat away freely to us young, inconsequential students as if we were proper cricketers. That impressed us as much as the runs, the wickets and the golden locks.

'Vale Tony Greig, a world-class all-rounder', by Kersi Meher-Homji, *The Roar*, Saturday 29 December 2012

The death of Tony Greig came as a shock to me as to all of us. An interesting character, it was always interesting discussing cricket with him in the SCG Press Box. He had that certain presence, that certain aura, a charisma that attracts. At six-foot-seven he was larger than life size but was very approachable.

Tall, fair, handsome and articulate, Greig has gone through the gauntlet and emerged unscathed. Born in South Africa, he shone out as an all-rounder for England, later captaining his adopted country to success, and was one of the key figures in the formation of Kerry Packer's World Series Cricket in 1977. His voice was recognised internationally as the cricket commentator on Channel Nine in Australia with that typical 'Greigy' unflappable style.

He was a leader of men, charming and multi-talented He knew what he wanted and got it. According to Christopher Martin-Jenkins in *World Cricketers* (1996), '[Greig] was a brave, determined and skilful all-round cricketer who seldom failed in Tests and many times seemed to be holding England's fortunes on his shoulders.' At times ruthless, he relished challenges, imposing his personality on matches and on events.

He usually batted at number six and showed to the bowlers who the boss was. And who would argue with his tall frame? He came out swinging his bat round his shoulders as he took the 'middle' from the umpire. Mostly a front-foot batsman, he specialised on the off-drive and lofted straight drives which went over the ropes and within the stands. Like Keith Miller before him he had 'six appeal' and he was a crowd favourite, especially in India. Many of his best innings were played on his two tours to India.

He loved India and India loved him. In 1972–73 he shone out as a batsman playing unbeaten innings of 68 and 40 (and accepting five catches) in the Delhi Test which England won by six wickets. In the final Test in Mumbai, he hit 148. During this innings he added 254 runs with Keith Fletcher.

Greig achieved all-round success when England toured the Caribbean the next season. He scored 430 runs (including two centuries) at 47.77 and captured 24 wickets at 22.62 runs apiece. In the third Test in Bridgetown, he made 148, his joint top score and bagged 6–164, becoming the first to record a hundred and take five wickets in an innings of the same Test for England. Inspired, Greig scored another century in the Georgetown Test and captured 8–86 and 5–70 in the final Test in Port of Spain.

Both his 8–86 in that innings and 13-156 in the match were records for England against the West Indies at that time. On this tour he had switched from swing to quickish off spin which may explain his success. This bowling bonanza enabled England to win the Test and draw the series.

However, his copybook was blotted somewhat by a controversy in the first Test in Port of Spain. When West Indian batsman Bernard Julien played the last ball of the second day down the pitch, Greig picked it up. Then observing that Alvin Kallicharran was out of the crease, he threw down the stumps and appealed. Kallicharran was given run out by umpire Sang Hue and the crowd was furious. After long consultations between captains, umpires and administrators, the appeal was withdrawn. Greig apologised and peace was restored.

He carried his fine batting form in Australia in 1974–75, playing a buccaneering innings of 110 against Dennis Lillee and Jeff Thomson at their peak. This was the first century in a Brisbane Test by an England player since 1936–37. He put in an impressive all-round performance in the third Test in Melbourne, scoring 60 in the second innings, lofting off-spinner Ashley Mallett for a monstrous hit in the outer and taking valuable wickets.

Appointed captain, Greig led England to a successful tour of India in 1976–77. England won the Test series 3–1 as he totalled 342 runs at 42.75. His 103 in the Kolkata Test, his

49th, was memorable as he became the first one to achieve the double of 3000 runs and 100 wickets for England.

He led England in the historic Centenary Test in Melbourne in March 1977 which attracted the largest collection of international cricketers in history. Although England lost, Greig remained a very popular player on and off the field. At that time he was 'earning upwards of £50,000 a year from various cricket contracts and allied business activities', according to Christopher Martin-Jenkins in *World Cricketers* (1996). He was also certain of leading England for many years.

Then was born Kerry Packer's rebel World Series Cricket (WSC) with Greig as one of the key figures and he lost credibility with the establishment. Although he was the captain of England, he travelled the world between March and May 1977 to sign up many of the world's best cricketers on Packer's behalf including some of his own teammates. The WSC was born soon after and Greig was dismissed as captain of England for what was regarded as 'his betrayal of trust' but he continued to play for them successfully under Mike Brearley in 1977.

In 58 Tests he scored 3599 runs at a healthy average of 40.43 with eight centuries and took 141 wickets at 32.20, claiming five wickets in an innings six times and pouched 87 catches. He was one of the four cricketers who averaged more than 40 with the bat and under 35 with the ball in the Test arena, others being Aubrey Faulkner of South Africa, the West Indies legend Garry Sobers and South African Jacques Kallis.

And in 350 first-class matches, he amassed 16,660 runs at 31.19, took 856 wickets at 28.85 and held 345 catches.

As a slip fielder he was superlative, the safest and the most brilliant of his era. Well, his height helped too.

Greig migrated to Australia in 1978 and started as a chairman of an insurance company and a successful television commentator on Channel Nine. Along with WSC pioneers Richie Benaud and Ian Chappell, Greig has been broadcasting the game and presenting his views on the box for 30 years. He spoke his mind without fear or favour and remained popular with TV viewers from the time the coin is tossed (with his key in the pitch as his trademark) to interviewing the man of the match at the end.

One cannot speak for hours on end without a gaffe here and there and Greig is known for putting his foot in the mouth on occasions. He was once 'caught out' when commentating on Channel Nine during a one-day international between Australia A and West Indies on the Sydney Cricket Ground on 10 January 1996. When a batsman hit a sizzling six, he yelled in excitement 'It's a HUGE sh*t' instead of 'It's a HUGE six'.

A lively after-dinner speaker, he told a humorous story at a cricket function. He had just started playing county cricket for Sussex after leaving South Africa. The bowler steamed in and had Greig out plumb lbw. That was the first ball he had faced and to his relief the appeal was turned down. He took a single off the next ball which brought him near the umpire who whispered to him: 'Do you know Sandy Greig from Queenstown?' 'He's my father,' Tony replied. 'Damn good decision, then!' was the retort from the umpire who was Sandy's mate.

Greig went on to make 150-plus, captured newspaper headlines and never looked back.

Let me narrate a humorous anecdote involving Greig and Sunil Gavaskar. When Greig (six foot seven tall) and Gavaskar (five foot five) were batting together for Rest of World XI against Australia in a match in 1971, a woman asked ABC cricket commentator Norman May: 'How do they communicate with each other with such a difference in height?'. Norman May replied: 'By Morse code; one is a dash and the other a dot!'

Tony Greig will be remembered for his tall frame, tall hits and tall (but true) tales.

With the passing of Peter Roebuck, Vinay Verma and now Tony Greig, the SCG Press Box will not look the same.

Rest in peace, Tony Greig.

'Tony Greig – Sri Lanka's biggest overseas fan', by Rex Clementine, *The Island*, Saturday 29 December 2012

What's your Tony Greig moment? 'These Sri Lankans are giving the Aussies a real hiding' ('96 World Cup final), 'These Sri Lankans are very, very good, they catch everything' ('95 Benson and Hedges Series), 'Little Kalu has smashed that for four and the Sri Lankans are loving it' ('95 Benson and Hedges Series).

At a time when Sri Lankan cricket was nobody in the mid-'90s, Tony Greig was a dear friend. During that acrimonious tour of Australia in 1995 and the World Cup that followed Greig came up with several gems supporting Sri Lanka. Here are some of those.

'They have come such a long way in such a short period

of time and here they are taking away the ultimate cricket trophy.'

It was only fitting that Greig was doing commentaries with Sri Lanka on the brink of winning the World Cup. As Arjuna Ranatunga scored the winning runs, Greig said, 'This is a little fairytale. The thing that I like about these guys is that they not only win, but they win in style. It is only a small place, Sri Lanka. And what a moment this is for Sri Lankan people.'

Greig first caught the imagination of Sri Lankan fans during the tour of Australia in 1995. In a very pro-Australian commentary team, Greig's role was crucial as whatever he said helped form public opinion and won Sri Lanka admirers among the Australian public. One such Greig comment during the chucking controversy was, 'I have got to say that I have sympathy with the Sri Lankans here. They had enough,' he said as Arjuna Ranatunga took the team off.

There are some commentators [whom] you love to listen to. Benaud, Chappell, David Lloyd and Greig fed us with so much information, both technical stuff and some terrific moments in the past. But what made Greig such a popular personality was his love for Sri Lanka. Greig not only kept our cricketers on a high pedestal, but told everyone that our pineapple was the tastiest in the world and that our crab is the best in the world.

Once during a match some cricket fans put out a banner which said, 'Tony Greig – Born in South Africa, played for England, lives in Australia and supports Sri Lanka'. When cameras showed the banner, Greig had a laugh and said, 'Oh boy, these blokes are going to get me into trouble.'

Greig is known for his banter as a player and a commentator. Once in the late 1970s during a game at the P. Sara Oval when Greig called Sri Lankan cheerleader Percy Abeysekara 'a black b******', Percy sledged him. 'Hey Greigy, you've got your height, I have got my might. I will send you up like a kite if the air is right and I will have you for bite especially if I am tight.' Since that day Percy and Greig have been great pals.

Greig hosted Sri Lankan cricketers for dinner when they were playing in Sydney, his adopted home. And when he came to Sri Lanka he went out with current and ex-cricketers and Galle seemed to be his preferred destination.

His last commentary stint happened to be in Sri Lanka during the World T-20. He was struggling with bronchitis and when he underwent tests it was revealed that he had damaged his right lung. Upon returning to Australia he was diagnosed with cancer.

The Sri Lankan fans were shaken by the news and conducted Bodhi Pujas hoping for his speedy recovery. Star cricketers Kumar Sangakkara, Mahela Jayawardene and several others attended the religious ceremony.

It was a heart attack that claimed him at about 1.45pm, the day after the Sri Lankans had suffered a massive innings and 201-run defeat inside three days at the MCG. He was 66.

Born in South Africa, Greig came to England and went on to play 58 Tests, some of them as captain. Since abandoning the England captaincy and joining Kerry Packer's World Series Cricket, he remained loyal to Packer's Nine Network.

'You've no idea how much one misses getting to the cricket on a day like today. When you've been doing it for 33 years it's absolutely unbelievable. Even my little bloke who came home from school today was almost, "Dad what are you doing at home, you shouldn't be here", so it takes a little bit of getting used to, and I'm sure it's going to get worse as this Test match goes on,' Greig told his Nine commentary colleagues during the first Test between South Africa and Australia at the 'Gabba, where the traditional first Test of the Australian summer is played and Greig had not missed a game there for 33 years.

He was hoping to return to work for the Sydney Test involving Sri Lanka that gets under way on the 3rd of January.

Greig was the ultimate Sri Lankan fan. He loved Sri Lankan cricket more than some of our own cricketers do.

'Very Greig-arious and a master of gamesmanship', by Avijit Ghosh, *The Times of India*, 29 December 2012

He would appeal with abandon for a catch when the ball had clearly come off the pad and con the umpires into making a wrong call. He would pretend to be heartbroken and wronged when declared leg before but admit smilingly in private that he was out plumb. He would chat up the batsmen to break their concentration and often succeed too. But nothing could stop the Indian spectator from falling in love with Tony Greig.

On his first tour to India in 1972–73, the six feet, six inch tall cricketer charmed crowds across the country with his antics. When Gundappa Viswanath scored a century at the Brabourne Stadium, the all-rounder picked up the diminutive batsman in his arms and rocked him like a baby. The crowd roared in delight. Often, 'lambu' Greig would kneel before the spectators, as if begging their forgiveness, much to their delight. He even dropped his pants before a packed Eden Gardens once. Few, if any, visiting cricketer was such a darling of the spectators as the tall South Africa-born cricketer who played for England.

Greig was a master of gamesmanship. But off the field, he was an extremely easygoing bloke. Writes Sunil Gavaskar in *Sunny Days*, 'I was given out, caught by Greig, after the ball had come off my pads. The poor umpire got foxed by Greig and wicketkeeper (Alan) Knott, who began applauding the bowler with such gusto, that he declared me "out". When I met Greig in our dressing room in the evening, he laughed in characteristic fashion and started pulling my leg. I, however, swallowed all the choice bad words I had thought of, because, with Greig it is a love-hate relationship. On the field, he makes you hate him; but off it he is a wonderful chap, who doesn't bear you any grudge. He believes that whatever happens on the field should be left there and should not be allowed to sour one's friendship.'

Gavaskar also wrote, 'Throughout the tour Greig made use of his knowledge of Hindi expletives which he learnt from us and the Pakistanis during the Rest of the World's tour of Australia (in 1972). Often, he did not even know the meaning of the word and the Indian team were surprised to hear his Hindi vocabulary. His pronunciation was not perfect, but the meaning was clear. More than anyone else, Farokh (Engineer) and Ajit (Wadekar) suffered, because they often played long innings during the series. Yet, when the MCC (as the visiting England team called itself those days) left, all our players agreed that he was a likeable guy, off the field.'

And Greig's love for the Indian crowds was genuine. In his book *Cricket: The Men and the Game*, he lauded Indian spectators for their sense of fun. Enthusiastic spectators would blow conch shells in those days, and bells could be heard tolling, much like a temple, on the ground. Greig wrote that the sounds reminded him of films produced by the Rank Organisation, which always opened with a bare-bodied man striking a gong.

In 1976–77, Greig returned to India, this time as the captain of the team. The series, won 3–1 by England, is also remembered for the Vaseline controversy where medium-pacer John Lever was caught shining the ball with the stuff. Yet Greig managed to remain a popular figure. So much so that Mihir Bose writes in his book *A History of Indian Cricket* that Greig appeared to be more at home than Bedi. 'Greig, ever the showman, knew Indian crowds from his previous visit and used this knowledge so well that Bedi was always a step behind. In Calcutta, he so charmed the crowds that he became known as Greigda, a term of affection. Even in Bangalore, after he had lost, he led his team on a lap of honour.'

Describing his crowd-pleasing antics, Bose further writes, 'Greig used all this and more, carefully discriminating between the cheaper stands – where his impressions of a full-breasted woman went down well – and the pricier stands – where he was more decorous – to make Bedi and the Indian cricketers feel as if they were playing away from home. Some of his antics came close to the sort of gamesmanship that should have no place in cricket: if a batsman played and missed Greig, very often fielding at silly mid-on, he would snatch his bat and show him how to play the shot. The crowd would roar, but the batsman would lose his concentration.'

Gavaskar did manage to get the better of him once. The former India captain recounts in his autobiography, '[T]here was a funny incident when I survived a leg-before appeal off Arnold. Greig walking past me at the end of the over remarked, "It was close, wasn't it?" I replied, "Yeah sure. But the umpire is my uncle." Greig then asked what his name was. "I said, Gothoskar, but he had changed it, or else he would never get to be Test umpire." Within minutes word had gone round and I was asked with much consternation by quite a few people whether Gothoskar was really my uncle.'

'A champion of the players' cause', by David Tossell, *Cricinfo* Magazine, ESPN Cricinfo, 29 December 2012

With barely two of his enormous strides, Tony Greig crossed the Lord's hospitality box, into which his sister Sally Ann had invited me for tea, and stuck out his hand. 'So,' he said, smiling down in my direction, 'have you sold all of those books of yours?'

It had been a year since publication of my biography of the former England captain, a project in which he had generously participated without there being anything in it for him. He had even offered to do some interviews 'to create some headlines' in order to publicise the release date, and had duly taken swings at everyone from Dennis Lillee to the BCCI in the cause of publicity.

When I'd suggested he might want to see the book before helping to publicise it, he'd responded: 'I can't believe I wouldn't want it to do well.' After the interview time, the family contacts and photographs, and the endorsements he'd given on my behalf to doubtful interviewees, this really was above and beyond the call of duty.

As we chatted now, guests of his brother-in-law, MCC president Phillip Hodson, while England and Australia fought out an ODI below us, I ventured the question to which I dreaded the answer: 'You never did tell me what you thought of the book. Did you like it?'

'Well ... I have to admit I haven't read it from cover to cover,' he said, and in his reply was the implication that he'd probably read not a single word. It should have come as no surprise. Tony Greig, the South African-born captain who was accused of betraying English cricket, a man for whom controversy lurked at every turn of his career, had long since ceased worrying what people said about him.

Nor did he ever back away from the challenges that confronted him, whether it was the bouncers of Lillee and Thomson, Roberts and Holding, or the cricket authorities he defied by becoming a leading figure in Kerry Packer's World Series Cricket in 1977. It was why news of his death by heart attack early on Saturday as he fought cancer came as such a shock. If anyone was ever going to beat that most cruel of diseases, surely it was this greatest of competitors.

Born in Queenstown, South Africa, on 6 October 1946, Greig had a comfortable childhood, but it was never quite the idyllic upbringing that a white, professional family in the era of apartheid might have expected to offer.

That was due partly to the alcoholism that afflicted his Scottish father, Sandy, after a distinguished wartime RAF career that ended with his posting to South Africa as an instructor. Just as significant was the discovery, following Greig's collapse during a teenage tennis match, that he was epileptic. As a result, Greig began a lifetime of disciplined medication, keeping his condition from all but the closest of his team-mates over the years until acknowledging it publicly in 1980.

Sussex team-mate Peter Graves, one of those in the know, recalled the threat of an attack being a constant presence. 'You always worried whether it was going to happen,' he said. 'Tony was like this juggernaut and he used to get really tired and that was when it could strike. He used to take a lot out of himself. But he wasn't a boozer and he wouldn't be up late.'

Greig had arrived at Sussex in 1966, scoring a century against Lancashire on his Championship debut the following season. A striking six foot seven inch blond, he quickly established himself as an attacking middle-order batsman and purveyor of useful seamers off a jerky, pigeon-toed action.

Taking advantage of the opportunity denied his countrymen by South Africa's sporting exile but offered to him by his English residency and a British father, Greig won a place in the England team against the Rest of the World in 1970. The downgrading of that series meant it was not until the Ashes contest of 1972 that he played his first official Test, beginning an England career that lasted for

58 matches. During that time he dominated the team in a manner that few have done before or since.

His best performances were reserved for overseas tours, many of which are lost to cricket history due to the lack of TV coverage. On four consecutive tours – India (1972–73), West Indies (1973–74), Australia (1974–75) and India (1976–77) – Greig was England's outstanding player, proving himself Test cricket's pre-eminent allrounder.

It was not until 20 years after Packer that the MCC life membership traditionally afforded to former England captains came his way; not until the 2005 Ashes series that Greig was invited to commentate on a full England home series on a British station.

In the Caribbean, he set up a series-saving victory in Trinidad by taking 13 wickets after deciding to try his hand at offspin. He'd already scored two centuries in the series and now, according to his great friend Alan Knott: 'In that match he was the greatest offspinner I have ever kept to.'

In Brisbane, in the first Test of England's disastrous Ashes defence, he thrashed 110 off Dennis Lillee and new fast-bowling discovery Jeff Thomson. When he wasn't deliberately upper-cutting Thomson over the slips, he was driving Lillee through the covers and celebrating by signalling his own fours.

His marathon effort in Calcutta two years later, when he defied India's spinners, the stifling atmosphere of an 80,000 crowd and a temperature of 40 degrees, to score a match-winning 103, could not have been more different in character. 'I have two memories that qualify Greigy as a top-quality player,' said Derek Underwood. 'The hundred in Brisbane and then the century in India against the best spin attack of all time. It shows that against any attack he was very high quality.'

His Test batting average of 40.43, including eight centuries, and a bowling mark of 32.20 speak for themselves, placing him in the company of Ian Botham and Andrew Flintoff as England's great post-war allrounders. That he is not always acknowledged as such is because he was never a man of the people like 'Beefy' or 'Freddie' and that his exploits are not all over YouTube or retro TV sports channels.

Not to mention that two episodes as England captain tend to dominate popular memory of Greig.

Leadership of his country passed to Greig in 1975, in spite of reservations among those who felt his attempt to run out Alvin Kallicharran while stumps were being drawn at the end of play in the West Indies were indicative of an over-competitive nature unbecoming to the post.

When he announced on the eve of West Indies' visit in 1976 that he intended to 'make them grovel' it wasn't just those dissenters who were outraged. Michael Holding remembered: 'He was a white South African and 'grovel' was an offensive word for him to have used. It smacked of racism and apartheid.'

As Holding and his team-mates made England pay with a brutal 3–0 series victory, Greig, who acknowledged immediately that he had made a clumsy choice of words, even went on his hands and knees in front of the West Indies fans at The Oval to do his own piece of grovelling.

Greig always knew how to charm. As Sussex and England skipper, he was accommodating to journalists – which could also be a source of trouble – and understanding of how to get the crowds on his side. Nowhere was that more evident than in his team's 3–1 win in India, where he praised the umpires, encouraged his men to play up to the stands, and walked away a hero.

Yet it was soon after that tour that his crown slipped, when it was announced that not only was he defecting to Kerry Packer's World Series Cricket, but that he had been busy recruiting players for the Australian tycoon in his battle against established cricket over TV rights.

Greig was no longer English cricket's saviour; he was a money-grabbing South African. Alec Bedser, chairman of selectors, was one of many who said Greig had 'betrayed' his adopted country. When his children began getting abuse in the playground, Greig knew it was time to head permanently to Australia. His protestations that all cricketers would benefit were met by deaf ears and closed minds. One of the first players to understand that he had a commercial value to be exploited, Greg said in later years that he went to WSC primarily for himself and his family, and secondarily because the cricket establishment needed shaking up. He saw that England players merited more than £210 per match and that county players deserved better than to work as shelf-stackers in the winter.

Within a year, Test fees were up to £1000. And when, only a couple of years after WSC, his brother Ian showed him his new contract offer from Sussex, which was more than he'd ever been offered even while captain of his county and country, he knew he had been vindicated.

Forgiveness took longer. It was not until 20 years after Packer that the MCC life membership traditionally afforded to former England captains came his way; not until the 2005 Ashes series that Greig – an established and typically controversial commentator on Packer's Channel 9 – was invited to commentate on a full England home series on a British station, Channel 4. It was completed earlier this year when he was asked to deliver the MCC's prestigious Cowdrey Lecture at Lord's.

No one who heard that predictably forthright speech knew that Greig's rehabilitation had come just in time; that a few months later he would be gone. He had seemed invincible.

He leaves a wife, Vivian, and four children, Beau and Tom, and from his first marriage, Mark and Samantha. And to cricket, cricket lovers and cricketers he leaves a legacy of defiance and brilliance; images of an upturned-collar and long-legged cover drives; and a debt of gratitude that every young professional in his sponsored car should acknowledge.

Career Statistics

Full name Anthony William Greig
Born October 6 1946, Queenstown, Cape Province,
South Africa
Died December 29 2012, St Vincent's Hospital, Sydney
(aged 66 years 84 days)
Major teams England, Border, Eastern Province, Sussex
Batting style Right-hand bat
Bowling style Right-arm medium, Right-arm offbreak

Batting and fielding averages

	Mat	Inns	NO	Runs	HS	Ave	BF	SR	100	50	4s	6s	Ct	St
Tests	58	93	4	3599	148	40.43			8	20	437	19	87	0
ODIs	22	19	3	269	48	16.81	378	71.16	0	0	19	3	7	0
First-class	350	579	45	16660	226	31.19			26	96			345	0
List A	190	177	19	3899	129	24.67			3	21			88	0

Bowling averages

	Mat	Inns	Balls	Runs	Wkts	BBI	BBM	Ave	Econ	SR	4w	5w	10
Tests	58	93	9802	4541	141	8/86	13/156	32.20	2.77	69.5	6	6	2
ODIs	22	19	916	619	19	4/45	4/45	32.57	4.05	48.2	1	0	0
First-class	350		52513	24702	856	8/25		28.85	2.82	61.3		33	8
List A	190		8435	5650	244	6/28	6/28	23.15	4.01	34.5	12	3	0

Full name Ian Alexander Greig
Born December 8 1955, Queenstown, Cape Province,
South Africa
Major teams England, Border, Cambridge University,
Griqualand West, Surrey, Sussex
Batting style Right-hand bat
Bowling style Right-arm medium

Batting and fielding averages

	Mat	Inns	NO	Runs	HS	Ave	BF	SR	100	50	4s	6s	Ct	St
Tests	2	4	0	26	14	6.50	102	25.49	0	0	2	0	0	0
First-class	253	339	50	8301	291	28.72			8	40			152	0
List A	235	200	44	3136	82	20.10			0	6			55	0

Bowling averages

	Mat	Inns	Balls	Runs	Wkts	BBI	BBM	Ave	Econ	SR	4w	5w	10
Tests	2	3	188	114	4	4/53	4/72	28.50	3.63	47.0	1	0	0
First-class	253		25065	13023	419	7/43		31.08	3.11	59.8		10	2
List A	235		7993	5953	212	5/30	5/30	28.08	4.46	37.7	3	3	0

Source: www.espncricinfo.com

Bibliography

Eric Beecher, *The Cricket Revolution*, Newspress, Melbourne, 1978.

Mike Brearley, *The Art of Captaincy*, Channel 4 Books, London, 2001.

Peter Fitzsimons, *Tobruk*, HarperCollins, Sydney, 2009.

Cass Francis, *A Life Fulfilled: An Autobiography*, Quill Publishing, London, 2011.

Ian Greig Benefit Publication – various authors.

Gideon Haigh, *The Cricket War,* Melbourne University Press, Melbourne, 1993.

Alan Knott, *It's Knott Cricket*, Macmillan, London, 1985.

David Lemmon, *The Cricketing Greigs*, Breedon Books, Derby, 1991.

Peter McFarline, *A Game Divided*, Hutchinson, London, 1977.

Derek Randall, *The Sun Has Got His Hat On*, Collins, London, 1984.

David Tossell, *Tony Greig: A Reappraisal of English Cricket's Most Controversial Captain*, Pitch Publishing (Brighton) Ltd, Durrington, 2011.

Max Walker, *Caps Hats and Helmets: Cricket's a Funny Game!*, Tangle Press, Melbourne, 2006.

Wisden Cricketers' Almanack, 115th Edition of *Wisden*, London, 1978.

Index